YOU ARE VALUABLE

How winners achieve phenomenal success by recognizing and fully utilizing all the God-given abilities within themselves and others

Glisson J. Heldzinger

Johannesburg
South Africa

YOU ARE VALUABLE

How winners achieve phenomenal success by recognizing and fully utilizing all the God-given abilities within themselves and others

Soft Cover Paperback Edition

Second Edition (International)
ISBN 978-0-620-70163-1
Front and back cover photograph by Creative Photo Studio
Published by Joshua Crown Publishing, Johannesburg

This book is dedicated to ...

Elohim, the triune God who grants us our valuable lives and also the opportunity to grow and become more valuable;

my parents, **Leslie and Lena**, the two people who have made the greatest and most valuable investments in my life;

Mrs. Val Davids for being the most valuable teacher any student can have.

Acknowledgements

Thank you to Bishop Marcus Jacobs for graciously agreeing to write the foreword for this book. I am humbled by everything that he has written about me and this book.

Thank you to everyone who has invested in me, either directly or indirectly, through teaching, guidance, mentoring, coaching and ministry.

Thank you to all my students - at schools, churches, government departments and companies, who grant me the privilege to teach them by accommodating me with some of their valuable time.

Thank you to all my faithful relatives and friends who have rallied behind me in support of the promotion of this book.

Thank you to you - the reader who has invested both money and time to learn what is contained within the pages of this book.

Contents

Foreword

I have known the Heldzinger family since the 1980s, and I can attest to the fact that Glisson was raised in a God-fearing, Christian home. He is the eldest of four siblings.

Glisson is a thinker and someone who is of a sound mind. He is an asset to the broader body of Christ. He is a righteous, upright and humble man of character and integrity.
Whenever Glisson ministers, lectures, teaches or co-ordinates workshops, he encourages, inspires and brings out the value in people. We thank God daily for a man who loves to serve the broader body of our Lord and Saviour, Jesus Christ with his gifts, talents and abilities.

I have had the privilege to personally work with Glisson on numerous kingdom and spiritual projects and programs within our communities and the broader church, and it has been a blessing and pleasure to work alongside him. We have also worked closely together in the South African Christian Ministers Network and the Faith For Quality Education Program to ensure that prayer returns to all schools. We worked together to bring about the transformation of our communities where thousands of young men and women were caught up in drug and alcohol abuse.
We worked tirelessly on mass evangelism and revival within our local churches.

The author has put his thoughts on paper and has written this outstanding, must-read, must-apply workbook for the benefit of your personal life. This book is very thought-provoking and easy to read. I guarantee that it will move all readers to do more in God's kingdom and the nation.

I strongly recommend that all leaders, and people who are aspiring leaders, read YOU ARE VALUABLE with great urgency.
I want to encourage you to sit down and ponder after every chapter you have read and to look inward so that you can begin to see and bring out your own value and the great value in other people.

In the bible we read: 'As a man thinketh in his heart, so is he,' and in another place we read: 'Where there is no vision, people perish.' *(It is important that people learn the knowledge and thought-patterns that will make them see themselves as valuable.)*
With these verses in mind, I suggest that YOU ARE VALUABLE must be read by all generations – share it with your children and grandchildren so that they may know that they are valuable.

I believe that every reader will realise how valuable they are and that this book will inspire and bring out the untapped value in you and others who read it. I know that this book will make an enormous impact and contribution to the life of everyone who reads it.
My friends, as you read this well-scripted manual, may the Lord resurrect and raise you up in every area of your life, in the name of Jesus. May the Lord bless and prosper you as you read this wonderful book.

Yours in kingdom service
Bishop Marcus R. Jacobs - *December 2015*
President – SACMIN
(South African Christian Ministers Network)
President – GWM
(Global Word Ministers)

Forethought

A writer is a wordsmith and his tools are governed by the laws of communication. His raw materials are random words which he must assemble in a new and interesting way. The challenge of authorship is to find just the right words to convey the right message. That message must be original, relevant and useful.

Regarding originality - I believe that most of what has been presented in this book has been presented in a new way. The arrangements of the words are new, but I have leaned on the thoughtful quotes of wise men and women who have stated what I wanted to state but in a more eloquent manner. One such quote was made by Samuel Johnson, the English writer.

Mr. Johnson said: "A man will turn over half a library to make one book."

This is true. We turn over books so that we can marinade our minds with the thoughts of great men and women, and then form new thoughts of our own. Eventually some of us decide to make a book, and we find ourselves referring to the quotes, expressions and maxims that have shaped our thinking.

Regarding relevance - I believe that the message contained within the pages of this book is one that is in-season because billions of people everywhere are living below their potential, since they have a diminished view of their own value.

Regarding usefulness – it was Benjamin Franklin who once said: "Either write something worth reading or do something worth writing."

When I began writing this book, I endeavoured to write something worth reading, as Benjamin Franklin advised. The challenge related to the authoring of this book has been interestingly ironical, because my message concerning the value of the individual must be a message that is of value to the individual.

Thus, I have spent thousands of hours in research and reading to present a message that is truly of value to people. It is my mission to awake the 'INNER WINNER' inside of people, and this book is an extension of that mission.

I trust that you will be enlightened as you read through its pages, and that your life will be positively impacted by it. However, in order to gain the maximum benefit from its contents, I recommend that it should not just be read one-time, but instead it should be used as a manual to refer to often.

As you read, please be aware that any reference made to 'him,' unless the context states otherwise, is meant to apply to the male and female gender. This has been used as a convention to make writing, and reading, easier and I hope that no-one will be offended by its use. In addition, I have tried to find a balance between British and American English, especially with regards to spelling, but I have in some cases chosen one over the other in order to avoid long explanations in each vernacular.

I commend you for taking up this book in order to read it, because it is an indication that you want to improve yourself. I pray a blessing upon you for life's journey, and although we may not have met and we might never meet, I thank you for permitting me to communicate with you through this book.

I hope that your search for greater value and effectiveness will be well-rewarded.

Awaken your INNER WINNER!

Release your brilliance!

Introduction

Recently, on a cold winter night, I went on a midnight tour of the inner city streets of Johannesburg with the Department of Health. We were accompanying health officials to distribute blankets to the homeless and inform them about shelters that are available to help them with accommodation and food.

I remember that I was feeling very cold despite being warmly dressed. Many homeless people die due to hypothermia in winter – they freeze to death, hence the reason for the distribution of blankets.

I came across Tony[1], a young man who was sleeping on and under cardboard boxes despite the severe cold. As we spoke, and I enquired about his circumstances, a few disturbing facts concerning this young man came to the fore. I had been under the impression that he came from another province, and was unable to find gainful employment, but I was wrong.

Soweto is the biggest black township in Johannesburg, South Africa. Most commuters in Soweto make use of minibus taxis for transportation. This young man did not grow up in another province, neither was his family in another province. He was raised in Soweto and the rest of his family was still in Soweto. He could easily get to his parent's home in less than 30 minutes in a minibus taxi. The cost of the taxi was less than R20, which is about $1.50 at the current R/$ exchange rate (2015).

According to Tony, earning this amount of money was no problem for him. On the streets, they **gereza**. Gereza, (pronounced *geh-reh-zah)* is a slang word meaning '*to hustle and sell; to make a way and a plan; to persuade someone to buy something.'* He easily earned about R100 on a good day, he claimed. He would pack all his belongings together in the morning when he awakes, and then he would *gereza* all day, while carrying his belongings with him. At sunset he would return to the place where he sleeps. His bed was a concrete slab next to a building in downtown Johannesburg.

---

[1] Not his real name

Tony was about 23 years of age. Heated conflict with his parents made him leave his home willingly. He said that his father always beat him and treated him abusively. He couldn't live with the abuse any more. He left his home to live on the streets, and hustled every day for something to eat. He had lived on the streets for about two years already. I asked him if he wanted to go back home, and he replied that he did. He would have to forgive and forget in order to go back home, I added. After giving him a blanket, directing him to a shelter and praying with him I had to leave. We were transported by a bus, and my transport almost left without me because I was chatting with this young man for a long time.

I never saw Tony again, and I don't know if he made it to the shelter or back home to his parents.

However, this I do know – this young man's story is one of low esteem and also low self-esteem. Low esteem stems from the fact that his family did not value him and treat him as valuable. If his family esteemed him a little more, he would not have felt the urge to move out.

Low self-esteem stems from the fact that he did not see and treat himself as valuable. If he had esteemed himself a little more, he would not have embraced and accepted the circumstances and standard of living which he found himself in.

A few weeks later I experienced a great deal of unfair treatment and verbal abuse by some people. My own personal experience, coupled with Tony's story brought me to the realization that nobody is immune to abuse by others. I also realized that nobody is immune to self-abuse.

As I began to ponder this encounter with Tony along with my own experiences, I began to study the impact of esteem and self-esteem on an individual's life. I discovered that volumes have been written about the subject. Philosophers and even authors of biblical books wrote about the subject. I concluded that if esteem and self-esteem are discussed in the bible, then it must be important.

I began to realise that in some way, all of us are Tony. Proverbially speaking each one of us has lost our way, and in losing our way, we've lost ourselves.

We all sleep on proverbial concrete floors at some point in our lives. In seeking solutions to our problems, we find ourselves facing worse problems. We run from one tough situation into another. We run and fall on concrete slabs. We make our bed in a place that is not our home. We settle for less – less than we are worth and less than we deserve.

We all gereza in some way, to survive and get by with what we have – we are all trying to make the best of a bad situation.

We all sometimes turn our backs on a better way, and the hurts of the past make us deny ourselves better opportunities. There is always a better way, but we don't know about it and if we do know, we don't take it.

Although we are not all living on the street, we all have been devalued by other people, whether they are relatives or friends. We all have been abused in some way and ostracized.

In addition, we all have devalued ourselves in some way, just like Tony. We abuse ourselves when we place ourselves in harm's way and when we live below our abilities. All of us have at some point lived below our potential and accepted conditions that are potentially dangerous. We also live below our potential when we accept circumstances that are not a true reflection of what we are capable of doing and achieving. We all live below our true value. We have all devalued ourselves.

We all have been devalued by other people.
We have all devalued ourselves.

These are the core focus-areas of this book.

This book was written to awaken people to their own worth and the worth of others. Life is an exercise in inter-dependence. Independence is about wanting to prove that you can stand on your own two feet without the help of others. Inter-dependence is about working hand-in-hand with others because we are more effective with the help of others.

Dr. Stephen Covey wrote that inter-dependence is a higher value than independence. If we aspire to realise our goals, we must then pursue inter-dependence. To this end, one must be keenly aware of one's own value, but simultaneously also be aware of the value of others.

I was born in Johannesburg, South Africa. South Africa is well-known for the racist legislation, known as *Apartheid*, which was in force during the latter half of the twentieth century.

Dr. H. F. Verwoerd, who is widely regarded as the architect of Apartheid, once described Apartheid as a "policy of good neighbourliness."

Apartheid laws were meant to cement the ideology of white (people of European ancestry) supremacy, whilst simultaneously suppressing non-white people. Apartheid was a set of laws which guaranteed the best jobs for minority whites. This system prevented and outlawed inter-marriage between whites and non-whites.

It imposed movement restrictions on black people through the Pass System. The Pass System was an internal passport system which forced black South Africans to carry valid documentation all the time. The pass laws were intended to control urbanization, movement and migrant labour.

Apartheid legislation gave police officers carte blanche to interrogate, by the most brutal means, anyone who was suspected of treason or opposing Apartheid and the white government. Some men were tortured until they died. On several separate occasions many black people, who were marching for freedom, were mowed down with gunfire from police officers.

Apartheid represented anything but *good neighbourliness*.

Apartheid was an abusive system that placed people on different planes of value. The colour of your skin determined the level of respect and esteem that you would engender. In this sense, Apartheid created a sense of unbalanced value where people are concerned.

Fortunately, Apartheid legislation is a thing of the past. It has been removed from the law books and relegated to the history books. People who were once unequal under the law have now become equal under new law. Enemies have become friends.

My country's dark past bares testament to the terrible consequences that flow from not seeing all people as being of equal value. However, when the winds of change blew strong, it has shown that a dark past can be illuminated with the light of hope so that through co-operation, people from diverse backgrounds and ethnic groups can, and should, work together for the common good of all. South Africa has shown the world that people from diverse backgrounds can and should be seen as being equally valuable. It was more than a mere political triumph when millions of people from diverse ethnic and cultural backgrounds voted into power South Africa's first truly democratically elected government. It was also a triumph of human spirits whereby diverse people were able to embrace each other, literally and figuratively, and recognize the value in others as if for the first time. So profound was this transition, that the first black president of South Africa, the world-famous, late Nelson Mandela, unofficially rechristened South Africa ***The Rainbow Nation***. Even after Mr. Mandela's passing, people in South Africa still refer to themselves as 'The Rainbow Nation' in recognition of the diversities of skin colours, ethnicities, ideologies, cultures and religions that make up the populace of this great nation – almost like the many different colours that abide side-by-side in tranquillity and yet they harmoniously make up a perfect rainbow which comes after the storm and which lies high in the sky for all to observe, appreciate and value as they look on its beauty.

There is only hope when we embrace the characteristics of others – especially if they are in contrast to our own, and work together peacefully for everyone's benefit – our own benefit, the benefit of our families and also of our nation. There is only hope when we value others.

YOU ARE VALUABLE awakens people to their true value.

> **There is only hope when we embrace the characteristics of others – especially if they are in contrast to our own, and work together peacefully for everyone's benefit – our own benefit, the benefit of our families and also of our nation.**
> **There is only hope when we value others.**

People have a *grass is greener on the other side mentality.* People are chronically dissatisfied and they believe that two things will make them happier. Those things are:

- having more of something, or
- having something else instead.

There are those who hope for more in order to solve their problems and be happier. They want more money to solve their financial problems. They want more material goods to feel successful. They want to be loved more so that they can feel worthy. They want to be more understood so that they can feel validated. They want more recognition so that their efforts do not go unnoticed.

There are those who want something different to what they have. Some want to change their spouse because they believe that someone else will be better. Some want to change their jobs so that they can be rid of their difficult boss. Some want to change their body and face so that they can be more attractive.

However, we need to realize that success does not lie in acquiring what you do not have, whether it be a greater amount of what you have available or something different. True success comes from using what you have available right now. Only when you identify and leverage what you already have, can you be more effective and successful.

We maximize success when we maximise our existing resources.

Resources are both internal and external. Internal resources are cognitive and spiritual abilities and physical activity.

Zig Ziglar once wrote: 'Success is the maximum utilization of the ability that you have.'

External resources are finances, tools, capital goods and other people.

King Solomon advised us that two are better than one, and that we should wage our wars by wise counsel. The waging of war is a metaphor for all the difficulties we must overcome as we progress towards fulfilling our goals.

We can only maximize resources that are within our power to use, and we can only exercise the powers of which we are aware.

The real key to success is knowing what you can do – what powers you have – and then using those powers to get what you want. In this sense, people are never really empowered – they are only made aware of their intrinsic powers. Change comes when they employ those powers.

When you read YOU ARE VALUABLE, you will be made aware of your intrinsic powers as you are taken on a how-to journey which reveals to you the great potency at your disposal and then you are shown how to put those powers to use for greater success and happiness. When you know and use all your powers, you will achieve phenomenal success. You will also learn to forge healthy and beneficial relationships by seeing the potential in others, and then capitalizing on that potential too.

YOU ARE VALUABLE

Each of us lives as a pauper in some way,
Untrue things about ourselves we sometimes say.
Everyone, at some time, sells themself short -
Because of incorrect things they have thought.
We have departed from home, where we belong –
From a place where we are happy and strong.
Each of us makes a bed on the street –
Religiously believing our own self-deceit.
We all have pushed away family and friends –
The relationships that to a man value lends.
"I don't need people," we often say –
But it is only ourselves we betray.
Every man is a mere fraction of what he could be –
What he is and can be, he does not really see.
He has accepted a diminished value of himself –
And has placed his worth on the discount shelf.
Lay aside the pain of every emotional scar –
Come home and be the winner that you are!
Rebuild the relationships damaged by what was said –
Come home and sleep in a winner's bed.
Awaken to the knowledge of the real you;
You deserve the best – you have great value!

Glisson J. Heldzinger

Chapter 1

Creating Greater Value

All philosophy lies in two words, sustain and abstain.
Epictetus

Life's Perplexing Questions

Have you ever thought that you should be further ahead in life than you are right now, but you don't know what it is that's keeping you back?
Do you sometimes dream of achieving something amazing, then your mind tells you that it's impossible, and that you do not have what it takes?
Have you ever asked yourself why some people succeed, and others don't ... why some people have phenomenal success and others barely get by?
Why does one woman file for a divorce from her husband and another actively seeks to be reconciled to her husband?
Why does one student devote hours to his studies and another plays games with his friends all day?
Why does a smoker die of a heart-attack at age 50 and the health-fanatic lives to age 90?
Why does the old guy at the company get overlooked by management for a promotion and the new guy is promoted several times in one year?
Why do some people acquire exceptional levels of wealth and others depend on a meagre government pension?
If these questions have crossed your mind ...
YOU'RE NOT ALONE!
People everywhere are desperately searching for the answers to these questions. The answer is this –

PEOPLE CHASE AND PURSUE ONLY THOSE THINGS THAT BRING FULFILMENT AND JOY TO THEM.

In this sense it can be said that people only build on and pursue those things on which they put a high premium – they pursue the things and relationships that are of value.

So then, the answer for all the above questions is exactly the same ... the answer is VALUE!

People only build on and pursue those things on which they put a high premium - so then, the answer for all the above questions is exactly the same ... the answer is VALUE!

People do not have phenomenal success because they have a diminished view of their own intrinsic value and what they are capable of doing, so they will not build on their dreams, and they will also not pursue anything that holds no great value for them.

Creating Greater Value

Everywhere and everyday people face problems, firstly on a personal level and secondly, on an organizational level. People are searching frantically for solutions to their problems.

As we begin to search for solutions to problems, we must begin at the root of the problem, using what is generally called Root-Cause Analysis. This process aims to identify the symptoms of a problem, and then identifies what the most likely causes of the symptoms are.

The Roman philosopher Epictetus once said that all philosophy lies in two words: "sustain and abstain."

It simply means that wise living entails keeping up certain activities whilst simultaneously discarding others. But how do we know what we must abstain from and what we must sustain? We begin by making a careful study of our behaviour patterns. This first step is a vital prerequisite if we are to uncover the underlying causes of our failures, our sadness, our unhappiness and distress. We look at what we have been doing up to now. When we look at what we've been doing, we can then, through analysis, determine what behaviour patterns have been working for us and which ones have not. In other words, we identify which activities are valuable and which are not.

It is here where we discover what is to be *sustain*ed and what must be *abstain*ed from.

It gives us a clear indication of what must be changed. However, willing change must be accompanied by a willingness to change. This means that we must embrace the need for change. It also means that we must be prepared to accept the necessity for change and then implement the necessary changes. Thus the first step is acceptance, and then the second step is transformation.

> **Willing change must be accompanied by a willingness to change.**
>
> **We must be prepared to accept the necessity for change and then implement the necessary changes.**

As we identify and earmark processes, positions, habits and resources which need to be kept, chopped and changed we must remember three important caveats, namely:

- "If it ain't broke, don't fix it."
- "Let it go."
- "Accept the things which cannot be changed."

Firstly, we must know what does not need changing. The late US President, John F. Kennedy once related a lesson which his father taught him, and it was this: "If it is not necessary to change, it is necessary not to change."
This advice holds true on an individual level as well as on an organizational level – it is imperative that we keep what should not be changed, regardless of the arena.
Secondly, we must also be willingly to let go of what needs to be changed, especially if we have a strong emotional bond related to this aspect of our lives – whether it be a relationship, an original creation, a project you have birthed and nurtured, an object you love, a position you love etc. Learning to let go is vital for change.
Thirdly, we will find that there are the things that we desire to change, but it is outside of our abilities and/or resources to do so. In this case we must accept this reality and move on.
But why do we go to such great lengths to bring about change?

As we implement change through keeping, letting go and accepting, we must have a very clear purpose in mind. The end of all change is to make something better of ourselves, our organizations and the world that we live in. The end is to leave a better place for our children and to ensure that future generations are better off.

> **Our purposes, when we implement changes are:**
> **to make ourselves more valuable,**
> **to make our organizations more valuable,**
> **to make our world more valuable, and**
> **to leave greater value for future generations.**

Our overall purpose is to create greater value. But, we've encountered this word 'value' before – it was used to identify the worth that is attached to ourselves and others, when I wrote about what must be sustained and what must be abstained from.

> **Our overall purpose is to create greater value.**

Identifying what must be kept, is really identifying what is valuable. Identifying what must be chopped is identifying what is not valuable. Thus we leverage existing value to create greater value – this is the premise of this book.

> **We leverage existing value to create greater value.**

In this book we study the process of identifying the existing value that you have within yourself and also the value that is contained in your relationships – people with whom you interact regularly such as relatives, friends and colleagues. I have discovered three important truths concerning the study of value of the individual and of a group, and they are *perception*, *identification* and *utilization*.

Perception relates to awareness. Most people are not aware of the abilities and resources that they have at their disposal. The truth related to perception is that people are not aware of the great value attached to themselves and others – people are ignorant of the value that they and others possess.

Identification relates to the recognition, naming and separation of resources. Identification can be best described as the discovery of hidden talents, abilities and resources. It is the investigative process that identifies exactly what we have that is valuable within ourselves and others. The truth I have discovered, concerning identification, is that people do not know how to identify the skills and resources, which are linked to themselves and others, and which can be of practical use.

Utilization refers to putting the value that we have identified within ourselves and others to use. When we employ resources that were once unknown, unused or under-utilized then we can create greater value at considerably less cost to ourselves. This refers to leverage. Leverage is nothing more than the ability to do more with less. The truth concerning utilization is that people do not know how to apply the resources, attached to themselves and others, so that maximum effectiveness can be attained with minimum resources.

We attain great success when we are able to use what we already have in order to attain what we do not yet have. We must capitalize on the value of what we already have in order to create the greater value of what we do not already have.

**We attain great success when we are able to use what we already have in order to attain what we do not yet have.
We must capitalize on the value of what we already have in order to create the greater value of what we do not already have.**

People do not know who they really are ...

People do not know who they really are ...
Because they do not know who they are –
For themselves they set a very low bar.
They do not know their own potentiality.
They do not know their own responsibility.
They do not know what they could be doing.
They do not know what they should be doing.

They walk around with a veil over their eyes,
And each his true self and identity denies.

Each man is just a fraction of what he could be.
They have all become like a little bonsai tree.
Being trimmed by opinions, they remain so small,
Never knowing that they're meant to be tall.

Words and actions of others trim them every day,
And the things about themselves that they say.
Memories of failures past keep them back,
When they start something, eventually they slack.

They have accepted this is how things should be,
They embrace that they're just a bonsai tree.
Their real nature has from them been hidden,
To live up to their true nature seems forbidden.
What a man really is has been concealed,
Every man to his own self must be revealed.

To his true identity and value every man must awake,
Then in God's universe his rightful place he may take.

Glisson J. Heldzinger

Chapter 2

The Beginning And End Of Fulfilment

> **How we value ourselves is the beginning and the end of all achievement and fulfilment.**

How We See Ourselves

> **Most men lead lives of quiet desperation and go to the grave with the song still in them.**
> *Henry David Thoreau*

Every man and woman starts out in life with big dreams and aspirations. They have lofty and romantic ideas and visions, but as time passes they abandon their pursuits. They give up. They trade in their hopes and dreams for something that is more easily achievable or for something that just falls onto their laps because they begin to believe that they cannot achieve their dreams. For many people these dreams and hopes become more and more distant as they grow older, and eventually they breathe their last breath without having achieved that dream which they once held so dear, and which once held them. Henry David Thoreau described this as a state of desperation and continued to say that these desperate men 'go to the grave with the song still in them.' The song is a metaphor for every unfulfilled dream that a man may have had. This beckons the question:

Why are most men desperate and then ultimately die with unfulfilled dreams?

The answer is simple - most men are desperate because they possess dreams, but they do not truly belief that they can accomplish those dreams. They do not possess belief that equals their dreams and so they fail to take action on their dreams or any action taken is not sustained until the dream is achieved. What they are actually acting out is the belief that they are not capable of achieving and having the things which they desire. They really do not believe that they possess the knowledge, skill, talent, tenacity, and resources to build their dreams. They don't have belief, but more importantly, they don't have much self-belief. At the very core of low self-belief is the information that they have received and believed.

> **We are shaped by what we have received and believed.**

Throughout their lives they have been discounted by the words and actions of others. By sub-consciously, and even consciously sometimes, accepting the biased opinions of others, people are indoctrinated to believe that they are not valuable.
When people have a positive self-value their confidence goes up, and when confidence goes up achievement goes up, and when achievement goes up fulfilment, joy and peace go up. It is here where we discover the timeless truth about the direct relationship between how we see ourselves and what we see ourselves being able to achieve. Self-value is linked to fulfilment.

> **There is a direct relationship between how we see ourselves and what we see ourselves being able to achieve.**

When an individual has high self-value then fulfilment goes up, but then miraculously the individual's self-value goes up too. Thus self-value not only influences achievement and fulfilment but it is also influenced by achievement and fulfilment. As one goes up, so does the other.

> **Self-value not only influences achievement, it is also influenced by it.**

So the end brings us back to the beginning and the beginning brings us to the end. If you have high self-value then you will achieve the blissful end of fulfilled dreams and desires, and when your desires and dreams are fulfilled then your self-value increases and the start is then influenced by the end. We then see that how we value ourselves is the beginning and end of all achievement and fulfilment.

How we value ourselves is the beginning and the end of all achievement and fulfilment.

The contents of this book will help people re-align with accurate images of themselves and thereby elevate their level of self-value. When someone's self-value goes up, their confidence goes up. They automatically forge new relationships easier and maintain lasting and fulfilling relationships. Increased self-value nudges people to pursue new dreams without the debilitating effects of self-doubt. A man with increased self-value actively and diligently judges the actions and opinions of others to see if they are in alignment with how he truly sees himself. Such a man would dismiss those opinions which break down his self-value but will still assess if there exists room for improvement within himself. A man with high self-value bases his personal worth on intrinsic factors and not on extrinsic factors. Such a man carries the knowledge of his value with him and is not influenced by the factors which easily cripple the value of people. His self-worth lies deep inside of him ... within his very core. This core is unshakeable and strong. He nurtures this core with positive affirmations and feeds it with positive and inspiring information. A man of high self-value is secure in the knowledge that he can take on new challenges, and even if things do not work out as planned, he is still confident of his ability to adjust and change as the environment requires. Thus, it is his unchanging core that permits him to face his changing circumstances.

It is a man's unchanging core that permits him to face his changing circumstances.

The man who has a high self-worth understands that he is not defined by his environment, but rather that he defines his environment. A man of high self-worth understands that the seeds of greatness are nurtured by the fruitful soil of high self-value and high self-confidence. His confidence lies not in the prospect that he will never fail, but that he has the ability to get up and continue moving on despite setbacks and unplanned blockages in his path. His confidence lies in his inner strength and in the knowledge that he knows what he wants and will stop at nothing to get it.

Thus, the measure of a man's success in any area of endeavour is largely based on how good he feels about himself.

> **The measure of a man's success rises and falls on the criteria by which he measures himself.**

The criteria by which a man measures himself will affect his self-worth. For example if you value yourself according to the
opinions of other people, your self-worth will always be at the mercy of people's fickle notions. It then follows that if an individual endeavours to have high self-worth, then he must have a good opinion of himself, and he must also associate with people who generally have good feelings and opinions towards him. This can be summarized as having good relationships with oneself and with others.
There are two primary needs which an individual requires to be met in order to have healthy relationships with himself and others, and to feel whole and complete. Those needs are:

1. **rendition, and**
2. **recognition.**

Let us look at rendition and recognition more closely.

1. Rendition

> **Low self-esteem is like driving through life with your handbrake on.**
> *Maxwell Maltz*

Self-image is how you see yourself. It is a picture that the individual holds of himself.
Self-esteem is how you value yourself, based in your self-image. Self-esteem is the measure of how good or bad an individual sees himself and feels about himself. It was Maxwell Maltz who said: "Low self-esteem is like driving through life with your handbrake on."
If this is what low self-esteem is like, then high self-esteem must be like driving through life with your handbrake down and your foot firmly on the accelerator with the engine

burning high-octane fuel and propelling you through life at breath-taking speeds.

If you have a good self-image then you will have a positive self-esteem.

While self-image is the definition of self and the answer to the question: "Who am I?" self-esteem is the value of self. Self-esteem is also the individual's interpretation of his relative value. Relative value is the comparison of one's own perceived value to that of others with whom we interact.

As was previously mentioned, there exists a direct correlation between an individual's success and their self-value. Self-value and self-esteem are synonymous terms. The higher a person's self-esteem, the greater their level of achievement and the more successful they are at forging and maintaining healthy inter-personal relationships.

People can only behave in a manner that is indicative and reflective of their self-image and self-esteem. In the performing arts, rendition is the interpretation of a dramatic role or piece of music. Rendition is acting. For the purpose of this text, I suggest that rendition is the way that people act because of how they see and value themselves. How you present yourself is always a reflection of how you perceive yourself. Rendition is the behaviour that stems from your self-image and self-esteem. It is impossible for an individual to achieve anything significant without a positive rendition. Positive rendition is a critical component for success.

> **Rendition is the way that people act because of how they see and value themselves. Rendition is the behaviour the stems from your self-image and self-esteem.**

People with very low self-esteem tend to be less successful at building strong inter-personal relationships and achieving their personal goals. Negative rendition can only produce negative results.

> **Whether your rendition or personal sense of value is low or high, your achievement follows the same direction.**

2. Recognition

> **No man is an island.**
> *Thomas Merton*

A child is born into the world because of the intimacy between two people. That child is then nurtured and raised in a family environment. As the child grows, he will develop new friendships in addition to his existing relationships with relatives. In adulthood that child will then seek out a life partner and they will begin the process all over again. That small baby then knows intuitively that it needs its parents, especially its mother. It knows that it needs a relationship with its mother. As the child grows, he will eventually develop an independence from his parents and avoid the type of intimacy that was once shared with his parents in pursuit of new relationships with other people. One of the major reasons, but certainly not the only reason, people marry is that they do not want to grow old alone. Furthermore, most people claim that they want to be surrounded by their loved ones when they die.
We are thus born into relationships because of the intimate relationship of our parents, and throughout our lives we crave relationships, with varying degrees of intimacy, with different people. We crave these relationships throughout our lives right up to the very end.
Humans are thus by nature, intuitively social creatures. It is our social nature that drives us to forge meaningful relationships with other people, because our very existence is justified by the social structures that we belong to. We are justified and defined by our family and friendship circles. The people with whom we are connected to in our social circles are the ones who qualify our existence and define our value.

> **The people with whom we are connected to in our social circles are the ones who qualify our existence and define our value.**

They qualify our existence because ultimately we live for others and not for ourselves, and so they provide a definition for our lives from a social perspective. They provide us with the "why" of our existence.

They define our value because we see ourselves through the collective eyes of others, and so they provide us with the value that we have of ourselves. They provide us with the "what" of our existence.

We know intuitively that we are defined by our associations and affiliations. We feel a sense of happiness and fulfilment when we are in meaningful relationships with those individuals and groups we desire to be with, because we feel accepted. However, we feel rejected and worthless when we are ostracised by the ones we care about. What we really need is recognition from others. We want recognition from others to whom we render recognition. Thus, this is a reciprocal recognition because we want to be recognized by those individuals and groups who we regard as being valuable. However, recognition is not sought for recognition's sake only. The ultimate desire of recognition is to be publicly acknowledged and also be accepted for who we are. This type of recognition is a very basic human need.

> **Being recognized, acknowledged and accepted are basic human needs.**

On 23 December 1888, Vincent Van Gogh sliced off a portion of his ear after he discovered that his friend, Paul Gauguin, was about to leave Arles and abandon him. Van Gogh held Gauguin in high esteem and craved the recognition that his counterpart had been receiving from art collectors.

Whilst recovering from his self-inflicted wound, Van Gogh repeatedly asked for Gauguin but the latter refused to visit Van Gogh. On 27 July 1890, at the age of 37, Van Gogh shot himself in the chest. He was treated for the wound, and although he initially appeared to recover, he succumbed to his wound about 29 hours after shooting himself. According to Theo Van Gogh, his brother, Vincent Van Gogh's last words were "The sadness will not end."

Indeed it is sad when a man of considerable talent is not recognized in his lifetime. Although some of Van Gogh's paintings are now worth of millions of dollars, I believe that if the troubled artist had received this form of recognition and value for his work during his lifetime that he would have had a great reason to hold onto life.

People also want to be acknowledged for who they are and what they do. When others acknowledge our existence and our efforts and achievements, we begin to feel that our efforts carry some weight and that we have not moved from birth to death without having left some sort of memorable impression in the minds and hearts of others. This desired acknowledgement is usually tacit ... it is implied. It is not the type of acknowledgement that is as bold as an award ceremony (although many people love and crave this sort of public acknowledgement), but rather it is displayed by the manner in which we are treated by others. When others care about our health, our circumstances, our safety, our family and all the things which are important to us, they subtly acknowledge us.
Just beyond acknowledgement lies acceptance. Just as no man is an island, according to Thomas Merton, no man is exactly the same as another. We all have differences. We want to be accepted for our differences whether they are based on ethnicity, gender, appearance, talents, social standing and religion. Regardless of our differences to others, we desire to be part of the crowd ... one of the guys (or girls) ... part of the pack.
The ultimate end of being accepted is value. When others accept us for who we are, we feel a tremendous sense of value and self-worth. We also feel whole and complete.

The ultimate end of being accepted is value. When others accept us for who we are, we feel a tremendous sense of value and self-worth. We also feel whole and complete.

King Solomon once wrote: 'What a person desires is unfailing love.' [i]
In this text from the Holy Bible, King Solomon expressed the idea that every single person desires to be loved. To be loved means to be ***valued*** and ***accepted***.
We can thus restate King Solomon's wise proverb as follows:

What every person desires is to be valued.

YOU ARE VALUABLE

King Solomon considered being valued by others of such extreme importance that he also wrote: 'Being held in high esteem is better than silver or gold.' [ii]
Esteem is simply another word for ***value***, thus we can rephrase this text as follows:

> **Being held in high value is better than silver or gold.**

In the final analysis, to be valued for who you are and what you do, is better and of far greater worth and benefit than any riches that you may procure. Your value, which is way above material possessions, hinges on your associations – the people you spend time with and dedicate your time to.

> **In the final analysis, to be valued for who you are and what you do, is better and of far greater worth and benefit than any riches that you may procure. Your value, which is way above material possessions, hinges on your associations – the people you spend time with and dedicate your time to.**

Since we are established or demolished through the eyes of others, we should be careful who we associate with and what relationships we build.

Let us then begin by looking at the three distinct categories of relationships which will have an influence on your self-value.

Every human being's self-value will be influenced by:
1. how others see them,
2. how God sees them, and
3. how they see themselves.

The relationships that we have with other people, with God and with ourselves will have an influence on how we value ourselves.

> **The relationships that we have with other people, with God and with ourselves will have an influence on how we value ourselves.**

You may consider it obvious that we have relationships with other people and with God, but may find it obscure that your relationship with yourself is included in the list. This is not a typographic error or an editorial oversight. Your relationship with yourself or, stated differently, how you relate to yourself is just as important as how others relate to you when it comes to shaping your self-value. This is the relationship category which covers your rendition. The relationship that we have with other people and with God covers our recognition.

These three categories of human relationships are the basis for the format of this book.

In the chapters contained herein we will investigate the dynamics of these relationship categories and I will provide some insights and suggestions on how you can improve your self-image and your perceived self-worth. Since there is room for improvement in every individual's life, whether you consider yourself successful or not, you will benefit from the contents of this book.

King Solomon wrote: 'Above all else, guard your heart, for everything you do flows from it.' [iii]

> **Above all else, guard your heart,**
> **for everything you do flows from it.**
> *King Solomon*

Another translation of this text reads as follows: 'Keep your heart with all diligence, for out of it spring the issues of life.' [iv]

The word ***'heart'*** in this proverb does not refer to your literal heart which pumps and circulates blood in your body, but instead it refers to your mind, which is the seat of your thoughts and emotions. Thus, King Solomon was advising us to be vigilant and careful about the thoughts and feelings that we permit to occupy our minds. This proverb from the wise king is a reminder that we should be careful about the thoughts we think and also the things we desire because

they lead to the problems we face and the problems we avoid – they also lead to the failures we must endure and the successes we enjoy.
The contents of this book have been collated and presented in a manner that is intended to change some of the contents of your thoughts so that the issues of life that spring from them will be more rewarding and satisfying.

If you have been experiencing failure, you can begin to chart and follow a new course of success by following the suggestions in this book.

If you consider yourself to be successful already, you too will benefit from this book and place yourself on a higher trajectory of success by growing in the areas of relationship-building and self-confidence because even successful people sometimes feel lost, worthless and forgotten. Even successful people can reach higher and be more successful.

I hope that this book will be the beginning of an exciting new journey of self-discovery and that it will ignite a positive self-appraisal within you because **YOU ARE VALUABLE!**

Chapter 3

People In Our Lives

> **The greatest good you can do for another is not just to share your riches but to reveal to him his own.**
> *Benjamin Disraeli*

Our Lives Revolve Around Relationships

We feel happy and fulfilled when we are accepted by others. On the flip-side, our lives carry no real significance if we are ostracised and shut out by other people.
Inter-action with others is essential for normal human functioning. We go insane without other people around us. We live *for* and *because of* other people.
In addition, it is not normal for an individual to isolate himself deliberately from the company of other people. King Solomon wrote that a man who isolates himself rages against all wisdom.[v]

We live for and because of other people.

The mother delights in being able to nurture and care for her baby. She experiences great joy in feeding, cleaning and communicating with her child. Her womanhood is confirmed through her ability to conceive and deliver a child and her motherhood is confirmed through the deep love and care that she expresses for her child. In the book of I Samuel in the bible we read about Hannah, the barren woman who craved to have a child and she petitioned Yahweh on many occasions to bless her and her husband with a child. She desired to love and care for her own child.[vi]
Every virtuous woman will make tremendous sacrifices for her husband, her children and people who work for her. In the biblical book of Proverbs, King Lemuel wrote that a woman of virtue gets up early to feed her family and her maidservants.[vii] A virtuous woman lives for and loves others.

A virtuous woman lives for and loves others.

A husband and father willingly goes to work to provide for his family. King Solomon wrote that a man's mouth compels him to work[viii] and that a Godly man provides an inheritance for his children's children.[ix] His desire to care for and feed his family, and himself will let him wake up in the morning, go to work in traffic, put in a full day's labour, and then go home and still attend a school parents meeting at night. His actions are sparked by a deep inner desire to see his family being healthy, happy and safe. He works to provide the best education for his children. He lives for his family.

A husband and father lives for his family.

A man associates with friends who like similar things as he does. They enjoy watching sports together and having a meal together. They share in the joys of each other's achievements and also in carrying each other's burdens. King Solomon wrote that a friend loves at all times and a brother is near for adversity.[x]

A friend is near for adversity.

The business person understands that the doors of his business are kept open by traffic ... the feet of customers. Without the patronage of customers a business cannot survive and thrive. In the biblical book of Proverbs, King Lemuel's mother instructs him that a good wife manufactures and supplies clothing to merchants.[xi] The supplier and the merchant are in a relationship for the mutual financial benefit of both parties. Our economic survival depends on relationships with other people and organizations.

Our economic survival depends on relationships with other people.

We need people in our lives to guide us in our thinking and mould our character. King Solomon wrote that a child should not forsake the teaching of his parents, but should adorn himself with these teachings as if it was precious jewellery.[xii] We also need mentors in our lives to counsel us and advise us to make right and appropriate choices. We need to consult with people who have specialised knowledge and experience so that we can avoid unnecessary mistakes and accompanying headaches and heartaches. King Solomon confirmed the need for mentors in our lives when he wrote that we find safety when we have many counsellors.[xiii]

> **We need mentors and counsellors to teach and guide us for safety sake.**

When you want to build a house, you need to engage the services of a qualified builder to complete the project. When your house is completed and the plumbing is faulty, you need the services of a qualified and experienced plumber to fix the problem. We read that Moses called upon skilled artisans to build the Tabernacle and Ark of the Covenant in the desert.[xiv]
Many years later, King Solomon called upon King Hiram, who was a highly skilled artisan, to supply the masonry and carpentry materials for the Temple.[xv] We need relationships with skilled individuals to help solve the problems and challenges that we face.

> **We need relationships with skilled individuals to help solve the problems and challenges that we face.**

We need people to execute justice and equality in society. Sometimes we experience disagreements with others and this may lead to legal proceedings. In the bible we read that King Solomon had to judge when people brought their grievances before him. In one incident two women brought a baby to him with each woman claiming that the child was hers. With wisdom and skill, King Solomon quickly established who the true mother of the child was and justice was served.[xvi] King Solomon wrote that by justice a ruler gives stability to a country. [xvii]
We need people in government and fair and honourable legal practitioners to execute and expedite justice, judgement and equity.

> **We need people to execute justice and equality in society.**

We need to associate with people and groups who share the same values and some common goals with us. When we belong to clubs and various organizations such as a church or a board or a committee we can interact with like-minded people to bring about organizational goals but to also simultaneously receive strength, encouragement, acceptance and a sense of belonging. In the bible we read that Jesus visited the synagogue regularly from childhood and he learnt[xviii], read[xix] and taught in the synagogue.[xx] He interacted regularly with people at weddings, funerals, in the market and even at a well. He had a close group of friends, whom we now call the twelve disciples, who walked with him wherever he went. They ate, preached and prayed together.[xxi] Jesus and His disciples shared a common purpose, which was to preach the good news of God's love for man to the lost.

Paul the Apostle wrote that we should not neglect the gathering of the saints.[xxii] When like-minded individuals gather they can encourage, help and sustain each other. King Solomon wrote that two are better than one and a three-fold cord is not easily broken.[xxiii] He also wrote that as iron sharpens iron, so one man sharpens the countenance of his friend.[xxiv] We need to associate with individuals and groups who share a common purpose and who will sharpen us and build us up.

> **We need to associate with people and groups who share the same values and some common goals with us.**

Pierre Teilhard de Chardin once said: "We are not human beings having a spiritual experience. We are spiritual beings having a human experience."

Human beings have a spiritual aspect in their make-up. Just as we need physical food to sustain the physical aspect of our make-up, we also need spiritual food and guidance to sustain our spiritual aspect. The Apostle Paul wrote that apostles, prophets, evangelists, pastors and teachers are for the building up of the saints.[xxv] We need relationships with these people to understand spiritual matters, to pray for and with us and to build us up spiritually.

> **We need relationships with apostles, prophets, evangelists, pastors, teachers and fellow Christians to understand spiritual matters, to pray for and with us and to build us up spiritually.**

We can see clearly that God did not create human beings to live in isolation. Our very nature compels us to seek out meaningful relationships with others for the purpose of survival and fulfilment.
We instinctively pursue these relationships with individuals and groups from whom we endeavour to gain support, love, recognition, acknowledgement and acceptance. In this pursuit, throughout our lives, we will build fulfilling and disappointing relationships. We will encounter people who make us feel good and happy, but we will also meet people who disappoint and hurt us. There are those who will support us through thick and thin and others who will push us down and demean us. Whether people are good towards us or they are bad towards us, their opinions invariably affect our self-value. Other people will make or break us because we see ourselves as others see us. We therefore constantly reflect the views and opinions of those who are closest to us. This reflection is both conscious and sub-conscious. Each of us reflects the worth that others place on us. This is the **mirror effect**.

The Mirror Effect
Little Rosey was only five years old, and when she heard from her kindergarten teacher that the carnival was in town, she decided to ask her parents to take her there. When she asked her parents, they agreed that she could go the following Saturday with her dad because her mom had to work.
Little Rosey was excited about the idea of going to the carnival and she reminded her dad of his promise every day as she counted down the days to Saturday ... which she had dubbed "Carnival Day."
When Little Rosey and her dad entered the carnival, she was in awe of all that there was to see. She saw people selling different things, food stands and wild animals like lions and elephants performing tricks. Then Little Rosey saw a place

that caught her attention. It had bright, multi-coloured flashing lights around the door and strange music came from inside.
"Daddy, what is that place over there?" she asked as she pointed to the door.
"That is the House of Illusion Sweetheart," responded her dad as he read the sign above the door.
"What is a house of illusion, Daddy?" she asked curiously.
"Well Sweetheart, it's a place where you can see things that seem real but they are not. An illusion is something that is not real," he answered.
"Wow! That sounds so cool. Can we go in there please Daddy? Please can we go in there?" she asked in an excited tone.
"Sure, we can go in if you want," he answered.
They walked through the door and entered a room with mirrors. Little Rosey and her dad stood in front of one mirror, and she started laughing.
"Look Daddy, we look so tall and skinny," she said giggling. "We look so funny!" she added.
They moved onto another mirror and Little Rosey laughed louder than before.
"Daddy, see. My head looks big and funny. This is awesome," she shouted.
Little Rosey and her dad stood in front of many mirrors and she was amazed at the images that she saw.
"Daddy, I'm so glad that I don't really look like I do in these mirrors," Said Little Rosey as they walked past the last mirror.
"Why Sweetheart?" asked her dad curiously.
"These mirrors don't show the real me but when I look in my proper mirror at home, I can see the real me," she responded politely.

In the same way, many people, in a proverbial sense, are looking into mirrors that are producing distorted images. Only when people view themselves through accurate mirrors will they have an accurate picture of themselves. Those mirrors are the opinions of other people. Only when we align ourselves with accurate pictures can we hope to be successful. Thus in this sense, other people will either make or break you. They will either establish or demolish you.

Other people will either make or break you. They will either establish or demolish you.

We must then learn how to build healthier relationships with people who see us as valuable, and whom we also see as valuable. Let us then look at the seven foundational disciplines for building healthy relationships.

The Seven Foundational Disciplines for Building Healthy Relationships

1. Start every day with a clean slate

I sat in the patient's chair next to the desk in the old doctor's surgery as he warmed his hands with the heat from the electric heater. The doctor was approximately 70 years old at the time, but he was still very involved in the running of his medical practice. I was not visiting him as a patient. I was providing him with a service and we were discussing some issues related to our business. He proceeded to relate to me his travel agenda for the next few weeks. He was scheduled to travel abroad to meet, for the first time, the family of the young lady whom his son was marrying. The topic then shifted to first encounters. He proceeded to explain that he and a few learned friends meet once weekly to discuss philosophical matters. Their most recent discussion was about first encounters with strangers. It was also about subsequent encounters with people after an initial meeting. They debated a few deeply philosophical questions related to interaction with other people.

Here are some of the questions he mentioned:

Can you treat people as if you are meeting them for the very first time?

Can you start with a clean slate every day with no remembrance of past offences, no continuation of yesterday's conflicts, yesterday's misery, misunderstanding and no continuation of resentment?

When you see someone you know, can you treat them as if you are meeting them for the very first time?

When I left the old doctor's surgery, I was in awe of the wisdom that I had been exposed to. I began to realise that we can only build worthwhile relationships when we are able to forget about people's past mistakes and see every individual as being valuable.

> **We must see people as being worth much more than the sum of their past mistakes.**

2. Perfection versus perpetuity

When we begin to consider the mistakes of others, it becomes apparent that forgiving and forgetting are hard principles to adhere to. They are hard because we struggle to let go of the pain and injury we have suffered as a result of the words and actions of others. We often seek to punish those people for their mistakes. The only people who do not suffer the consequences of our wrath are those who are perfect. Perfect in a manner where they behave as we desire for them to behave – all the time. However, nobody is perfect. Nobody will do the things and say the words that meet with our approval all of the time. Desiring perfection in others carries many negative consequences. One of the results of seeking this form of perfection in others is estrangement. People drift away from relationships when unreasonable expectations are placed upon them.
Catherine* was a caring person whom I had met and had grown very fond of. We dated for a short while, and during this time we had many disagreements. I soon began to see a pattern emerge. I would be criticised for something I had done or not done, or I would be criticised for something I had said or not said. Sometimes I would be made an offender for a single word. The punishment took the form of broken communication and other times heated arguments. Although I defended myself by arguing the validity of my actions and/or words which were under scrutiny, we were not able to reach consensus on most of our disagreements. I eventually began to feel that unreasonable expectations were being placed on me and I walked away from the relationship.

*Not her real name

Perfection carries a different meaning for everyone. Perfection is personal. Since desiring perfection in others is an imposition of personal standards, conflict will inevitably arise. When people are expected to walk the line without offending in word or deed, the stage is set for arguments and battles. People do not want the values of others imposed upon them. They do not want to conform to behaviour patterns which are considered by someone else as perfect but are most likely in conflict to their own personal definition of perfection.

How then do we deal with these disagreements which occur in relationships?

The answer lies in the changing of focus. When we are focused on ensuring that people always act according to our acceptable perfect standards, we are focusing on something which cannot be achieved ***directly***. Please note that I have stated that perfection cannot be directly achieved, thus implying that it can be achieved indirectly. The most interesting fact about indirect perfection is that when it is achieved, that its qualifying criteria are vastly different to those we impose when we pursue direct perfection.

When we change our focus from ***seeking perfection*** to ***seeking perpetuity*** of the relationship, the ballgame changes completely. When we begin to focus on ensuring the longevity of the relationship, we then have to value others for who they are and not for whom we want them to be. The focal point then becomes the perpetuity, or continuation, of the relationship and not the behaviour of others relative to our own opinions. Only when we experience this paradigm shift, will we begin to enjoy more rewarding relationships.

I recall watching the televangelist Joyce Meyer on television recently and she was talking about how her relationship with her husband, Dave Meyer, had evolved over the years. She mentioned how she would often, in times past, become very agitated at some of the things that Dave did. Dave, in turn, had a few reservations about some of the things she did. Their differences often led to heated arguments. This situation persisted for many years until the day they made a pact to not try to change each other and instead accept each other as they are. Their relationship changed completely from that day. She no longer fussed about the amount of time he spent on the golf course and he didn't object to some other things that she did. They now have a greater appreciation for each other's attributes than before. Ironically, their relationship changed when they stopped

trying to change each other. Appreciation improved when they stopped focusing on each other's flaws. They achieved a sort of perfection in their relationship, but it was vastly different to the type that they had sought before.
This story reveals to us how indirect perfection can be attained.

> **When we seek perfection in a relationship, we will find neither perfection nor perpetuity, but when we seek perpetuity, we will find it and perfection will miraculously appear.**

3. Showing kindness

Healthy relationships do not happen overnight. They are the result of hard work and sacrifice. Only when we are determined to build our relationships, and are prepared to pay the necessary price, will we reap the rewards of healthy and fulfilling relationships with others.

> **Too often we underestimate the power of a touch, a smile, a kind word, a listening ear, an honest compliment, or the smallest act of caring, all of which have the potential to turn a life around.**
> *Leo Buscaglia*

Leo Buscaglia once wrote that: 'Too often we underestimate the power of a touch, a smile, kind word, a listening ear, an honest compliment, or the smallest act of caring, all of which have the potential to turn a life around.'
The tiniest act of kindness towards another human being has the potential to turn that person's life around. In addition to that, I have seen that it can turn your own life around. This is the phenomenon of ***Reciprocal Kindness***. Many times it does not come back to you only from the person to whom you showed kindness first. I have experienced this phenomenon many times in my life.

Jenny* runs a ministry that aids many financially challenged individuals. She often gives away food parcels and money to struggling families. Many of these people just needed to be reminded that they are special through acts of generosity shown to them. On several occasions Jenny asked me to assist her with a few of these community outreach programs. I volunteered my time willingly for this worthwhile cause. Although I did not seek payment for what I had done, there were times when I needed some resources and/or service and Jenny would come to my door and provide the resource without me having asked her. She would come in response to the convicting voice deep inside of her. I believe that when I opened the door of benevolence to others, I also opened it for myself. The smallest act of caring has the potential to turn a life around.

*Not her real name

4. Choose your company wisely

All human beings are endowed with the ability to express themselves in a creative manner, with each individual having been bestowed with different talents and gifts. Along with these gifts we all also have a strong natural need to express, or live out our creativity.

Creative expression consists of two phases, namely:

1. production, and
2. promulgation.

Idea production is the first phase of creativity and it is also the **private phase** of creative expression. The production phase is when you mentally create your artistic work or solution to a problem in your mind and then plan how you will convert it into reality.

Idea promulgation is the second phase of creativity and it is also the **public phase** of creative expression. The promulgation phase is when you physically create or express your idea or solution so that you and others can observe and enjoy it.

You may be tempted to ask what relevance a brief discussion on the aspects of creative expression has in relation to choosing your company. It has everything to do with choosing your company. Each of us will encounter two categories of people in our social circles, namely:

1. those who **promote** our creative expression through:
    a. *inspiration*, such as a love interest;
    b. *encouragement*, such as a mentor, coach or teacher; and

    c. *involvement*, which can occur in the form of:
        i. *support*, which is indirect involvement such as a supportive relative or friend, and
        ii. *collaboration*, which is direct involvement such a fellow-member of a team who works hand-in-hand with us to achieve a specific goal.
2. and those who **prevent** or impede our creative expression through:
    a. *mediocrity*, such as a complaining or nagging friend who drains your emotional and spiritual energy;
    b. *criticism*, such as a critical manager or co-worker who constantly dismisses as bad any suggestions from others that contradict their own;
    c. *sabotage*, which can occur in the form of:
        i. *visible damage* to you or your property, which is direct sabotage such as a destructive person who smashes what you've created or assaults you, and
        ii. invisible damage or unseen damage to your joy and happiness, such as a cheating spouse who erodes his partner's feeling of acceptance and steals her desire to creatively express love to him because of his infidelity.

I have had to eliminate people who disturb or interrupt my creative expression through their destructive criticism and by the imposition of restrictions on me for their own selfish reasons.

It is very possible to be a creative criminal and to abuse your endowment of creative expression for wrong. In this regard, King Solomon advised each of us to decline the invitations of wrong-doers who seek our collaboration to execute elaborate plans to steal from and harm other people. Such individuals will ultimately bring doom and destruction upon themselves.

Tommy* was a bright young high school student with a promising future. Tommy had a few friends at school who regularly engaged in criminal activities to support their lascivious lifestyle. One day on his way home from school Tommy's friends asked him to be the driver of a getaway car. They planned to execute an armed robbery at a local store. When Tommy declined, they called him a chicken and a coward. However, Tommy did not want to be seen as a chicken or coward. Despite the pleadings of one of his wiser friends to not go, Tommy acquiesced to the peer pressure and went along with his criminal friends. Tommy sat in the car while his mates robbed the store but the armed store-owner chased after the robbers as they exited the store and fired several shots at the car as it sped off. Tommy was fatally wounded by a bullet that struck him in the head. The lessons learnt from this true story of the death of a foolish young man are that we can be destroyed if we choose our company wrong, and that we will suffer the same fate that we wish to exact on the innocent. King Solomon wrote that those who wish to harm others will suffer the very fate that they endeavour to exact on the innocent.

* Not his real name

5. Goodwill

King Solomon wrote: 'He who seeks good finds goodwill.' Goodwill is a feeling of friendliness and kindness. Goodwill is also perceived worth. When we seek to see the good in others, and when we are friendly, kind, generous, and patient towards others then we automatically procure goodwill for ourselves.

> **He who seeks good finds goodwill.**[xxvi]
> *King Solomon*

6. Guard your speech

> **A man who lacks judgement derides his neighbour,**
> **but a man of understanding holds his tongue.**[xxvii]
> *King Solomon*

A man who insults, ridicules and demeans his neighbour through his words displays a lack of judgment. Wise judgment rests not in assessing and criticising others by what we say, but in knowing when not to say anything.

> **Wise judgment rests not in assessing and criticising others by what we say, but in knowing when not to say anything.**

7. Guard your thoughts and actions

> **The beginning of love is to let those we love be perfectly themselves, and not twist them to fit our own image. Otherwise we love only the reflection of ourselves we find in them.**
> *Thomas Merton*

As I am writing this manuscript, leaders of the SADEC Region are discussing the acts of violence and murder committed by South African citizens against foreigners living in South Africa.

The president of South Africa, Jacob Zuma, has had to explain the situation and the South African government's response to his foreign counterparts. As I watched the story unfold, two thoughts came to my mind.

The first is that the government has now been held accountable for the rogue acts of a few citizens who seem to ignore the very essence of the South African constitution, which guarantees the government's commitment to freedom of movement and speech to everyone residing within the borders of South Africa. These few people who have harmed and killed foreigners have proven that love for your neighbour cannot be attained through legislation. President John F. Kennedy reminded us of this shortcoming of laws when he said: "Peace does not rest in the charters and covenants alone. It lies in the hearts and minds of all people." He went on to say: "So let us not rest all our hopes on parchment and on paper, let us strive to build peace, a desire for peace, a willingness to work for peace in the hearts and minds of all of our people."

> **Peace does not rest in the charters and covenants alone. It lies in the hearts and minds of all people. So let us not rest all our hopes on parchment and on paper, let us strive to build peace, a desire for peace, a willingness to work for peace in the hearts and minds of all of our people. I believe that we can. I believe the problems of human destiny are not beyond the reach of human beings.**
> *President John F. Kennedy*

These statements highlight the need for peace and tranquillity to be resident in the hearts and minds of people so that they can then act in a peaceful and considerate manner towards their neighbours. These ideals are within reach.

It is ironic that here in South Africa foreigners residing within our borders are being killed, beaten and displaced whilst in another part of the world people from all over are rushing to Nepal with foreign aid to assist with rescue-operations, as well as medical and food supplies, in the aftermath of the 7.8 magnitude earthquake that struck that country on Saturday 25th April 2015. Here we see the international community showing their care for others even though they are not in the same country, whilst here in South Africa we were not able to protect the lives of those killed and hurt during the attacks on foreigners in April 2015.

Only when we consider the safety of our neighbours - whether they be from a foreign country or not – as being our God-assigned and human responsibility will we be able to achieve peaceful co-existence. King Solomon wrote: "Do not devise evil against your neighbour, for he dwells by you for safety's sake."

> **Do not devise evil against your neighbour, for he dwells by you for safety's sake.** [xxviii]
> *King Solomon*

King Solomon advised us that our neighbours live close to us for safety. We must all learn to act in a manner that values the life and dignity of others. These acts should include, but not be limited to sharing and caring as well as generosity and benevolence. We must show love and not hatred, peace and not war, valuing and not devaluing others! Let our actions esteem others.

The second thought was related to the strong influence that the media has displayed in defining the problem. On television news channels, on the radio, on the internet and on newspapers these heinous acts are called *xenophobic attacks.*

Everywhere you go people are talking and debating the *xenophobia* that is taking place. I was disturbed by the term that is being used to describe the recent events. People should be made aware that xenophobia is simply the fear of foreigners. Xenophobia is not the correct term for what has happened here in South Africa. The correct term is *xenocide.* Xenocide is the murder of foreigners. The media has been instrumental in the skewed perception created by its use of a wrong term.

> **A problem well-defined is a problem half-solved.**
> *Charles F. Kettering*

An important part of doing damage-repair is to properly define the problem. Charles F. Kettering taught us that we are half-way to a solution when we accurately define the problem that we face. Only when we are truly honest with what we are dealing with can we deal with it accurately.

> **Only when we are truly honest with what we are dealing with can we deal with it accurately.**

Conclusion

If you want to be a winner, you must learn to see yourself and other people in a new light, and you must treat people in a manner that promotes goodwill. The process of goodwill promotion starts with being kind and generous towards other people with your words, actions and resources. When you regularly practice **The Seven Foundational Disciplines for Building Healthy Relationships**, then establishing goodwill will be easy.

Benjamin Disraeli once said: "The greatest good you can do for another is not just to share your riches but to reveal to him his own."
Let us each then be generous in sharing what is ours with others and then go a step further to reveal, by whatsoever means we may find appropriate, the riches that a man possesses to himself, as Benjamin Disraeli so wisely advised.

Chapter 4

Lilies And Sparrows

> **God cares so wonderfully for the lilies of the field...he will certainly care for you.**
> **You are worth more than many sparrows.**
> *Jesus of Nazareth*

How are things valued?

In order to accurately determine the value of a thing it is important firstly to establish exactly where it comes from because the point of origin will give clues related to the characteristics and purpose of the thing.

Let us compare two familiar vehicle brands in order to understand the seven aspects of how things are valued.

The Seven Aspects of How Things Are Valued

1. The manufacturer places its unique insignia on the product.
Aston Martin vehicles are distinctly different from Toyota vehicles. These vehicles can easily be recognized by the logo or badge and the design of the vehicle. The badge is the trademark of the manufacturer.

2. The manufacturer places unique markings and attributes on the product as distinguishing features which indicate the origins of the product.
The environment in which a thing is produced will determine its characteristics. The Aston Martin is a different product to the Toyota because they were manufactured in different places. An elegant Aston Martin luxury sports car which is hand-made at its manufacturing facility in Gaydon, Warwickshire in the United Kingdom, is distinctively different to the mass-produced Toyota vehicles which are assembled at any one of Toyota's many state-of-the-art facilities which

are located in North and South America, Europe, Russia, Africa and Australasia. One of Toyota's oldest manufacturing plants is situated in Prospecton, south of Durban in South Africa, which is the country of my birth. Most South Africans who drive a Toyota vehicle are probably driving a locally manufactured product. Each of these vehicle brands is marked with a tag indicating the manufacturing facility where the vehicle was assembled.

3. The manufacturer of a product dictates its value.
Since these vehicles do not come from the same place, they possess different features and are consequently valued differently. Thus who the manufacturer is will have an impact on the value of the vehicle.

4. The level of personal care that goes into manufacturing a product contributes to its value.
We read that Aston Martin vehicles are hand-made. These vehicles are assembled by highly-skilled artisans, thus the culture of the Aston Martin facility hinges on the personal touch and consequently more care goes into the assembly of its vehicles whilst Toyota plants utilize robotic machinery to assemble its vehicles. Hence, an Aston Martin vehicle is more valuable than a Toyota vehicle. Thus, the level of personal care and attention that goes into a product determines its value.

5. The intended purpose of a product contributes to its value.
Aston Martin vehicles are built for a completely different purpose than Toyota vehicles. Whilst Toyota builds reliable and affordable cars for average people, Aston Martin builds status symbols for wealthy people who do not concern themselves with such things as acquisition and maintenance costs.

6. The manufacturer of a product is most suited, equipped and qualified to perform maintenance and servicing on the product.
The respective manufacturer of each of these two vehicle brands will be most suited for routine maintenance and servicing of a vehicle, because of specialised knowledge,

skill, diagnostic equipment and spares which are available at designated service centres. You will not take your expensive Aston Martin to a Toyota service centre or a bicycle-shop, neither will you take your Toyota to an Aston Martin facility or a household appliances repair facility.

7. The manufacturer of a product is most suited to recreate and upgrade the product, and will distance itself from the product if it drastically deviates from the manufacturer's original design in form and function.

When any of these two vehicles require repairs, the manufacturer will be most suited to remake and restore the vehicle to a complete state. Any form of remodelling and restoration should be done with spares and tools which are approved by the manufacturer in order for the vehicle to look as it should and operate optimally and safely. Whenever drastic changes are effected on any of these vehicles and the vehicle no longer conforms to the manufacturer's strict standards, the manufacturer is within its full right to request the removal of its name from the vehicle and distance itself from any consequences stemming from such modifications.

We will use the seven criteria necessary to value a vehicle, all of which are stated above, as points of reference as we investigate the value of people.

Let us begin by establishing the origins of man, and we will commence by asking the pertinent question:

Where do human beings come from?

Many debates have existed through the ages concerning the origins of human beings and the creatures with which we share this beautiful planet.

We will investigate the two common explanatory beliefs which pertain to this question. As you read the next section I wish to warn you that I will be explaining the commonly-held belief of creation through **evolution** which is propagated by atheistic and agnostic scientists although this **is not my personal belief.**

A Scientist's Valuation Of Mankind

In the 1859 Charles Darwin presented his ***theory of evolution*** to the world in his book ***On the Origin of Species***, and in it he suggested that all life forms evolved from a common ancestor.
The word ***evolve*** first started being used in the English language in the 17th century. It developed from the Latin word **ex** which later became ***e*** and which means *'out of.'* When ***e*** is combined with ***volvere,*** another Latin word meaning *'to roll,'* we get the word ***evolvere*** which became ***evolve*** in the English language. Evolve means *'to make more complex; to develop.'*
Darwin's theory is based on the premise that all life forms on Earth developed from a single living molecular structure which came into existence by accident. Stated in very simple terms, Darwin suggests that a self-replicating molecule developed on Earth through highly energetic chemical reactions. This self-replicating molecule ***evolved*** into a more complex molecular structure, which formed the earliest and simplest genetic material such as RNA (ribonucleic acid), and then formed the first simple cells.
All living organisms evolved from a common genetic pool or ancestor about 400 billion years ago. A prokaryotic single-cell organism (an organism with no membrane) developed into a eukaryotic cell (a cell with a nucleus and organelles enclosed in a membrane) and when these eukaryotes were engulfed by bacteria a simultaneous evolution of the two organisms occurred and produced the first multi-cellular organisms such as brown algae and sponges about 610 million years ago.
During a period called ***The Cambrian Period***, which lasted approximately 10 million years, the majority of animal types appeared. About 500 million years ago plants and fungi colonised the land and were soon followed by invertebrates (animals with no backbone) such as arthropods (animals with an exoskeleton, segmented body and jointed appendages) and other vertebrates (animals with an internal skeletal structure and backbone).
Although Charles Darwin's book ***On the Origin of Species*** did not address human evolution, one of his contemporaries Thomas Huxley argued for human evolution through various

illustrations depicting the similarities and differences between humans and apes in his book ***Evidence as to Man's Place in Nature.*** [xxix]

All hominids (orang-utans, gorillas, chimpanzees, bonobos and humans) are said to have had a common extinct ancestor. About 6 million years ago the human and chimpanzee lineage split, but hominid lineage did not move straight on to *Homo sapiens* (humans).

The chronology of the evolution of man is said to have begun with ***Ardipithecus ramidus***, who was bipedal (had two feet) and was most-likely a forest-dweller, and then evolved by a process known as ***natural selection*** (organisms which adapt to the environment tend to survive and produce more offspring) through the developmental stages listed below.

Australopithecus anamensis displayed advanced bipedal features but retained the distinctive ape-like skull.

Australopithecus afarensis possessed an apelike face with a sloping forehead, a ridge over the eyes, flat nose, and a chinless lower jaw with his head and face being much larger than that of a human although still bearing a resemblance to humans.

Australopithecus africanus was similar to the afarensis but was much larger in size and was a herbivore with a large jaw.

Australopithecus robustus lacked a forehead and had a huge, flat face and he lacked speech capabilities.

Australopithecus boisei was smaller than robustus but had a bigger face.

Homo habilis used tools and had some speech ability.

Homo erectus had a rounded face with small features; he cooked his own food, made his own clothing, travelled, was a hunter and definitely had speech abilities.

Homo neanderthalensis (also known as Neanderthal man) had a brain that was much larger than man and was more muscular; he had a large nose and a longer skull than modern man.

Homo sapien (modern man) is said to have appeared approximately 120 000 years ago.[xxx]

Here I wish to point out that although all hominids have 48 chromosomes (24 pairs) humans have only 46 chromosomes (23 pairs).

Chromosomes are the thread-like structures resident in the nucleus of the cells of living creatures. These thread-like structures contain genetic and hereditary information in the form of genes.

When we look at evolution as a proposition of man's origins and consider man's value in accordance with the requirements set out in the beginning of this chapter, we find that we have no manufacturer to consult or look to. If man came about by chance, and man is merely an animal who is a little more evolved than his ancestors, then man has very little worth, if any, in relation to the other creatures on planet Earth. Furthermore, if man is not subject to the rule of a higher being then moral aptitude becomes unnecessary and, consequently, we lack the need for a conscience. If evolution were true, we would have no creator to turn to when our bodies are dying and in need of healing. These conclusions are inadequate for our search of man's value and we must thus continue to look for the right answers.
Now that we have investigated the proposed origins of man from a scientific perspective we will investigate the origins of man from a theocratic, or God-centred, perspective.

Different from the beginning

The biblical account of creation reveals to us the sequential steps in which God produced the world and all living organisms here on Earth.
God created day and night on day one; clouds, oceans and continents on day two; trees, plants and grass on day three; celestial planets, stars and moons on day four; marine, avian and all terrestrial animals and insects on day five.

> **And God said, "Let there be light," and there was light.** Genesis 1:3a NIV
> *Moses the Levite*
> **For from him and through him and for him are all things.** Romans 11:36a NIV
> *Paul the Apostle*

Under inspiration of the Holy Spirit, Moses recorded an account of Earth's creation in the first book of the

Pentateuch, called Genesis. Combined with Paul the Apostle's account, we understand that God, who is a spirit, blew out a physical world from within Himself. As God conceived the planets, stars, moons, living creatures and plants, He gave none of these the attention that He gave to man. As opposed to simply exhaling a complete man, God's creation process included seven distinguishing differences which were not part of the creative process of things made during the first five days of creation. I refer to these distinguishing differences as The Seven Unique Attributes of Man's Creation.

The Seven Unique Attributes of Man's Creation

The Seven Unique Attributes of man's creation are:

1. man's nature was spoken (prophesied) by God before man's creation,
2. man would have God's appearance,
3. man would have God's nature,
4. man would have dominion over the earth and all creatures living in it,
5. man would have free will or freedom of choice,
6. God *personally and meticulously* formed man's physical body out of the dust of the earth, and
7. God exhaled man's spirit into man's physical body.

The Seven Unique Attributes of Man's Creation show that God dedicated much more time and effort into the planning and execution of man's creation. With God's different creative strategy, man was different to the rest of creation from the beginning.

> **God has had a special affinity for man from the very beginning.**

Let us look more closely at **The Seven Unique Attributes of Man's Creation** so that we may gain an accurate understanding of man's value relative to other creatures and things.

❶ Man's nature was spoken before his creation

> **Then God said, "*Let us make mankind* in our image, in our likeness, so that they may rule over the fish in the sea and the birds in the sky, over the livestock and all the wild animals, and over all the creatures that move along the ground."** Genesis 1:26 NIV
> *Moses the Levite*

God is an excellent planner. He knows what He wants to achieve, then He speaks it prophetically as if it already exists and then He creates it. God is the creator who thinks great thoughts and then gives those thoughts form.

> **God is the divine creator who gives form to His thoughts.**

The Mosaic account of creation tells us that God spoke, or prophesied, about His desire to create man before He began to assemble the first man's body from grains of sand and dust. Thus, man's creation was not an afterthought that slipped into God's mind when He had completed the creation of the earth. Man's creation was intentional and purpose-driven.

❷ Man would have God's appearance

> **So *God created mankind in his own image*, in the image of God he created them.** Genesis 1:27 NIV
> *Moses the Levite*

God fashioned man after His own image. Every aspect of man, including his facial features, his limbs, torso and general appearance are a direct copy from God's personal appearance.

God has a face - Moses wrote that God said: "you cannot see my face, for no one may see me and live." Exodus 33:20 NIV

God has a mouth and a voice and He speaks through his mouth - one psalmist wrote: 'By the word of the Lord the heavens were made, their starry host by the breath of his mouth.' Psalm 33:6 NIV

God has a nose and nostrils, and He breathes and smells through His nose - Eliphaz, the Temanite spoke to an ailing Job and said: *"By the blast of God they perish, and by the breath of his nostrils are they consumed."* Job 4:9 NIV
God instructed Isaiah, the Prophet to write a stern warning to the people of Judah saying: "The incense you bring me is a stench in my nostrils!" Isaiah 1:13 NLT

God has eyes - King Solomon wrote: 'the eyes of the LORD are everywhere, keeping watch on the wicked and the good. Proverbs 15:3 NIV

God has hands and fingers - Moses received two stone tablets with The Ten Commandments which had been inscribed thereon by the finger of God. Exodus 31:18
When King Belshazzar gave a great banquet, God's hand appeared and wrote these words on a wall: "MENE, MENE, TEKEL, PARSIN." Daniel 5:5,25

God has legs and He walks - Adam and Eve heard the sound of God as He was walking in the cool of the day. Genesis 8:3

We can clearly see that man has been given everything that God has. We have been made in God's image in every respect.

❸ Man would have God's nature

God purposed in His heart to have a race of beings with whom He could have a personal relationship. Thus it was necessary that these beings should have the very same nature as God himself.

> **Then God said, "Let us make mankind in our image, *in our likeness*, ..."** Genesis 1:26 NIV
> *Moses the Levite*

God laughs and He becomes angry - King David wrote in a psalm: 'The One enthroned in heaven laughs; the Lord scoffs at them. He rebukes them in his anger and terrifies them in his wrath...' Psalm 2:4-5 NIV

God loves and hates intensely - King Solomon wrote that there are six things which God hates and seven things which are an abomination to Him. Proverbs 6:16
John, the Disciple wrote that God had such an intense love for every person in the world that He sent His only son so that whoever believes in Him should not perish but have everlasting life.

God smiles - King David asked God to: "Smile on me, your servant; teach me the right way to live." Psalm 119:135 The Message

God has given us all of His personal attributes such as the capacity for love and hatred and to smile, to name but a few.

❹ Man would have dominion

> **Then God said, "Let us make mankind ..., *so that they may rule over the fish in the sea and the birds in the sky, over the livestock and all the wild animals,and over all the creatures that move along the ground.*"** Genesis 1:26 NIV
> *Moses the Levite*

❺ Man would have free will

> **And the LORD God commanded the man, "*You are free* to eat from any tree in the garden; but you must not eat from the tree of the knowledge of good and evil, for when you eat from it you will certainly die."** Genesis 2:16-17 NIV
> *Moses the Levite*

❻ God *personally and meticulously* formed man's physical body out of the dust of the earth

> **Then the LORD *God formed a man from the dust of the ground* and breathed into his nostrils the breath of life, and the man became a living being.** Genesis 2:7 NIV
> *Moses the Levite*

God did not leave the creation of man up to chance, nor did He outsource man's creation to some other deity. Man was God's personal project. God created Adam's body from soil. He skilfully crafted Adam and formed all his biological organs and systems which make up his physical form and which enable and qualify man to survive, live and thrive in his earthly environment.
After having formed Adam, God created Eve, the female, from human tissue removed from Adam's side.
God made two people who were complete in every respect and they did not require additional evolution over time.

❼ God exhaled man's spirit into man's physical body

> **Then the LORD God formed a man from the dust of the ground and *breathed into his nostrils the breath of life*, and the man became a living being.** Genesis 2:7 NIV
> *Moses the Levite*

How God sees man and feels about man

Most people are not aware of the love that God has for each and every human being. No human being is excluded from the love of God, but the devil has progressively convinced people that God does not love them or care about their well-being. People foolishly believe this lie. We have seen that God devoted much more time to man's creation.

> **"And why worry about your clothing? Look at the lilies of the field and how they grow. They don't work or make their clothing, yet Solomon in all his glory was not dressed as beautifully as they are. And if God cares so wonderfully for wildflowers that are here today**

> **and thrown into the fire tomorrow, he will certainly care for you."** Matthew 6:28-30 NLT
> **"Are not two sparrows sold for a penny? Yet not one of them will fall to the ground outside your Father's care. And even the very hairs of your head are all numbered.**
> **So don't be afraid; you are worth more than many sparrows."** Mathew 10:29-31 NIV
> *Jesus of Nazareth*

Jesus taught that King Solomon, in all his regal magnificence and splendour was not clothed like the lilies of the field. He also said that God considers sparrows as valuable and that He cares for them. He added that two sparrows can be valued at a penny, but every human being is worth more than many sparrows.

> **God considers your worth to be more than the lilies of the field and the sparrows in the air.**

However, the devil has progressively eroded man's confidence and faith in God through lies. If God, the Creator, holds you in such great regard and has such a special affinity for you, should you not then value yourself as He values you?

God and the devil

The theory of evolution, or Darwinism, is contradictory to creationism or what I refer to as ***theolution*** - creation by God.
Evolutionary theory is the devil's concoction of presumptions and assumptions based on archaeological skeletal findings which have been connected to form a very complicated lie. That a lie of this magnitude should come from the devil should not surprise us. Jesus said that the devil was a liar from the beginning.
If we can believe that we came into existence by accident, then we do not have to acknowledge a creator who formed us, thus paving the way for man to be a god unto himself. If we can acknowledge that we share a common ancestor with apes and monkeys, then we are really glorified animals, and

if we are glorified animals then we really do not have much greater value than the animals to which we are related. However, we are not related to apes, chimpanzees and monkeys. As I stated earlier, humans have two less chromosomes than hominids, but humans also possess something that animals do not have ... a spirit. This is expounded further down in this chapter. It is tragic that many people have been convinced that the lie of evolution is the truth. The purpose of this great deception from Satan is to devalue people.

God justifies and the devil condemns. The devil's primary function is devaluing people. God's job is to value people.

> **God values people.**
> **The devil devalues people.**
>
> **The thief comes only to steal and kill and destroy; I have come that they may have life, and have it to the full.** John 10:10 NIV
> *Jesus of Nazareth*

In the Garden of Eden, the first thing the devil did was to cause Eve to question her own value. He made her think that she was not like God, although she already had God's image and likeness. She was already like God. She was already perfect, but she believed someone else's opinion of her. She believed the devil's opinion of who she was. Her actions attempted to achieve a level of self-value that was being defined by someone else. Unfortunately, her actions were also in defiance of God's direct instruction. When God gave Adam his mandate, He was telling him that he was a king and that he should not allow anyone or anything to usurp his position and/or make him see himself as being anything less than a king. He was indirectly instructed to not let anyone devalue him. But, we all know how the story ends. Adam and Eve were deceived when they believed the lie about the value that God had placed on them, and many of their children still believe that lie. The consequence for believing the lie is still the same as it was in the Garden of Eden – death! We die when we do not know the worth that the Creator places on us. We die when we are ignorant of the

great gifts he has placed in us and bestowed upon us. We die when we do not know our value!
This **death** is not first a physical death. It is a spiritual, psychological, emotional and intellectual death. Death is nothing more than the cessation of activity and expression. It is also the departing of the life-giving force.
In the dimensions of the spirit, the psyche, the feelings and intellect, **life** is a sense of well-being, confidence and positive growth of these characteristics. In the physical world, movement and physical expression are proof of life, but when death occurs, movement and expression cease.

> **Many people die at twenty five and aren't buried until they are seventy five.**
> *Benjamin Franklin*

Most people are spiritually and psychologically dead. They have no true movement and expression in the areas of creativity, thinking, reasoning and personal development because they do not live up to their creative potential. Even when they are aware of their attributes, abilities and endowments, they do not use them to their fullest capacity. So most people, although they are physically alive, are already dead. This is what Benjamin Franklin meant when he said: "Many people die at twenty five and aren't buried until they are seventy five."

> **The spiritual and psychological death of a man precedes his physical death.**

Thus the spiritual death of a man precedes his physical death. Unfortunately for many, the physical death comes about as a direct result of the spiritual and psychological death. Some live lives of mediocrity by merely existing and plodding along until the day they expire. Some seek an escape from reality by pursuing addictive practices such as substance, food and sexual abuse. Some simply give up and commit suicide. Some cover and compensate for their own weaknesses by preying on the weaknesses of others. These are all examples of the behaviour that stems from spiritual death. However, spiritual and psychological death displays itself in many other behavioural patterns in the realm of the physical.

What God wishes to give to mankind

The man who gives a diamond ring to the girl he loves shows his love for her by the gift. The gift usually expresses the love he has for her. In the same way God expresses his love for mankind when He bestows gifts upon His people.

The giving of a gift has two distinct purposes, namely:

1. to show to the recipient how strongly the giver feels about him/her (it is an opportunity for the giver to express his feelings and thoughts: the giving is an outer expression of the giver's inner thoughts and feelings). The gift is an indication of the magnitude of the value that the giver places upon the recipient, and
2. to build a stronger relationship between the giver and the recipient (to ensure longevity in the relationship).

Thus, it is love that gives, but hatred takes away.

> **Love gives. Hatred takes.**
> **God gives. The devil takes.**

We read in the gospels about the prodigal son who convinced his father to give him his inheritance so that he could spend it immediately and in a manner that he saw fit. The son left his father's home with his share of his inheritance and squandered his money on a lascivious lifestyle. Finally, with no money and no friends, the son was forced by circumstances to seek employment and he was granted the unenviable task of looking after pigs and also ate of the food which was fed to the pigs. Eventually, when he could not endure the humility, shame, loneliness and hunger any longer he purposed to return to his father's home and propose to take up the position of a slave in the home in which he was raised. He lifted himself up and travelled many days and nights, with no food to eat and his strength waning with every passing day. Then one day, he came to the gate of his childhood home, and suddenly saw a man behaving like a mad man. This man came running to him with arms outstretched and shouting with elation ... it was his father. With tears in his eyes and uncontrolled excitement the father embraced his son whose sandals were walked through and he was dressed in torn clothes and smelled like a pig's mire. However, above the nauseating stench of pigs the father smelled the sweet aroma of repentance. Before, on the day when his son had left with much money, he was perfumed with the sweet smell of aromatic oils, but with his departure he had carried the horrible stench of rebellion and disobedience. In contrast, this day was different because repentance paved the way for restoration. It didn't matter to the father that his son was barely strong enough to hug him back, but his actions spoke volumes. His actions spoke of a deep regret for the pain he had caused his father and himself. The father called on the servants to tend to him. The son was bathed and shaven and anointed with sweet-smelling aromatic oils. He was given new clothes, shoes and a ring was placed on his finger. The father instructed a fatted calf to be slaughtered and instructed for the banquet hall to be prepared. Friends and relatives were invited to the celebration. The father wanted to share his joy of the return of his long-lost son with as many people as possible and he wanted his son to again feel welcome in the home of his youth. At the celebration the father proposed a toast and said: "My son who was lost has now returned. He was homeless but has now found his home. He wished to be placed as a servant in the home where he grew up, but I will have no such thing. **You are valuable! You are valuable because you are my son.**"

This parable from the Gospels expounds very clearly the things which God our creator wishes to give to us. There are seven things which the Creator desires to share with, or attribute to His creation. I shall refer to them as The Seven Attributions God Desires to Bestow on Mankind.

The Seven Attributions God Desires to Bestow on Mankind

The Seven Attributions God Desires to Bestow on Mankind are:

1. recognition,

2. redemption,
3. realization,
4. reconciliation,
5. recreation,,
6. remuneration, and
7. relation.

Let us look at those things now.

1. Recognition

> **My people ... are called by my name.** 2 Chronicles 7:14
> **I said, You are "gods"; you are all the sons of the Most High.** Psalm 82:6 NIV

We read in the introduction that people need recognition. God wishes to let His people know that He recognizes them as His own and as being very valuable.
The psalmist penned God's heart towards his people when he wrote: "I have said you are gods."
The word *gods* is the plural form of the Hebrew word *Elohim.* Elohim as applied in this sense refers to individuals who have deity and might and who assume the positions of heavenly beings, judges and magistrates.
Jesus reiterated this when said: "Did He (Yahweh) not say that you are gods? He said this to those to whom He sent His word." John 10:34
We see clearly that God the Creator sees man as gods. This should not be a surprising revelation, since we have been created in the image and likeness of God Almighty.
God also said that His people are called by His name.
The original Hebrew word for ***name*** is ***shem*** (pronounced shame) and it means *'a memorial of individuality; a position of honour, authority, character and renown.'*

> **God, our magnificent creator, has recognized His people as being gods who carry His unique name, and because we bare His name we also have honour, authority and renown.**

2. Redemption

To err is human, to forgive divine.

When we look at the universe, with its many constituent galaxies and focus our attention on our small galaxy called the Milky Way, we cannot help but stand in awe of the brilliance of its creator. We marvel at stars which are made up of gases burning at unbelievably high temperatures and which radiate their heat and light to the far reaches of our galaxy. We stand in awe of stars, moons and planets which appear to hang unsuspended in space, yet they diligently stay in a fixed orbit as if they are entrenched in an invisible path. Clearly, the creator of this universe is an individual who displays the highest levels of order and excellence. It is then a natural conclusion that the God who created the universe would require the highest levels of order and excellence from man. It is not an unreasonable proposition that man's ultimate aim in life should be to live up to the standards prescribed by God, and that we should acknowledge the necessity for punishment especially when we have been warned of the possible punitive actions when we are disobedient to our Creator's instructions.

When we look at God we find that He is a just God because He has laid out a constitution and a set of unequivocal laws by which we must conduct our lives. His laws are unequivocal because He does not chop and change them as He goes along, but instead He adheres strictly and diligently to what He has said. One psalmist recorded God's observation of His spoken words and commandments when he wrote: "I honour my word even above my name." Psalm 138:2 These laws were given to Moses, a man of Jewish descent who was raised as an Egyptian prince during a period when the Jewish people were held captive as slaves in Egypt. God liberated his people from Egyptian slavery and later issued Moses a series of five books, called **The Pentateuch**, which contained the true account of the creation of the universe and man and also contained the Jewish Law (called The Torah) with specifications of religious feasts and strict commandments which prescribed acceptable behavioural practices for God's people. A further investigation into scripture reveals to us that God's law has been meant for adherence by all people and not only Jews. Unfortunately, people all over the world have violated God's laws. Paul the Apostle attested to this when he wrote: 'for all have sinned and fall short of the glory of God,' Romans 3:23 NIV

Since every man, woman and child ever born has sinned, or contravened God's laws, we all have been judged as sinners. God's judgement is fair and just. The consequence of being found guilty of sin is death. In a letter to the church in Rome, the Apostle Paul wrote: 'for the wages of sin is death.' Romans 6:23 KJV

Thus we are all condemned to suffer death as a result of our sinful acts. I'm sure everyone would agree with the idea that God's judgment is fierce. Even though His judgement is fierce, it is still just. However, since God is a prognosticator, He saw man's shortcomings even before He created man, and He devised a plan of redemption for man. The plan involved an elaborate scheme whereby He himself would bare the punishment for the sins of every man, woman and child who will ever be born. The Apostle John, when he was imprisoned on the island of Patmos, received a revelation from an angel who declared: "the lamb of God *was* slain before the foundations of the world." Revelation 13:8

God devised this plan of redemption before He created anything.

God's plan was implemented when a young Jewish virgin became pregnant by miraculous conception and then later, gave birth to a little boy in a manger in a town called Bethlehem. The boy was called **Immanuel**, which means '*God with us*,' and he was also called **Yeshua** in his Hebrew tongue (**Jesus** being the Greek equivalent). The name **Jesus** means '*the Lord saves, Jehovah redeems.*'

Jesus lived for 33 years and he taught and did things that the world had never seen before. Some people said of him: "No one ever spoke like this man!" John 7:46 NET

He performed signs, wonders and miracles which attested to His divinity. In one place He said: "If you do not believe that I am sent from the father, then believe because of the miracles." John 14:11

This tender-hearted, forgiving and compassionate man was murdered by crucifixion (being pinned on a cross made from tree stumps and which is then planted in an upright position). This was God's act of redemption. This was God's act of mercy. The scripture states that we were slaves to sin, and that while we were slaves God gave His son, the man Jesus Christ, to die for us. Romans 5:8

I have often contemplated the method by which Jesus died and when I asked God for revelation concerning this matter I discovered an encouraging truth.

I was prepared to concede that we must be punished for our sins, but then I questioned why Jesus did not die a natural death or by some less brutal means. God then revealed to me that when the charge of the murder of His only son is added to our already long list of offences, that the judgement is much higher. With a greater offense greater mercy is required for redemption and it pleased God that He would be able to bestow greater mercy upon His people.

God's redemption plan hinged on one critical factor: that His great and just judgement would be superseded only by his great mercy. James, the brother of Jesus testified of this when he wrote: 'Mercy triumphs over judgement!' James 2:13 NIV

When I consider my past experiences with other people, I have found that people can be the most unforgiving creatures ever. People can be indescribably cruel when it comes to the manner in which they treat those who have offended them in word or deed. They can hold onto the memory of a past offence for eternity and will continue to treat the offender with great animosity and contempt.

Despite His creation being remarkably unforgiving of his fellow-man, we find that God displays a characteristic that appears to be uniquely divine. That divine characteristic is forgiveness. God's redemption is made complete in our lives when we believe and accept by faith that Jesus is the son of God and that He died in our place for our sins.

3. Realization

> **"For I know my plans for you," declares the Lord, "plans to prosper you and not to harm you, plans to give you a hope and a future."** Jeremiah 29:11 NIV
>
> *Jeremiah, the Prophet*

We must come into the full realisation of how God sees us and embrace an accurate image of ourselves.
We re-evaluate our worth when we come into the full realisation of who we are, and how precious we are in the eyes of our maker. When we accept that the human race does not owe its origins to some freak chemical accident which supposedly occurred millions of years ago, and when we refuse to acknowledge that we share a common primate ancestor with other hominids but that we are the proud product of the most highly skilled craftsman, then we will come into the full **realization** of who we really are.
God knows every aspect of man's make-up and is the final authority on who we are. When you align your self-image and self-esteem with His thoughts of you, then you can begin to operate at your highest potential. However, if you are operating without God, you will always be operating below your potential.
The Jewish prophet Jeremiah declared that God's intentions for every man and woman are only for good. God purposes to enrich the life of every human being on Earth, and to ensure that they have a certain and happy end.

King David, the son of Jesse, contemplated man's value in context of God's perpetual thoughts about man. The truth is that you are constantly on God's mind. Everything God does is focused on you. He sees you as having immense value and potential.

> **Of what importance is the human race, that you should notice them? Of what importance is mankind, that you should pay attention to them?** Psalm 8:4 NET
> *King David*

4. Reconciliation

In accounting practice, businesses often have to create statements that compare the records of accounts against that of its service providers, bankers, creditors and debtors. The process entails the tracing of transactions and the ultimate purpose is to ensure that the final figures on both ends are firstly, accurate and secondly, equal. Such a statement is called a reconciliation statement. Since the reconciliation statement shows the exact financial value of the transactions between two parties it can be best described as a document which expresses the true value of a relationship. Paul the Apostle revealed to us that God made Jesus Christ to be the reconciliation document by which He (God) would express the true value of His relationship with us. Paul wrote: 'For it was the Father's good pleasure for all the fullness to dwell in Him *(Jesus),* and through Him to reconcile all things to Himself, having made peace through the blood of His cross; through Him, I say, whether things on earth or things in heaven.' Colossians 1:19-20 NASB

When a man and woman have gone through a separation and they get back together, we say that they have **reconciled**, and the relationship is restored to its former state. God wants to restore His relationship with us to its former state.

5. Recreation

Recreation has a dual meaning. The first meaning refers to the re-making and rebuilding of something, and the second meaning refers to rest and leisure. God wishes to bestow both types of recreation upon His people.

Let us look at recreation in the sense of re-making and rebuilding.
Man is made up of a spirit, a soul (the seat of thought, and emotions) and a physical body. God wishes to recreate (remake, restore and heal) His people on all three levels.

Firstly, God wishes to recreate every man's spirit.

> **If any man is in Christ, he is a new creation, old things are passed away and all things are become new.** 2 Corinthians 5:17 KJV
> *Paul the Apostle*

Paul the Apostle wrote that if any man is in Christ (Jesus), he is a new creature, old things are passed away, behold all things have become new."

When someone receives Jesus, God recreates that man's spirit. The term ***new creation*** as it was penned in Greek means *'a type of species that has never existed before and of which the manufacturer holds sole proprietorship.'*
When God recreates you, then you are unique. This recreation is a **spiritual recreation** which occurs when you become born again. Jesus said to Nicodemus,
"unless a man be born again, he cannot enter the kingdom of heaven," and he also said,*"unless a man is born of water and of the spirit he cannot enter the kingdom of heaven."* John 3:3,5

Secondly, God wants to recreate your soul.

> **For God has not given us a spirit of fear, but of power and of love and of a sound mind.** 2 Timothy 1:17 NKJV
> *Paul the Apostle*

Paul the Apostle wrote that God has not given us a spirit of fear, but of power and love and a sound mind. The ***love*** aspect refers to our ***emotions*** whilst the ***sound mind*** aspect refers to our ***thoughts.***
In recreating your soul, God addresses your ***thoughts*** (thinking patterns) and your ***emotions*** (feeling patterns).

Recreating our thoughts

> **Therefore, I urge you, brothers and sisters, in view of God's mercy, to offer your bodies as a living sacrifice, holy and pleasing to God—this is your true and proper worship. Do not conform to the pattern of this world, but be transformed by the renewing of your mind.** Romans 12:1-2 NIV
> **Finally, brothers and sisters, whatever is true, whatever is worthy of respect, whatever is just, whatever is pure, whatever is lovely, whatever is commendable, if something is excellent or praiseworthy, think about these things.** Philippians 4:8 NET
> *Paul the Apostle*

Paul the Apostle urged us to escape conformity to worldly standards by having our minds renewed. He also wrote to the Corinthian church reminding them that: 'we have the mind of Christ.' 1 Corinthians 2:16 NIV

> **For as he *(a man)* thinks in his heart, so is he.** Proverbs 23:7 NKJV
> *King Solomon*

King Solomon wrote that a man is defined by his thoughts because as he thinks in his heart, so is he.
God wishes to recreate our thinking patterns because we are defined by the thoughts that we entertain.

Recreating our emotions

God wants His people to display positive emotions in their lives. He wants His people to exercise love, patience and goodness. He wants His people to exercise self-control and not be swung from side-to-side by changing emotions. God desires for His people to be emotionally stable.

> **But the fruit of the Spirit is love, joy, peace, longsuffering, kindness, goodness, faithfulness, gentleness, self-control.** Galatians 5:22-23 NIV
> *Paul the Apostle*

Thirdly, God wants to recreate your body.

All human beings are stained with the condition of mortality. Mortality carries a two-pronged curse because on the one side we have fallible bodies which progressively deteriorate due to ***sickness, disease and injury***, and on the other side we have the cessation of our bodies in an event we refer to as ***death.***

> **God wants to recreate (heal) our bodies from sickness, disease and injury while we are still alive.**

YOU ARE VALUABLE

We are constantly in need of healing or physical recreation. God wants to recreate (heal) our bodies while we are still alive.

> **He said, "If you will diligently obey the LORD your God, and do what is right in his sight, and pay attention to his commandments, and keep all his statutes, then all the diseases that I brought on the Egyptians I will not bring on you, for I, the LORD, am your healer."** Exodus 15:26 NET
>
> *Moses the Levite*

God promised Moses that He will heal His people, but only if they pay attention to his commandments and do what is right in His eyes. This is the sort of recreation that occurs while we are alive.

God wants to recreate your mortal body, after death, so that you can have eternal life. God desires to give immortality to the mortal.

> **Listen, I tell you a mystery: We will not all sleep, but we will all be changed— in a flash, in the twinkling of an eye, at the last trumpet. For the trumpet will sound, the dead will be raised imperishable, and we will be changed. For the perishable must clothe itself with the imperishable, and the mortal with immortality.** 1 Corinthians 15:51-53 NIV
>
> *Paul the Apostle*

God wanted to bestow mercy upon us through the death of His son Jesus, but mercy is not all that man would benefit from the death of Jesus. Jesus arose from the dead after three days with a recreated immortal body.

The physical recreation occurs when the children of God are raised from the dead.

In his letter to the Corinthian church Paul the Apostle explains that we will be transformed in an instant and our bodies will be changed. All believers will follow the pattern of the resurrection of Jesus, because He is the first of all God's children to awaken from the claws of death.

This resurrection from the dead has been reserved for those who have accepted and verbally confessed that Jesus is the son of God and that He arose from the dead after three days.

> **God wishes to recreate your body from mortality to immortality. All believers will follow the pattern of the resurrection of Jesus.**

Let us now look at recreation in the sense of rest and leisure.

God is not unfamiliar with the challenges that we face on a daily basis. In one text it is written: 'This High Priest of ours understands our weaknesses, for he faced all of the same testings we do, yet he did not sin.' Hebrews 4:15 NLT

> **Then Jesus said, "Come to me, all of you who are weary and carry heavy burdens, and I will give you rest. Take my yoke upon you.**
> **Let me teach you, because I am humble and gentle at heart, and you will find rest for your souls.** Matthew 11:28-29 NLT
> *Jesus of Nazareth*

Jesus declared that we can cast our burdens onto Him and he will give us rest. The word for ***rest***, which was used in the original Greek manuscript means '*intermission, recreation and to be refreshed.*' Through a deep intimacy with Christ Jesus we will be refreshed and He will assist us to carry the burdens which life imposes on us.

> **God wishes to bestow recreation upon His children: recreation of remaking and recreation of rest and being refreshed.**

6. Remuneration

Each of us will be repaid according our deeds and actions. God wants to give us crowns of glory, honour and immortality when Jesus judges us for our works that we did while we were alive.

> **And when the chief Shepherd appears, you will receive the unfading crown of glory.** 1 Peter 5:4 ESV
> *Peter the Apostle*

> **God "will repay each person according to what they have done." To those who by persistence in doing good seek glory, honour and immortality, he will give eternal life.** Romans 2:6-7 NIV
> *Paul the Apostle*

Accessing God's wonderful gifts
All seven gifts which God wishes to give to people are available to everybody who has the key to open the storehouse of God's gracious benevolence. That key is faith. Faith will unlock the door to salvation and the path to pleasing God. However, if you do not have faith and you walk in doubt, it does not change what God can do, it simply changes what God can do for you.
God can do nothing for the person who does not believe that he exists and that He rewards those who seek Him.

> **If you walk in doubt and unbelief, it does not change what God can do, it simply changes what God can do for you.**

7. Relation

> **But as many as received him, to them gave He power to become the sons of God, even to them that believe on his name.** John 1:12 KJV
> *Paul the Apostle*

Although we were slaves to sin, God wished to bestow upon us the rights of sons by offering up His only son. God wants to bestow **sonship** upon His people. Through this offering of one son God would obtain many sons. The word ***sons*** refers to both male and female human beings. In a letter to the church in Rome, Paul the Apostle stated that we were slaves for a short while but now we will come into full maturity as children of God. Ephesians 4:13
In another place He wrote: 'praise be to God of whom the whole family in Heaven and Earth is named.' Ephesians 3:15

Before ascending into Heaven, Jesus prayed this prayer: "that they *(the followers of Jesus)* all may be one, as You, Father, are in Me, and I in You; that they also may be one in Us, that the world may believe that You sent Me." John 17:21 NKJV
We are elevated to the position of children of God when we receive Jesus and believe on His name.
In the parable of the prodigal son we saw that the father desired nothing more than to restore his lost son to his former position because the son's restoration will lead to a stronger relationship between father and son. In one text Paul the Apostle wrote: "we are co-heirs with (Jesus) Christ." Romans 8:17
Thus our elevation from slaves of sin to sons permits us to be equal heirs with Jesus of all that the Father has.

> **God seeks a stronger relationship with all of mankind and He wishes to bestow all the benefits of sonship on them.**

God wishes to spend eternity with his children. The relationship that He desires is one that will last into all eternity.
What higher value and self-esteem can a mortal man ever wish to have? There is no greater esteem that a man can hope for than to be loved by Almighty God and to be called a child of Almighty God, the creator and keeper of all things. John the Apostle testified of the great love that God has for mankind by allowing us to be called His children. The true believer's self-esteem is secure in the knowledge that he is a child of the living God, although he cannot see God with his natural eyes.

> **How great is the love the Father has lavished on us, that we should be called children of God! And that is what we are!** 1 John 3:1 NIV
> *John the Apostle*

The Seven Aspects of Man's Value

When we look at **The Seven Aspects of How Things Are Valued**, in relation to man's creation, we clearly see that:

1. God placed His image on man – this is God's trademark or ***unique insignia placed on man.***

2. God placed an eternal spirit inside of man – the sort of spirit that animals do not possess, and it is this eternal spirit that is that ***unique marking and attribute which man possesses and which is the distinguishing feature which indicates the origins of man and also man's uniqueness relative to other creatures.***
3. When God sent His son to die for all of mankind, He placed His valuation on every human being that He created ... ***the Creator dictated the value of His creation.***
4. God put His personal touch on man, when He created mankind. ***The high level of personal care that God invested in man contributes highly to man's value.***
5. God made mankind to dominate and control all life forms on Earth – this was man's God-ordained function and purpose. ***The intended purpose of man contributes highly to man's value.***
6. God is most suited to heal our broken bodies and broken hearts, because He alone has all the right knowledge and tools which are needed for our healing. ***God is the manufacturer who is most suited, equipped and qualified to perform maintenance and servicing, in the form of healing, on man.***
7. God has the power to restore us completely to our original, creative state, if we desire it, but He will distance Himself from anyone who refuses to live in the manner that He intended. ***God is the manufacturer of man who is most suited to recreate and upgrade any human being, and He will distance Himself from any person who drastically deviates from His original design, in form and function.***

There is no-one who understands your value as much as God, the Creator. He knows everything about you, and wants to have a relationship with you.
Furthermore, He wants to awaken you to your true worth, because **YOU ARE VALUABLE!**

God Values You

The greatest love is the love that God has for every woman and man;
If you didn't know it - God loves you and God is your biggest fan.

He sent His beloved and valuable son, from His throne up high;
So that in the place of every woman, man and child He should die.

Jesus, the Saviour, fulfilled God's prophetic promise from millennia before -
That through His death, God will man to his former glory restore.

Your worth has been made equivalent to the life of God the Creator -
There is no value on a person's life that could be greater.

All God's promises and gifts for man are wrapped up in Jesus, the Messiah;
The Creator gave you all of Himself - no-one can value you higher.

There is nothing in all of creation for which God shows more care;
We are worth more than lilies in the field and sparrows in the air.

Jesus taught us that we are the light of the world and salt of the earth -
Every single person ever born carries great value and worth.

Jesus warned us that every man must properly value his own soul -
To gain all the world's riches and lose your own soul is heavy toll.

As you love yourself, so you must love your neighbours far and near -
This is the sum total of God's Law, and every prophet and seer.

Jesus also taught us many wise and practical principles for a happy life -
How to value others by exercising forgiveness and avoiding strife.

He said we must show mercy and loving-kindness, even to a stranger -
Be a Good Samaritan to those who have fallen prey to danger.

Jesus promised that we will do greater things than he has done;
Because through the baptism of the Holy Spirit, with Christ we are one.

Through obedience to the Holy Spirit, with divine wisdom we are led;
And we are filled with the same power that raised Christ from the dead.

God has given you everything to be happy, healthy and completely well;
And He desires that all His children will with Him for eternity dwell.

To God, the Creator, you are not just the average rung of the mill;
To God you are loveable, costly, expensive and ... **You Are Valuable!**

Glisson J. Heldzinger

Chapter 5

Precious Stones

> **The story of the human race is the story of men and women selling themselves short.**
> *Abraham Maslow*

People sell themselves short

Little Rosey hopped and jumped as she was walking hand-in-hand with her father at the carnival. Her father told her that she can have anything that she wanted to eat and drink. She was excited at the prospect of being able to buy whatever her heart desires.
As they walked pass the different food stalls, she saw all the delicious pies, hot-dogs, burgers, fries, cookies, sodas and milk-shakes on display but when her eyes fell on the bright-coloured cotton-candy (candy floss) she knew exactly what she wanted.
"I want the cotton-candy. It looks so delicious...mmmmmm!" she shouted as she pointed and jumped up and down.
"Alright Sweetheart, if cotton-candy is what you want, cotton-candy is what you'll get," her father answered.
After having paid and the little girl was holding the stick with a huge mountain of cotton-candy wrapped around the end, the father asked:
"Are you sure that you can finish all that candy, Sweetheart?"
She looked up at her father, with her left hand holding the stick, a handful of cotton-candy in her right hand and a mouth full of the sweet treat and answered while chewing:
"Don't worry Daddy I'm alot bigger on the inside than I am on the outside."

This chapter was written to show you that you are a lot bigger on the inside than on the outside, and that there is a lot more to you than meets the eye.

Diamonds

When coal is exposed to high temperatures and high pressure for millions of years deep underneath the earth's surface, it is transformed into diamonds. These stones may have had humble beginnings but they are celebrated and highly prized. Each and every human being is just like a like a piece of coal – we may not start out resembling what we can be, but through a long process of change, eventually we become a diamond. Even a diamond needs attention in order to let its brilliance shine through. When a cutter and polisher takes a rough stone through a process of cleaning, cutting and polishing, the diamond becomes a gemstone and its brilliance shines through. That's a long way to travel for a little piece of wood – from being a piece of wood, to being a piece of coal, then being a rough stone and then finally a gemstone.

Developing human potential can be equated to the process of the formation of a gemstone from a seemingly insignificant piece of wood.

We must all begin to see ourselves as diamonds in the making, and we must also see others in the same way.

As you read through the pages of this chapter, I dare you to embrace higher possibilities for yourself. I dare you to see yourself as the shimmering, extremely valuable diamond that you are. You have greatness inside of you – RELEASE YOUR BRILLIANCE!

You have greatness inside of you – RELEASE YOUR BRILLIANCE!

How you see yourself

> **A gift is as a precious stone in the eyes of him that hath it: whithersoever it turneth, it prospereth.** Proverbs 17:8 KJV
> *King Solomon*

Each man is precious and valuable. When you appreciate and cherish your own unique physical, intellectual, emotional and spiritual attributes then you begin to value yourself. This sense of self-worth is one that is not wavering and inconsistent, but instead it is a self-worth that is stable and consistent. It is like holding a handful of brilliant diamonds and regardless of where you travel and what you may face, those diamonds are still valuable. A handful of diamonds are a metaphor for the valuable and unique gifts that God has given to everyone. Every man should see each of his unique characteristics and talents as a precious stone with unwavering value and that these stones remain valuable and precious regardless of the opinions of others and the circumstances that the holder faces.

The Gideon mind-set

In the biblical book of Judges we read about a young man named Gideon. We read that Gideon was hiding in the mountains because he feared being attacked by Israel's enemies. Gideon was threshing corn in a winepress. An angel sent from God startles Gideon when he says:
"The Lord is with you, mighty warrior."
To this Gideon replies:
"If the Lord is with us, why has this happened to us? ...The Lord has abandoned us and put us in the hand of Midian."
The angel responds to his unbelief by saying:
"Go in the strength you have and save Israel out of Midian's hand. Am I not sending you?"
"But Lord, how can I save Israel? My clan is the weakest in Manasseh, and I am the least in my family,"
Gideon replied. Judges 6:1-15
We read further that Gideon becomes more courageous as time passes. He tears down the altar of a foreign God and he and an army of only three hundred men eventually defeat the many-thousand strong Midianite army.

Gideon possessed an inferiority complex related to his family and also himself. Furthermore, he regarded himself as the proverbial "black sheep" of his family. Gideon had a very poor self-image. He had a negative rendition. Gideon assumed a self-devaluing approach to life. Although Gideon lived approximately 1100 years before Christ, the phenomenon of self-devaluation displayed by Gideon is still common. Tragically, every individual on earth feels inferior or inadequate in one or more areas of their life. Self-devaluation is a characteristic that is an integral part of the human psyche. The celebrated psychiatrist, Abraham Maslow said that "the story of the human race is the story of men and women selling themselves short."

Maslow was right. All human beings have been infected by the virus of low self-worth and self-discounting. If we are to find a cure for this viral infection, we must do a thorough diagnosis of the problem. A thorough diagnosis begins with symptoms and then looks at the causes. We know the symptoms. The symptoms are low or no confidence, achievement and fulfilment. Then we go to the place where it all starts.

> **The first symptoms of low self-value are low or no confidence, low achievement and low fulfilment.**

Where does this self-discounting start?

People develop these deep-rooted negative feelings and images of themselves from their first inter-actions with others. From the time babies develop and start exploring their environments and as they grow into teenagers, many of them are bombarded with negative affirmations which eventually sink into the child's subconscious mind. Adults carelessly say things like:

"Don't do that! You are naughty!" and

"This is a miserable child."

Sometimes adults will say:

"You are not like your brother," and

"You are stupid! You can't do anything right. You are going to fail in school because you are dumb!"

Sometimes these statements are made by parents, relatives and teachers. As these recurring statements take root in a child's subconscious mind, he begins to shape his image of himself around these perceived truths. They are not truths. They are only perceived and imagined truths. We readily accept these perceptions of ourselves on a deep, subconscious level. We then become the victims of the interpretation of others. We therefore see ourselves through the eyes of others.

> **We see ourselves through the eyes of others.**

Our rendition then becomes an acting-out of the indoctrination of others. In the story of Gideon we see that many years of Midianite persecution and fear linked to the small size and the poverty of Gideon's clan had indoctrinated him into believing that he was worthless and impotent compared to other people. This was just the first symptom. A second symptom of low self-value displayed itself. Gideon justified his low self-worth by arguing for his shortcomings. Gideon seemed determined to hold onto his negative perceptions of himself. Gideon was saying to the angel that the evidence supports the conclusion that he is nothing and that he will never achieve anything significant and will never become anyone significant.

> **People of low self-value argue for their perceived shortcomings by providing past evidence and this allows them to continue believing the lie and holding onto the lie.**

This symptom has a terrible backlash because you can only achieve that of which you are convinced of being capable of achieving. Whatever you argue for becomes a self-fulfilling prophecy.
Henry Ford, the industrialist who revolutionised automotive manufacturing and the production line, was someone who had to overcome many obstacles in his life. Mr. Ford had a very simple philosophy and this philosophy served him well throughout his life. Through its understanding and its use he became one of the wealthiest men in the world during the mid-1900s. Mr. Ford believed that whether you think you can or think you can't, either way you are right.

> **Whether you think you can, or you think you can't – you're right.**
> *Henry Ford*

The story of Gideon reveals to us a young man who was convinced that he can't. He argued vehemently to substantiate this claim. The strength of Gideon's argument lies in his memory of past events and the opinions of others. His argument was based on historical recollection. He recalled how the Israelites had been continuously attacked by the Midianites and he recalled the sneers of other people directed at him and his family. Gideon's thinking was highly flawed. People in modern times still display this flaw in their thinking, reasoning and arguments. The flaw lies in using the experiences from your past to predict your future. It is a thinking habit which states that if I've consistently failed, and I've been consistently ridiculed and attacked in the past, then I must be a failure, and if I am a failure now then I will still be a failure in the future. People incorrectly believe that past failures are a guarantee of future failures, and inversely that past successes are a guarantee of future successes. This was Gideon's philosophy. He believed it and lived it. People today believe and live that same philosophy.

> **People incorrectly believe that past failures are a guarantee of future failures, and inversely that past successes are a guarantee of future successes.**

It is a fallacious lie! Your past failures are not a seal of future failures. The truth is that every man and woman's life represents an array of successes and failures. No individual is so fortunate as to have never failed at anything and no individual is so unfortunate as to never have succeeded at anything.

> **Every man and woman's life represents an array of successes and failures.**

The only way to overcome self-depreciating thoughts is to start thinking positive thoughts about yourself. When you change your thought patterns, you will say more positive words about yourself.

Changing thought patterns

> **Men simply don't think.**
> *Dr. Albert Schweitzer*

Reshaping your thought patterns is not an easy process. Undoing years of negative indoctrination and ineffective cognitive habits requires more than just a quick motivational seminar or self-help book. Reshaping your perceptions of self is not a goal which can be accomplished overnight because it is a process, and the process is difficult.

When things are going well, it is easy to say:
"I'm beautiful," or
"I'm smart and articulate," or
"I'm wealthy and successful."

However, when things do not go well, it is very easy to slip back into old self-depreciating patterns of thinking and say things like:
"I'm just too unattractive to find a life partner," or
"I'm just dumb and stupid," or
"I'm not good with money...I'm a failure."

Since actions follow thought, when you slip into old patterns of thinking you slip into old actions.

The process of change follows seven steps. They are the steps which are necessary for an adjustment in your thoughts. Let us look at those steps briefly.

The Seven Steps of Change

1. ***Dissatisfaction***

   You must be dissatisfied with the way you see yourself and the results that you've attained thus far. Without a sense of dissatisfaction related to who you are, the results that you've attained thus far and your level of effectiveness, you will never move beyond where you find yourself. People who are complacent will never move - only those who are dissatisfied will move themselves into action.

2. ***Desire***

   Even if you are dissatisfied, you must also have a strong desire for change – the changing of yourself and your circumstances. You must have a burning desire to make something better of yourself – desire is the fuel that will propel you towards your dreams.

3. ***Depart***
   In order to leave your circumstances, you must first leave your old self behind - you must depart from set thinking habits. Only when you are willing to leave behind the old person who is satisfied with mediocre results, and who is lazy and complacent will you be able move forward. In order to get to where you want to be, you must first depart from where you are.

4. ***Displace***
   The only way to get rid of bad thinking habits is to displace them. 'In order get out of something old, you must get into something new,' is the maxim that you must learn and apply in the area of your thinking patterns. Expose yourself to positive, uplifting and valuable knowledge and skills so that you can begin to entertain new thought patterns.

5. ***Decline***
   Decline any thoughts that entertain the notion that you are not valuable or worthy. Be vigilant about the thoughts that you entertain. When you notice that you are sinking back into old thinking patterns, block out those thoughts immediately and then think about something positive and uplifting. Think thoughts that will produce quality actions – quality thoughts produce quality actions and quality actions produce quality results.

6. ***Discipline***
   Develop the thinking habits that are necessary for your success. Success in any endeavour is the result of regular disciplined action of mind and body. Discipline requires commitment. When you combine commitment and discipline in the area of your thinking, it will begin to manifest as greater effectiveness in every area of your life.

7. ***Daily renewal***
   Every day, expose yourself to uplifting and positive material which will shape your perceptions in a

positive manner. Read material that builds you up. Listen to empowering teachings. Associate with people of value. By exercising these routines daily, you will be renewing your mind by flushing away all negative thoughts, ideas and perceptions.

Prescriptions for overcoming low self-value

Below are some inspiring quotes to help you embrace new thought-patterns concerning your identity, your value and your potential. When you believe and act out these prescriptions, your thoughts will change and your actions will then change and then your results will change.

Someone else's opinion of you does not have to be your reality.
How someone else sees you does not have to be how you see yourself.

Improvement in action can only come from improvement in thought.

Your life's path is not set in concrete - you can choose to belief different and be different.

Only a diamond can cut a diamond, so only a mature and strong man can make another man mature and strong.

To mould yourself on the opinions of others is to believe a lie,
Continue doing this and your self-value will most certainly die.

Chapter 6

Value Redefined

> **For a man to achieve all that is demanded of him he must regard himself as greater than he is.**
> *Johann W. Von Goethe*

Self-actualization

In an earlier chapter I discussed the concept of *rendition.* Rendition was defined as the way that people act because of how they see and value themselves.
Related to rendition is actualization. Rendition is acting out who and what you believe yourself to be while actualization refers to becoming what you believe you could be and should be. Every man is perpetually realizing the person who he believes he is meant or destined to be – this is referred to as self-actualization. The term self-actualization was popularized by the distinguished psychiatrist, Dr. Abraham Maslow. According to Dr. Maslow this process of actualization is present in every human being, from the time that the individual is born.

> **All the evidence that we have indicates that it is reasonable to assume in practically every human being, and certainly in almost every newborn baby, that there is an active will toward health, an impulse towards growth, or towards the actualization.**
> **What a man can be, he must be. This need we call self-actualization.**
> *Abraham Maslow*

Self-actualization begins with the self-image. Stated differently, actualization of the individual begins with how the individual sees himself. If an individual does not have an accurate picture of himself, he will always be falling short of who he could be. This is especially true where concerns the individual's picture of his abilities. Short-sightedness of what you can do translates into short-sightedness of what you can be. When you believe that you cannot do something, you limit the value of what you can manifest.

> **Short-sightedness of what you can do translates into short-sightedness of what you can be. When you believe that you cannot do something, you limit the value of what you can manifest.**

You will still realize your belief of who you are, but it will be way below your potential value. Potential is an ability that can be applied. Potential is what you could do and could be. Dr. Maslow wrote that a man must be what he can be, and this is what self-actualization entails. It then follows that if a man does not know what he can be, that he can never apply himself to actualize his true potential. Applied potential is of great use, but unapplied potential is a waste.

If someone has an accurate view of himself, he is constantly moving towards a true version of himself. He is actualizing someone who is aligned with the greatness, dominion and authority that he possesses.
We all are moving towards a version of ourselves. For some people that version is a genuine one, and for others it is a fake one.

I was involved in the movie rental industry for many years. Piracy has always been a major problem in this industry, even when video-cassettes were being used. Advancements in computer technology dealt a death-blow to the traditional video rental industry worldwide because pirate movies were more easily accessible. Through the internet people are able to download content and then write it onto a blank DVD (digital versatile disc) or other storage devices like hard drives, memory cards and flash drives. Through our licensed suppliers we were given access to information that highlighted the dangers of pirated content to a user's electronic equipment. When you insert a pirated DVD disc into a DVD player you risk damaging the software and sometimes the hardware of your valuable equipment. Piracy is also stealing because it violates the rights of copyright holders by denying them their due income. In addition, the sale of pirated goods is a criminal offence that robs any country of valuable tax revenue. Here in South Africa many informal vendors sell pirated DVD discs at malls, shopping centres and at traffic intersections. Oftentimes people buy from these vendors and when they watch the movie it is not what is presented on the sleeve.

The quality of pirate movies is so bad, that it will deny the discerning viewer a truly satisfying viewing experience. The viewer is not getting the maximum benefit because he did not make the effort to invest in a better version of the motion picture.

Just as some people invest in fake motion pictures, many people invest in a fake picture of themselves. Human beings do not get the maximum benefit from their lives when they do not make the effort to invest in a better version of the picture they have of themselves.

> **Human beings do not get the maximum benefit from their lives when they do not make the effort to invest in a better version of the picture they have of themselves.**

In a proverbial sense, people easily buy into the perceptions that they pick up on the street from punters and hawkers of inferior pictures. These hawkers can be a parent who called you stupid or abused you when you were growing up. A teacher who does not understand a child's unique learning style may have called the child dumb and stupid. A mean spouse who is verbally and/or physically abusive could also cause people to buy into inferior pictures of themselves. Sometimes you can pick up an inferior picture from a work colleague or from your boss.

There are tyrants in the dark chapters of the history of mankind who were able to establish certain laws that make people from one race inferior to another.

As you can see, it is possible to acquire an inferior picture of yourself in any environment.

When people buy into these inferior pictures they see themselves as less than adequate, less than capable and less than worthy. The greatest danger of buying into an inferior picture of yourself is that you can hold onto it for many years. An inferior picture can have disastrous consequences for many years into the future. For example, a child who was called stupid by a teacher could grow up seeing himself as stupid, and then manifest that belief as an adult. A battered wife may accept the idea that she is unattractive and unlovable and this may prevent her from walking away from the abusive relationship because she does not belief that someone else will want to be with her.

One of the indicators of the quality of the picture that individuals have of themselves is their conversations relating to themselves. One line that I have heard often being said by people who have not been able to realize a goal is: 'It was probably not meant to be. If it was, then it would have happened.'

This statement has several implications. Firstly, it implies that success is something that is guaranteed for some and not for others. Secondly, it implies that your efforts cannot secure success if it is not meant for you. Thirdly, it implies that the speaker is prepared to settle for something less than what he desires because it is just according to the order of things that he should not have that which he seeks.

To people who have made such a statement, or a similar one, concerning the picture that they have of themselves, I want to pose this question:

Who decided that it was not meant to be?

Was it God? Was it the stars? Was it the universe? Was it nature?

Before you read further, please ponder these questions and formulate the answers in your mind. Don't read ahead until you have satisfied yourself with the answers.

The correct answer to the question posed in the previous paragraph is *none of the above.* The only person who decides what's possible for you... is YOU!

It is important that you know what picture of yourself you have bought into because it is the foundation of your self-value.

Let us now look at the concept of value.

What is value?

In this section we will be looking at value from two perspectives. Firstly, I will investigate the traditional definition of the word ***value***. Secondly, I will redefine the concept of value as it pertains to people.

The word ***value*** comes from the Latin word ***valere*** which means '*be strong, be well; be of value, be worth.*'
It refers to the quality of something. It also refers to the measure of importance of something.
Value also refers to the fair monetary worth of something offered for its exchange. In short, value refers to the measure of the worth of an item.

Value is a ***perception concept***. It is the price-tag that we assign to people – including ourselves, organizations, things and circumstances. The process of valuing is nothing more than the assigning of a measure of worth onto someone or something. Stated differently, valuing is the process whereby we put a price-tag indicating the cost of a person or item.

Life can be defined simply as the searching, acquiring, maintaining, developing, expressing, bestowing and enjoying of value. It is ***searching*** because we look for value in people, organizations, circumstances and things and we only associate with the people we see as worthy and worthwhile. It is ***acquiring*** because we acquire what we desire through taking, buying and exchange. It is ***maintaining*** because we want to hold onto what is precious and dear to us and we want to preserve the state of what we have. It is ***developing*** because we want to grow and increase the quantity and quality of what we have. It is ***expressing*** because we convey to people what we think and feel about them. It is **bestowing** because we readily give of ourselves and our resources, to others by blessing them with the best of ourselves for reasons that vary from person to person. It is ***enjoying*** because we find satisfaction, fulfilment and happiness through the appreciation of value in ourselves and others, by ourselves and others.

In human terms, value is individual and relational.
The ***individual aspect*** refers to the value that the individual places on himself. The ***relational aspect*** refers to the value that that the individual places on others as well as the value they place on him.

As it pertains to the individual and relational aspects stated above, value refers to **worth** and **worthiness**.
The Seven Aspects of the Value of an Individual refers to the combination of all following seven aspects listed below:

1. the worth of his life;
2. his equal worth to other people, regardless of differences;
3. the worth of his ideas and dreams;
4. the value of his contribution;
5. the worth of his presence;
6. the value of his needs; and
7. the value of his freedom.

The value of an individual refers to worth in respect of: his life, his equality to others, his ideas and dreams, his contribution, his presence, his needs and his freedom.

Worthiness refers to the right of the individual to have things of value as well as being seen as a valuable individual. Worthiness says that I deserve good things. We must see ourselves as having just as much right to the good things that life has to offer as the next person. Worthiness speaks about the individual's right to have everything good that the next person has because he is not less worthy than the next person. Value is about seeing. Unless you see yourself as worthy, you will never pursue any thing worthy.

Worthiness refers to the right of the individual to have things of value as well as being seen as a valuable individual.
Unless you see yourself as worthy, you will never pursue any thing worthy.

Valuing yourself and others

Value is useful because it defines the parameters of our relationships with other people, organizations and things. This can be defined as ***contribution***, because it relates to how much we will contribute of ourselves and our resources to other people, groups, organizations and things. We express the level of value we assign to any of these groups through such things as acts of love, spending time with, caring for, looking out for and protecting the people and things we have in our lives. In this sense, the more we ***love*** something (or someone), the more resources we will devote to it (or them). Thus, the love can be restated as value. We can then say that the more we ***value*** someone or something, the more resources we will devote to it.
If I do not value ***myself*** very highly, I am highly critical of my flaws, shortcomings, mistakes and weaknesses, and I will not like my own company. However, if I value myself highly, I will be comfortable in my own skin.
If I do not value ***someone else*** highly, it will be easy to be critical towards that person, and I will see no need to associate and spend time with that person. Whereas, in contrast, if I value someone highly then I will constantly seek out opportunities to spend time in that person's presence.
If I do not value the combined and common purpose of a ***group***, I will not align myself with it and its people. However, if I value what the group purposes to achieve, I will align myself to it.
If I do not value the product-offering and market position of an ***organization***, I will not support it. However, if the organization's products appeal to my needs, I will gladly spend money to acquire its products. It is plainly obvious, in these statements, that value defines the parameters – the length, width and breadth of all our social interactions. It defines the parameters of our level of ***contribution***.

The assigning of value should have an ultimate end. The end of all value is the receiving of something that brings pleasure, happiness, enjoyment, fulfilment and satisfaction to yourself and others. This end is the ***remuneration*** that we receive. Usually, remuneration is a direct function of contribution – the more you contribute, the more you are remunerated with. It can also be seen that contribution and remuneration are directly proportional – as one goes up so does the other, and as one goes down so does the other.

> **The value of your contribution determines the value of your remuneration.**

We are remunerated when we receive a reward for our contribution. In relationships that reward can be the privilege of being able to spend time with a loved one. For organizations, reward is the financial gain for our marketing efforts. The reward can be the degree that we receive for years of studying. The reward can be the pretty lady who says yes to your marriage proposal because you have proven yourself to be a viable prospect as a life-partner. The reward can be a promotion to a higher-rank with more money because you are a dedicated employee who delivers above-average work. It can thus be said that the value of your contribution sets the bar for your worthiness for remuneration so that your level of remuneration is determined by the level of your contribution.

> **The value of your contribution sets the bar for your worthiness for remuneration so that the level of remuneration is determined by the level of your contribution.**

However, the value that is assigned to people is not solely related to what they have contributed. Value is also related to what people are, and what they have inside of them. When we consider an individual's contributions, we are looking at his value as it pertains to the past. However, we must also look at the prospective value of the individual – what his value is related to the future. Contribution considers someone's past activities but ***potential*** looks at their prospective future activities.

> **Contribution considers someone's past activities but potential looks at their prospective future activities.**

It then becomes clear that an individual cannot simply be assigned a level of worth and usefulness on face-value. As has been mentioned in this chapter, we need to consider an individual's past and future in order to determine their value. But, that is still not sufficient. We must look at everything that pertains to the individual – we need a holistic approach. The holistic approach considers the value of an individual from the key areas pertaining to his life, and gives one an accurate assessment of the individual's true value. Let us now look at those important aspects of the individual's persona so that we can value ourselves and others accurately.

The Aspects of Individuality

> **Every man is unique and possesses individuality and peculiarity, recognizing this grants him value and dignity.**

In order to value ourselves and others accurately, we must first look at the constituent components, or aspects, that make up the persona of an individual. It is only when we recognize the individuality and peculiarity of ourselves and others that we can gain and give value and dignity to ourselves and others. There are seven aspects, which I refer to as ***The Aspects of Individuality*** and they are:

1. physical
2. position
3. purpose
4. potential
5. problems
6. performance
7. personality

1. Physical

Physical refers to the features of your body. Physical differences exist amongst all people. No two people are exactly alike and no two people, including identical twins, look exactly alike in every respect.

In 1903 a prisoner by the name of Will West arrived at Leavenworth State Penitentiary, in the state of Kansas in the USA. When Will West was asked if he had ever been incarcerated at Leavenworth, he said that he had not. The clerk was suspicious of West's answer because she had learnt from experience that inmates were not always honest regarding the matter of previous incarceration at prisons. Her suspicions prompted her to look through the prisoner records. Back then all prisoners had their body measurements recorded and stored according to a method known as the Bertillon system. The clerk found a file of an inmate which matched Will West's Bertillon measurements and the photographs were similar, but the names were different. The oddity was that the file which she located was for a prisoner who was already being held at the prison. The prisoner's name was William West. An investigation into the matter revealed that Will West and William West were identical twins.

The William West and Will West case provided the impetus for the transition from the use of body measurements to the use of finger-printing to record and identify individuals in the criminal justice system in the United States of America.

William and Will West were identical or monozygotic twins. The term monozygotic refers to the splitting of a single zygote (fertilized egg) into two and then forming two embryos. The babies are identical in their genetic make-up and will therefore look alike and have the same gender. The shared genetic make-up was the reason for the identical appearance and body measurements between the West twins. However, their finger-prints differed.

All fingerprints consist of three basic features, namely:

1. **loops**, which start and end at the same side and which is the side of the opening;
2. **arches**, which go from one side to the other; and
3. **whorls**, which are almost circular with the ridge lines going all the way around.

There are billions of people on planet Earth today, and each person has a unique combination of loops, arches and whorls making up their fingerprints.

Even when people look similar, they still have uniqueness or peculiarity in some aspect. These peculiarities are physical, as in the case of our fingerprints, facial shape, body shape, skin colour, height, hair type and colour. Thus each person is a monotype and not a stereotype. Unless we understand the monotypic nature of the individual, we will never really appreciate him.

2. Position

Everybody occupies some sort of position in the groups and organizations that they belong to. That position is unique to every person. In every position the individual will play a different role.

In your family you occupy positions that are unique to you, such as that of being the father in the house, relative to your children as well as the husband in the house, relative to your wife. In the same way, only your firstborn child will hold the unique position of being the oldest sibling amongst his/her brothers and sisters. If you are the oldest living female in your family, you will occupy the position of the matriarch. These are all familial positions.

In your organization you may hold a leadership position, such as being the chief financial officer of the organization, or you may be an ordinary clerk. These are organizational positions.

You could also be the spokesperson for an organization which fights for a specific cause such as the cessation of the killing of an endangered animal species or perhaps the scrapping of unreasonable laws in a country. You may also be a famous singer who is followed, admired and emulated by millions of fans worldwide. These are public positions. Those people who hold influential public positions are able to shape trends and the opinions of other people on a worldwide scale.

Every person occupies more than one of these three types of positions simultaneously throughout their lives. When you consider your familial, organizational and public positions you must be aware that each carries with it different types of responsibilities and rewards. To explain this, let me use the example of a woman who is a wife, mother, corporate executive and she is also a member of the board of the local church's fund-raising committee as well as being a Sunday school teacher.

As a wife she will ensure that her husband always has cleaned and pressed clothing for work. She will also ensure that her husband and children are fed good food. These are her familial responsibilities. The rewards she receives from performing these responsibilities are a sense of joy and happiness from knowing that she can show her love for her family through her actions and support.

At the company where she works as an executive her responsibilities are different to her responsibilities at home. Whereas she cares for her small children at home, at work she has to manage large groups of adult employees who report to her on a daily basis. She is also less emotionally attached to the people at work. Her presence in the company is primarily for financial reward – she puts in the time at work and she is rewarded appropriately. Her reasons for going to work are different to the reasons that she has for going home.

As a member of the church's fund-raising committee she is volunteering of her time to raise funds to ensure that the church's services bill and the minister's salary are always paid on time by co-ordinating various income-generating activities. As a Sunday school teacher she has the privilege to shape young minds by teaching them valuable life lessons. She does not receive a financial reward for her efforts at church, but she gains a sense of accomplishment knowing that she has made a small, but meaningful difference in the lives of other people.

King Solomon wrote: "A friend is always loyal, and a brother is born to help in time of need."

> **A friend is always loyal, and a brother is born to help in time of need.** Proverbs 17:17 NLT
> *King Solomon*

We all occupy positions which make us indispensable to others, both in friendship and family circles. Every individual plays a valuable role in his family, organization and in society.

> **Every individual plays a valuable role in his family, organization and in society.**

3. Purpose

Purpose relates to those things that you pursue, live for and dedicate your life to. King Solomon wrote that where there is no vision, the people perish.

> **Where there is no vision,**
> **the people perish.** Proverbs 18:29 KJV
> *King Solomon*

Stated differently, people fail when they lack purpose in life. Every individual has unique dreams, goals and aspirations which he wishes to realize. This is the unique purpose of an individual. A purpose is a dream or goal.
Earl Nightingale defined success as the progressive realization of a worthy goal.

> **Success is the progressive realisation of a worthy goal.**
> *Earl Nightingale*

From Mr. Nightingale's definition we see that a goal must be 'worthy.' A worthy goal is a valuable goal. Success is the progressive realisation of a valuable goal. We must be progressively realising a goal that is of value.
Purpose also relates to what we want to achieve and make of ourselves.
Albert Einstein recommended that each of us should be more concerned with becoming a person of value than a person of great success.

> **Try not to become a man of success, but rather try to become a man of value.**
> *Albert Einstein*

I believe that Dr. Einstein was telling us that inner value is worth more than outer value. The truly valuable individual is not defined by his assets but by his inner character and strength. Jim Rohn, the American philosopher once said: "The major value in life is not what you get. The major value in life is what you become."

> **The major value in life is not what you get. The major value in life is what you become.**
> *Jim Rohn*

As we pursue success in our endeavours, we must become more aware of the impact that the pursuit of our goals has on us than we are of the goals themselves. We must pursue goals that are truly worthwhile and worthy, as Earl Nightingale taught. Since our goals define us, we must know that only worthy goals create worthy people. Valuable people set valuable goals because the value of the goals you pursue determine the value that you will become.

> **Valuable people set valuable goals because the value of the goals you pursue determine the value that you will become.**

Jim Rohn also wrote: 'The major reason for setting a goal is for what it makes of you to accomplish it. What it makes of you will always be the far greater value than what you get.' In this statement, Mr. Rohn reinforced that goals determine your value.

> **The major reason for setting a goal is for what it makes of you to accomplish it.**
> **What it makes of you will always be the far greater value than what you get.**
> *Jim Rohn*

Related to purpose is passion. Passion is a deep love for something or someone. Every individual has passions for things that are dear to him. Our lives would be empty if we did not purposely pursue the relationships and things that bring us joy, happiness and fulfilment. Passion also speaks about unrivalled commitment and enjoyment. Every person possesses a unique combination of valuable purposes and passions. We must pursue our purposes with intensity and commitment.

> **You've gotta dance like there's nobody watching,**
> **Love like you'll never be hurt,**

> **Sing like there's nobody listening,**
> **And live like it's heaven on earth.**
> *William W. Purkey*

4. Potential

The Oxford Online Dictionary defines ***potential*** as '*latent qualities or abilities that may be developed and lead to future success or usefulness.'*

Potential deals with the abilities and other qualities resident within an individual.

Let us look at a branch of science to gain a broader understanding of potential.

Physics is the branch of science which deals with the study of matter, energy, motion and force. Energy comes in two forms, namely:

1. potential energy, and
2. kinetic energy.

When an object is stationary, the earth's gravitational force gives ***potential energy*** to that object, but when the object moves and falls toward the earth, *kinetic energy* (or motion energy) is produced.

Just like an in animate object has potential energy, human beings have a type of potential energy deep inside of them. Every human being has potential. It was Ralph Waldo Emerson who said:

"What lies behind us and what lies ahead of us are tiny matters compared to what lies within us."

Potential is something that lies within you.

It has nothing to do with your past failures or successes.

> **What lies behind us and what lies ahead of us are tiny matters compared to what lies within us.**
> *Ralph Waldo Emerson*

Each individual has been endowed with both *common potential* and also *unique potential.*

Common potential is what everybody can do. Common potential is the ability to perform physical functions such as clean-up and walk to the store to buy something, and also

mental functions such as calculate the result of a simple mathematical problem like 3x3x3.
Unique potential is the extra-ordinary potential that people possess such as unusual physical strength and endurance or mental functions such as creativity and also problem-solving. Just as the potential of a stationary body is useless unless harnessed, the potential of human beings must be harnessed in order to be of any value. You have a choice as to what you will do with what is inside of you. A choice is deciding in which direction to employ resources. Potential is an employable resource.

> **You have a choice as to what you will do with what is inside of you. A choice is deciding in which direction to employ resources. Potential is an employable resource.**

When we believe in our own potential we are more likely to be successful. Likewise, when we believe in someone we permit them to exercise their common potential and unique potential and we give them expressive and creative air, and we thereby tacitly encourage them to be successful.

Thomas Edison had only three months of formal schooling. In school, the young Edison's mind often wandered, and his teacher, the Reverend Engle, was overheard calling him "addled", which means '*barren, useless and troubled*.' Nancy Edison immediately removed her son from the school and this ended young Tommy Edison's three months of official schooling. Edison recalled later, "My mother was the making of me. She was so true, so sure of me; and I felt I had something to live for, someone I must not disappoint."
She home-schooled her son and encouraged him to read up on physical science and philosophy. She also taught him to read the bible, placing a strong emphasis on the book of Proverbs by King Solomon. His mother's strong belief encouraged the young man to pursue his dream to be an inventor. This maternal belief paid off handsomely for Edison. Thomas Edison accumulated 2332 patents worldwide for his inventions, of which 1093 were held in the United States of America. The world would not have had such wonderful inventions like the incandescent lamp, the

phonograph and movie projectors if Edison had subscribed to the Reverend Engle's assessment of his potential.
Thankfully, Edison's mother disagreed and her son's story is now an example of how belief in someone's potential can set them on the high road of achievement, self-fulfilment and success. Edison's expressive and creative air came from his mother's unwavering encouragement and this permitted the young man to fully exercise his potential and develop into the prolific inventor that he was to become.

> **Strong belief in someone's potential can set them on the high road of achievement, self-fulfilment and success.**

Each human being is endowed with immense potential.
It has been said that human beings use less than 10% of their mental capacities. If you can achieve amazing things by applying only a fraction of your potential, imagine what you can achieve if you commit to utilizing more of your potential through skills development and education. The possibilities are endless.
Since most of us have a less than accurate assessment of our potential, we have to begin to regard ourselves as greater than we are. This is what Von Goethe meant when he wrote:
'For a man to achieve all that is demanded of him he must regard himself as greater than he is.'
When life makes demands on you, you must value yourself beyond your present assessment, because if you don't, you will never rise to the occasion and meet those demands. But worse of all, you will never exercise the great power resident within you and realise your limitless potential. Value is about becoming. To never, ever become who you could be and should be is life's greatest tragedy.

> **Value is about becoming.**
> **To never, ever become who you could be and should be is life's greatest tragedy.**

Abraham Maslow wrote that if an individual plans to be anything less than what he can be, he will probably be unhappy for the rest of his life. Put differently, it can be stated that you can only be really happy when you plan to live up to your maximum unique potential.

> **If you plan on being anything less than you are capable of being, you will probably be unhappy all the days of your life.**
> *Abraham Maslow*

Dr. Maslow added that our only true rival is our own potentialities, and that failing to live up to our possibilities is our greatest failure.

> **One's only rival is one's own potentialities. One's only failure is failing to live up to one's own possibilities. In this sense, every man can be a king, and must therefore be treated like a king.**
> *Abraham Maslow*

Dr. Maslow was absolutely correct when he claimed that every man can be a king, and must be treated like a king because of his inner potential. The word ***king*** in this case is a metaphor for a respected, honoured and valued leader regardless of their gender. This statement made by Dr. Maslow is a truth that applies to our views of ourselves and also our views of others. We must each see ourselves as a king and therefore treat ourselves as kings.
The greatest problem with human beings where potential is concerned, is that people do not see themselves as a bundle of unlimited possibilities. People limit themselves in their thinking – they sell themselves short. Dr. Maslow said that the story of the human race is the story of men and women selling themselves short.

> **The story of the human race is the story of men and women selling themselves short.**
> *Abraham Maslow*

Dr. Maslow also suggested that an individual will only change when he changes his awareness of himself. In order to stop selling himself short, the individual must be more aware of what he is capable of doing and then he can begin to see himself in a new way. When he sees himself in a new way, he can maximise his potential. In addition, we must also see other people as kings and treat them as kings.

> **What is necessary to change a person is to change his awareness of himself.**
> *Abraham Maslow*

The R.E.A.C.H. Formula for developing potential
You will never rise to the very pinnacle of your potential if it is not nurtured. The nurturing of potential is not about a once-off task but instead it is an on-going process. The R-E-A-C-H Formula is an excellent step-by-step process which can be applied to develop not only one's own potential but also the potential of others.

R = Recognize
E = Educate
A = Affirm
C = Capitalize
H = Hold On!

Recognize
You must know the potential that you have inside of you. Remember, potential is linked to purpose. Your life purpose is linked to your passion.
Ask yourself these questions:
What am I very, very good at? What do I love doing? What brings me peace and satisfaction? What will I do even if I don't get paid? What makes me sad? What makes me happy? What am I passionate about?
These questions will give you an idea as to what your life's purpose is and will show you where your potential lies.

> **Recognition of the individual's potential is the vital first step towards its activation and fulfilment.**

In 1940 Benjamin Elijah Mays became the president of Morehouse College in Atlanta, Georgia. In the same year, in his very first speech to an incoming freshman class, Mays

said: "If Morehouse is to continue to be great; it must continue to produce outstanding personalities."
In 1944, a young 15-year old African-American boy passed the Morehouse entrance examination, and was accepted at the college. This young boy caught the attention of Mays. Mays saw in the young boy a potential that exceeded that of his peers, and someone who could be one of the "outstanding personalities" that Morehouse could produce. The young man did eventually become a truly outstanding personality, not only at Morehouse, but also around the world, proving that the assessment of Mays was 100% correct. He recognized potential in the young man before the young man saw it in himself and before the rest of the world saw it. That young man was Martin Luther King Jr.

Unless the potential in an individual is first recognized, it cannot be nurtured and developed thus giving us the vital first step for the process for the development of potential. We saw earlier that Nancy, Thomas Edison's mother, recognized the young boy's potential. If she did not **recognize** her son's potential he probably would never have developed into the great inventor that he eventually became.
Sometimes someone will see our potential first, and sometimes we have to see it for ourselves first, but we must recognize it in ourselves eventually.

> **Only when we develop the potential that in a man is cast,**
> **Will he exceed and supersede his performance in the past.**

Educate

T. S. Elliot once said: "We shall not cease from exploration, and the end of all our exploring will be to arrive where we started and know the place for the first time."

It is through exploration that we discover who we are and also what we were born to do. Keep exploring until you return to where you started and you know the place. Without education, the musician will never become really great.

We shall not cease from exploration, and the end of all our exploring will be to arrive where we started and know the place for the first time.
T. S. Elliot

My people are destroyed from a lack of a desire to learn and accumulate knowledge.
Hosea (Ancient Jewish Prophet)

A human being is not attaining his full heights until he is educated.
Horace Mann

In 1889 a young Jewish couple befriended a struggling medical student by the name of Max Talmud. Talmud was immediately impressed by the curiosity of the couple's young son. The 10-year old boy wanted to know what caused the needle of a compass to move and he also enquired about chemistry. Talmud mentored the young boy by exposing him to articles and books related to his enquiries. At the age of 16 the young boy wrote a scientific paper called *The Investigation of the State of Aether in Magnetic Fields.*
The young couple's names were Hermann and Pauline, and their son was Albert Einstein. Albert Einstein's informal education at home was the precursor to the formal education that he would receive later. Without both forms of education the world would not have had the Theory of Relativity and the mass-energy equivalence formula $E=mc^2$. It is this formula which changed many age-old scientific theories and which has permitted us to harness nuclear energy.
As in Albert Einstein's case, once someone has recognized the potential in an individual, education becomes absolutely necessary.
The education must be specific and not just general. It must also be concentrated on a narrow range of topics. Although young Albert Einstein was also an avid violinist, his greatest passion was physics and, as we all know, he dedicated his life to the study of physics.

During his youth, until the age of 16, Alexander III of Macedon was personally tutored by the famous Greek philosopher Aristotle. The mentoring that the young prince had received prepared him for kingship to such a degree that he had conquered most of the known world by the time of his death in June 323 BC at the age of 32. This man is now known as Alexander the Great.

Martin Luther King Jr. made such a great impression on B. E. Mays that Mays personally mentored the young man. Mays had visited India in 1934 and had long conversations with Mahatma Gandhi. One of the topics Mays discussed with Gandhi was peaceful resistance and political transformation. Mays passed the lessons learnt from these conversations with Gandhi onto King, who later espoused it as a strategy to address racial segregation. Mays continued to teach and mentor King even after he left Morehouse. In fact, Mays mentored King up to the day he was killed and he also delivered the eulogy at King's funeral, on 9th April 1968 just 5 days after King succumbed to an assassin's bullet that wounded him in the jaw, neck and shoulder.

Education is pivotal if an individual's potential is to be realised. All the examples above bare testament to the impetus and acceleration that education provides in realising an individual's full potential.
Horace Mann, the American educator, wrote: "A human being is not attaining his full heights until he is educated." The attaining of the full heights of the human potential rests entirely on education.
Nelson Mandela once said: "Education is the most powerful weapon which you can use to change the world."
I believe that Mr. Mandela meant that education is, in the first instance, a tool to educate individuals so that they can realise the pinnacle of their potential and consequently make meaningful individual contributions to society, and in the second instance, it is a direct tool which can be used to change the paradigms of the masses for better social transformation.
When the correct education has been correctly applied, you can change the world.

> **When the correct education has been correctly applied, you can attain your full potential and then you can change the world.**

Education is also about practice. Through practice we hone our skills so that we can perform at exceptional levels.
There is the story of the man who was on his way to attend a performance at Carnegie Hall, but somehow he lost his way. He stopped and asked a musician who was performing on the pavement: "How does one get to Carnegie Hall?"
The musician answered: "Practice man, practice."
Through education and practice an individual can rise from mediocrity to greatness.

Through education and practice an individual can rise from mediocrity to greatness.

Affirm

By affirming the talents, gifts and abilities of others we give them confidence and room to express themselves freely. Through affirmations we also show people that we believe in them.
We all need people who tell us and show us that they believe in us. This support is vital for any individual to be able to manifest his potential. The belief of others is like the warmth of the Spring Sun which gently causes the flower to bloom from a tiny bud.
When you affirm your belief in the potential that someone possesses, you reinforce the idea just like a concrete slab is reinforced with steel. Eventually, the affirmations will take on a form in the natural, and the full potential of the individual will be realised.

Affirmations are to the bud of potential like the warm sun is to the flower bud - gently inviting it to come into full bloom.

We affirm people directly by giving compliments that are genuine. We can also affirm people tacitly by giving them responsibilities related to their talents and gifts. Perpetual direct and tacit affirmation builds belief in the eyes of the beholder and the holder of potential.

Perpetual direct and tacit affirmation builds belief in the eyes of the beholder and the holder of potential.

In March 1778, a man by the name of Johann advertised the first public performance of his 6-year old son. Although the posters lied about his son's age (his son was actually 7 years old) he had not lied about his son's unique musical abilities. He had ensured that his son was tutored in the use of the violin, viola and piano. At the age of 13, this young boy had written his first published composition with the guidance and assistance of the mentor which his father had appointed. Johann van Beethoven continuously affirmed his belief in his son Ludwig and because of his father's affirmations Ludwig van Beethoven became a celebrated composer during his lifetime and after, even though he became completely deaf at the age of 30.
The constant affirming behaviour that he received from his father gave Ludwig van Beethoven the confidence to manifest the musical genius that lay inside of him.

Sometimes you must affirm yourself, especially when people try to discourage you. Tell yourself daily that you are successful and you reach your goals. Do not associate with people who criticise or steal your dreams. Associate with people who affirm your dreams. If your friends don't like your dreams, don't change your dreams, change your friends.

> **If your friends don't like your dreams, don't change your dreams, change your friends.**

Capitalise

> **Carpe Diem – seize the day.**

The Latin aphorism ***Carpe Diem*** is translated into *'seize the day.'* It means to grab hold of an opportunity immediately and without delay. That's what capitalising is all about. Only when you seize the opportunity to exercise your potency will your potential be realised. Capitalisation is about being pro-active with regards to the exercising of your potential. Pro-activity involves seeking out opportunities to employ your inner abilities. Unless you vigilantly pursue these opportunities and are keenly aware of when and where you can perform, you may miss a golden opportunity. For some this opportunity may come once in a lifetime whilst others may be presented with many opportunities. Whatever the case may be, action will bring results.

When the young Thomas Edison borrowed some money from a friend to travel to New York in pursuit of better opportunities, he was not aware of how his fortunes would change. Edison had been in New York for three weeks, and he was starving. After begging for some coffee from a street vendor, he walked the streets of New York and found his way back to the building where he had been sleeping. He came across a crowd that had gathered around a man who was in a state of panic. The man was the manager of a stock brokerage firm and his anxiety was related to a stock-ticker that had suddenly stopped working. No-one in the crowd had any idea how the device worked or how to fix it. Edison drew on his telegraphy experience and he knew what the machine was supposed to do. Armed with his knowledge, Edison took a quick look at the device and replaced a tiny spring which had moved out of position. The device was again fully-operational. The manager was so delighted that he offered Edison a job to repair machines for the firm for a monthly salary of $300 which was twice the average salary of an electrical technician in New York. This incident was the turning point in the life of the aspirant inventor. Thomas Edison capitalized on the opportunity that was presented to him, and it changed the entire trajectory of his life.
Time and chance will create ideal opportunities for you to manifest your skill and knowledge, and you will reap immense rewards if you capitalize on those opportunities.

> **Time and chance will create ideal opportunities for you to manifest your skill and knowledge, and you will reap immense rewards if you capitalize on those opportunities.**

There is great potential to do great things inside of every human being. These potentialities, though they vary greatly from person to person, are extremely valuable in everyone. There are also great rewards available to those who capitalize on their potential. King Solomon wrote: 'The one who works his field will have plenty of food, but whoever chases daydreams lacks wisdom.'

In this little proverb, King Solomon is teaching us about the benefits that extend from working in your field. The field is a metaphor which represents your areas of interest, talent and expertise whilst the work entails those activities which capitalize on those interests, talents and expert skills. There are great rewards in store for those who work hard at their field of interest and expertise, according to King Solomon.

> **The one who works his field will have plenty of food, but whoever chases daydreams lacks wisdom.** Proverbs 12:11 NET
> *King Solomon*

Hold On!

Many people have turned around at the doorstep of the success that they would have obtained if they had held on a little longer. Holding on is about being persistent, even in the face of adversity and failure. People need a paradigm shift with regards to failure. Failure is only feedback, it is not final. Failure is life's response to your efforts. Through failure life is simply informing you that your approach is incorrect and life is simultaneously asking you to adjust your approach. Only those who respond positively to life's prompting hold on.

Holding on is about persistently believing in yourself and/or another person even if he has failed. Holding on is applying patience while the seed develops into the tree, and sometimes you must hold on a little longer, even when the tree is fully grown, before the tree bares any fruit. Jesus taught a lesson about holding on to his disciples when he said:

"A certain man had a fig tree planted in his vineyard, and he came seeking fruit on it and found none. Then he said to the keeper of his vineyard, 'Look, for three years I have come seeking fruit on this fig tree and find none. Cut it down; why does it use up the ground?' But he answered and said to him, 'Sir, let it alone this year also, until I dig around it and fertilize it. And if it bears fruit, well. But if not, after that you can cut it down.'" Luke 13:6-9 NKJV

In this parable we can see that the keeper of the vineyard was willing to hold on because he understood that fig trees sometimes need nurturing and patience in order to produce their fruit. Holding on is exercising patience, and while you are waiting you must nurture and nourish the tree. The fig tree is a metaphor in which the tree represents a human being and the fruits represent those products and services that they have the potential to produce. Only when we hold on can we see and enjoy the fruits of the potential resident in ourselves and others.

> **Only when we hold on can we see and enjoy the fruits of the potential resident in ourselves and others.**

In 1905 Franklin Delano Roosevelt married his distant cousin Anna Eleanor Roosevelt. In 1910 Franklin entered into politics by serving in the New York State Senate and thereafter as the Assistant Secretary of the Navy. In 1918, Eleanor discovered some letters in Franklin's luggage. The letters revealed an extra-marital affair between Franklin and Lucy Mercer, a lady employed by the Roosevelts as Eleanor's social secretary. Despite Franklin's unfaithfulness, Eleanor agreed to remain in the marriage. In 1920, Franklin D. Roosevelt and James M. Cox were the Democrat candidates for the U.S. presidential elections, but they lost to Republicans Warren G. Harding and Calvin Coolidge.
In August 1921, while on vacation in Canada, Franklin contracted polio. The disease caused permanent paralysis from the waist down. At this point, Franklin's mother insisted that he retire but Eleanor insisted that he remain in politics. Franklin wisely followed his wife's admonitions. Eleanor began to make public appearances and speeches on behalf of her disabled husband. His disability forced him to wear leg braces and eventually he had to move around in a wheelchair. Despite his disability, Franklin went on to serve as the governor of New York from 1929 to 1932, and then won the US presidential election in 1932. Franklin D. Roosevelt won the US presidential elections a record-breaking four times in succession. He died on 12th April 1945, while serving his fourth tenure as US president.

If Eleanor Roosevelt did not hold on, her husband would never have become the great statesman who led the United States of America through some of its most difficult years. He would also not have become the first man to win the US presidential elections four times in succession. She held on, and she stood by Franklin's side, even performing some of his duties for him, because she believed in his potential.

5. Problems

All people have problems and challenges. As human beings we have to face a mixture of challenges related to the different areas of our lives such as health, resources, time, relationships, survival, opportunities, dreams, happiness and fulfilment. This list is typical but it is by no means exhaustive because there are many other areas where people encounter challenges and problems. Just as our physical features are unique, we all have a unique mixture of problems that we have to deal with.

When we propose to help solve the problems that other people are facing, we tend to prescribe the solutions that have worked well for us. Unfortunately, due to the uniqueness of the individual's problems, what has worked very well over a long period of time for me may not be suitable for the next person. For example, I can easily recommend to someone who is having trouble reading small lettering in a book that they can use my reading spectacles because they've served me so well for a long time. The gesture may be noble, but the solution is useless. The other person's eyeball size and shape are different to mine and he will have to get a personal assessment in order to solve his problem. Just as problems that people face must be assessed and valued on an individual basis, solutions must be administered on an individual basis too.

> **Just as problems that people face must be assessed and valued on an individual basis, solutions must be administered on an individual basis too.**

It is clear that problems demand solutions. We must find workable solutions to the problems that we face if we are to attain and retain happiness and fulfilment.

Charles Kettering, the inventor once said: "Problems are the price of progress."
Kettering was instructing us about the important role that problems play in thrusting us toward greater progress.
Stated differently, problems are the price of greater value. That value can have varying degrees of worth. The worth can be for the individual only, and sometimes the whole world can benefit from it. The following true story illustrates that an individual can solve a problem for himself and then many others with the same problem can benefit.
In 1812, a 3-year old French boy was playing with an awl which his father used in his workshop. The boy was attempting to make a hole in a patch of leather but the awl slipped and struck him in one of his eyes. Although the boy received treatment for the injury, he became blind in the injured eye due to an infection. The infection soon spread to the other eye, and by the age of 5 the young boy was completely blind.
At the age of 10 the boy left home to attend a school for blind youth. At this school he was taught to read by the school's founder, Valentin Haüy. Haüy, who was not blind himself, had created a system comprised of embossed Latin letters which were prominent enough on paper to be read through touching. The boy learnt this system, but he was dissatisfied with it and he continued to seek a more convenient system.
His search led to a meeting with Captain Charles Barbier, who had invented a system of dots and dashes embossed on thick paper, as a means of communication for French soldiers during the night, or when light was dim. The system was called *night writing* and it provided a medium of communication for soldiers that eliminated the need for speaking. By the time the boy was 15 he invented a system which used some of the ideas from the night writing system.
That young boy was Louis Braille. His system is called the Braille System and it is used worldwide to create books and documents that can be read by the blind.
Louis Braille had a problem, and his tireless search led him to a solution that solved the problem for himself and many others.

We all face problems every day. Sometimes we do not share the immensity of the problems with others. King Solomon wrote: "Each heart knows its own bitterness, and no one else can share its joy."

> **Each heart knows its own bitterness, and no one else can share its joy.** Proverbs 14:10 NIV
> *King Solomon*

There are problems that are as unique as the individual facing them. When we take a closer look at a person, at some point we will gain a greater level of respect for them when we understand the battles that they have fought and are still fighting. In this sense, people become more valuable because of the problems they have faced. This was illustrated by the true story of Thomas J. Watson, the founder of IBM, who retained an employee after he had cost the company a sizeable sum of money.

> **Recently, I was asked if I was going to fire an employee who made a mistake that cost the company $600,000. No, I replied, I just spent $600,000 training him. Why would I want somebody to hire his experience?**
> *Thomas J. Watson*

6. Performance
Performance refers to an individual's activities. King Solomon wrote: 'Even a child is known by his deeds, whether what he does is pure and right.'
King Solomon was teaching us that we are defined by our actions, even from childhood. We are all judged according to our performance, from infancy.

> **Even a child is known by his deeds, whether what he does is pure and right.** Proverbs 20:11 NKJV
> *King Solomon*

Performance also refers to quality, speed and accuracy. King Solomon wrote: 'Do you see a person who is efficient in his work? He will serve kings. He will not serve unknown people.'

Other translations of this verse have replaced the word *efficient* with '*skilled*' and also '*competent*.'

> **Do you see a person who is efficient in his work? He will serve kings.**
> **He will not serve unknown people.** Proverbs 22:29 GW
> *King Solomon*

Thus people who are efficient, skilled and competent will be called upon to serve great leaders, and not ordinary men. Your level of performance will dictate the level of leader that you are called upon to serve.

> **Your level of performance will dictate the level of leader that you are called upon to serve.**

It is a generally accepted fact that people perform at different levels in the same arena. For example, if I were to run a long-distance marathon I will not perform well but someone who has a natural aptitude and strong desire for running will definitely perform much better than I will. The reason is simple: running marathons is not my thing!
The school class-room is another example of varying performance levels amongst people. In a learning environment, everyone learns in his own unique way and has a passion for a unique set of subjects. Remember that it was stated earlier that individuals are monotypes. There is a flaw in our modern schooling systems that stems from the standardisation of teaching materials and methods which are being imposed on non-standard, or monotypic individuals. The danger is that a stereotypical teaching approach to a monotypic individual casts learners into a common mould to which many cannot conform. Unless educators are sufficiently skilled to identify the unique attributes and performance areas of a learner and then align the teaching materials and methods with the learner's unique attributes, we will continue to produce under-performing and self-depreciating people from our schooling systems. We want our learners to be happy and to be effective contributors to society but we are creating automatons who must all produce the same type of results as per specified standards

set by a national teaching ministry to be imposed on non-standard individuals.
Fortunately, everybody in the world is not a terrible performer in everything. It is logical that you will not perform well in the arena of your weaknesses. We all have been endowed with strengths to compensate for our weaknesses. I therefore have the assurance that even though I may be a terrible athlete, that there is something at which I will perform exceptionally well. There are some things at which an individual will perform badly, but there are also some things at which an individual will perform exceptionally well.

> **There are some things at which an individual will perform badly, but there are also some things at which an individual will perform exceptionally well.**

Every person has that unique arena in which he is a superstar. Excellent performance is usually related to your natural gifting. It is important that the individual identifies his natural gifting because that will point the way to the arena in which he can be a star performer. It is not necessary that the individual is the best in that arena though, but what is necessary is that he finds peace and fulfilment because these are the great rewards we receive when we perform at our best with our best gift.

> **A musician must make music, an artist must paint, a poet must write, if he is to be ultimately at peace with himself.**
> *Abraham Maslow*

Performance is also about giving. Value is about giving. Unless you learn to give of yourself and your resources, you will never attain the valuable respect of others.

> **Unless you learn to give of yourself and your resources, you will never attain the valuable respect of others.**

A peak is the pinnacle or highest level of something. In geography it refers to the highest point of a mountain. In human terms, it refers to the highest point of your success, skills, knowledge, abilities and achievements.
A person's performance will always reach a peak. It may reach its peak when you are young, or when you're old. Many people accept that their performance will deteriorate when they grow older because society propagates that idea. However, you can exercise your power of choice even in the matter concerning when you will reach your peak.
You don't have to stop growing and developing in skill and knowledge as you age because you can decide when your performance will peak. You can continue to learn and earn even when you are old. Perpetual production comes through perpetual expansion.

> **Perpetual production comes through perpetual expansion.**

People usually make unique choices concerning when they will peak. Sometimes the choice is subconscious, especially when it comes as a result of popularity. Sometimes the choice is a conscious one. For example, in some rare instances people choose to peak at a very old age. There are also those few individuals who choose to never peak but rather to be on a constant upward spiral of skill and performance up until the day they breathe their last breath. In either case, it is must be remembered that people make choices regarding their performance, and as a result everyone's performance levels are unique.

7. Personality
There are four main personality types. They are also called temperaments. Let us look at them briefly.

Sanguine
The sanguine individual is an extrovert who loves to socialise and mingle. They are usually very vocal about their opinions, but are still caring and loving. They enjoy physical contact and love giving and receiving hugs.
The ability to get to know people quickly and their high levels of confidence are strengths of this personality type.

Lack of order, organization, ability to plan and the ease with which they become bored with tasks are weaknesses of this personality type.

Choleric

The choleric individual is the aggressive, take-charge and leader type of personality. These individuals are highly focused on their personal goals and they always want to be the best and have the best. They tend to flaunt their success.

The ability to take charge and provide leadership; the keen focus and unperturbed commitment to task-completion are strengths of the choleric personality.

The lack of consideration for the feelings of others; mood swings and the propensity for conflict are weaknesses of this personality type.

Melancholic

Melancholic individuals are usually introverted and can sometimes be seen as loners. These individuals are comfortable in their own skin and with their own company. They are usually well-educated and well-read.

The ability to plan and execute those plans; the exceptional general knowledge and a general sense of calmness are strengths of the melancholic personality.

The propensity to over-analyse facts and circumstances; the need for perfection and the tendency to worry are weaknesses of the melancholic personality.

Phlegmatic

The phlegmatic individual is sensitive and kind. These individuals are soft-spoken and they are not attention-seekers. These are the individuals who support humanitarian and animal anti-cruelty campaigns. They are usually very creative and are very gifted in the arts.

Displaying a deep sense of love and affection for people, animals and the environment; forming strong relationships and helping those in need are strengths of the phlegmatic personality.

A propensity to harbour feelings of hurt and then to explode when they can't handle the emotional pain and the ability to hold onto injuries inflicted by others, even in the distant past, are weaknesses associated with this personality type.

Similarities and Differences
Throughout this chapter we have seen that where the individual is concerned value exists both in similarity and in difference. We find value in those people who have similar interests to our own, but we also find value in those people who are different to us. For example, a young man will spend time with his teammates from the football team because they share a common interest in football, but he will also date a young woman because of her appealing gender differences.

> **Where the individual is concerned value exists both in in similarity and in difference. We find value in people who are similar to us, but we also find value in people who are different to us.**

What Value Entails

V = Visibility

A = Acceptance

L = Love

U = Understanding

E = Esteem

Visibility
An invisible man cannot be seen or heard. When you make a man visible, you make him seen, you give him a place and you give him a voice. It was stated earlier that people need recognition, and when you give a man a podium to speak, and you lend him your ears, you give him recognition. When you recognize a man, you make him visible.
Giving someone visibility is about making the unrecognized seen. When we recognize the individual along with his past and present contributions to our lives and/or the organization, we are adding value to that individual.

Making someone visible is about preventing anything that will overshadow that person or his contribution, because many people are often hidden under the shadow of someone else.
A man and his ideas are one. When you give a man's ideas visibility, you automatically give the man visibility.

Acceptance
When you receive someone into your company and you approve of who they are, you give them acceptance. Regardless of our obvious differences to other people, we all desire to be unconditionally accepted for who we are. Acceptance goes beyond mere tolerance – it is about embracing an individual for all his strengths and weaknesses. Acceptance dispels the need to change an individual, and instead it entertains the need to get to know the individual.

Love
Loving someone goes beyond having positive feelings about someone – loving someone entails that you treat them as being costly, all of the time. When Jesus taught us to love our neighbour as ourselves, he was giving us the definition of true neighbourly love. Genuine neighbourly love means to treat someone with the same level of care and respect that you invest in yourself. When we consider how we would like to be treated, and then treat our neighbour in that manner then we are exercising true neighbourly love.

Understanding
Understanding an individual starts with listening to the individual. When we listen empathically to someone, we will gain a better understanding about who they are. We can only really appreciate and value a person when we understand where they come from, and when we understand where someone comes from we can appreciate where they are standing. Where someone comes from is not referring to a geographic location, but instead it is referring to their life experiences. Understanding someone's life experiences and the battles that they have fought and are still fighting will give you a window of understanding related to that person's life.

Esteem

As was explained previously, esteem refers to the giving and the assigning of worth. In accounting terms, an appreciating asset is one that is increasing in value. When you esteem someone, you are appreciating him – you are permitting his value to increase. When you treat people with dignity, respect, honour, recognition and kindness you are esteeming them and making them feel more valuable.

Conclusion

The following story told by King Solomon expounds the importance of valuing people.

There was once a small city with only a few people in it.
And a powerful king came against it, surrounded it and built huge siege works against it. Now there lived in that city a man poor but wise, and he saved the city by his wisdom.
But nobody remembered that poor man.
So I said, 'Wisdom is better than strength.' But the poor man's wisdom is despised, and his words are no longer heeded. Ecclesiastes 9:14-15 NKJV

We all have ignored someone who seems to hold no value to us, and similarly we have all been ignored by others to whom we present no value. The value of an individual is not obvious to the eye.
Everyone has immense value, even the seemingly valueless person. The person you see as valueless may hold the key to your survival. You may hold the key to the survival of a person who sees you as valueless.

> **The value of an individual is not obvious to the eye.**
> **Everyone has immense value, even the seemingly valueless person.**

The Small piece of wood

"Hello little coal," said nature in a soft-toned voice.
"No," answered the wood, "I am a piece of bark, but not by choice.
I am only a small piece of wood, for that is my eternal plight."
Answered nature: "Time will show that you are not right."

Time went by slowly and Nature seemed quiet and still...
Yet secretly bending all to its purpose and will.
"Hello little diamond", said Nature as she passed by.

Said the wood: "First you called me coal, now you call me diamond;
I now am coal, my previous response apologetically I do rescind."

Time went by slowly and Nature seemed quiet and still...
Yet secretly bending all to its purpose and will.
"Hello little gem," said Nature as she passed by.

"No," answered the wood, "a gem I certainly am not.
A rough diamond I have become from my environment so hot."

Time went by slowly and Nature seemed quiet and still...
Yet secretly bending all to its purpose and will.
"Hello little jewel," said Nature as she passed by.

"No," answered the wood, "a jewel I certainly am not.
I started life as a piece of wood that began to rot.
A piece of coal I became: black, shapeless and soft.
I have no value: this I said to myself so very oft.
But over time into a diamond I began to permute,
And my opinion of myself nature did refute.
I was no longer soft: I was now a diamond strong and hard.
And I began to see myself with a totally new regard.
I was mined from deep inside the earth,
And so began this diamond's rebirth.
I was cleaned, shaped and polished by a master's hands,
Now I have been valued at millions of rands.
However, I am still alone: all by myself and on my own.
A precious jewel I am not, I am just a lonely gemstone."

Time went by slowly and Nature seemed quiet and still...
Yet secretly bending all to its purpose and will.
"Hello little jewel," said Nature once again, as she passed by.

"Yes, I was once a gem, but now I am set in a ring of gold.
I am now a jewel, which for many millions has been sold.
Thank you Nature for seeing my potential deep within.
You showed me that I am not a loser and that I was meant to win.
I thought that I was only a useless piece of coal,
But I actually possessed a precious jewel's soul.
Never again will I devalue and demean myself:
By placing myself on a discount shelf.
I have repented of this self-destructive crime,
Because what was within me has been revealed over time.
To all self-depreciating thoughts I say: "Nay!"
And I will always embrace the greatness that within me lay.
From a piece of wood into a jewel I have evolved,
And now to continually tap into my potential I am resolved.
I certainly am not what I was before:
I will continue to embrace my hidden potential forevermore."

Glisson J. Heldzinger

Chapter 7

Elements Of Self-esteem

> **The reputation you have with yourself – your self-esteem – is the single most important factor for a fulfilling life.**
> *Nathaniel Branden*

Definition and relevance of self-esteem

What is self-esteem? The word ***esteem*** comes from the Latin word ***aestimare*** which, like *estimate,* meant '*to asses, or judge the value of something.'*
That sense lingers on today. [xxxi]
The term ***self-esteem*** means '*the individual's estimation, assessment and judgement of his value and personal worth, how the individual feels about himself, how much the individual likes and respects himself.'*
An individual's self-esteem is an indication of his sense of worth. Since it is an opinion he holds about himself, it is called self-worth. Self-esteem and self-worth are synonymous and interchangeable terms.
The American psychologist, Dr. Nathaniel Branden defined self-esteem in the following way: 'Self-esteem is the reputation we acquire with ourselves.'

> **Self-esteem is the reputation we acquire with ourselves.**
> *Nathaniel Branden*

Every person has a measurement of himself that is based on *an estimation* of who he is and can be. This estimation can be seen as a personal calculation of self and it is influenced by internal and external factors. These factors are called influencers. The influencers are discussed in-depth later in this chapter.

> **Every person has a measurement of himself that is based on an estimation of who he is and can be.**

Based on his estimation of himself, an individual exercises his judgement to assess himself. He judges himself based on his alignment with or deviation from the attributes and possessions of other people as well as his ability to attain personal goals. Based on this comparative information, he forms an opinion of himself. It is at this point where the individual will begin to see himself in a good or bad light. He can either see himself as being acceptable, to himself and others or as being inadequate, unsuitable, unsatisfactory and insufficient. He can see himself with disregard, dishonour and criticism or alternatively he can see himself as a person who is valuable and worthy of respect, honour and dignity. The opinion that the individual forms of himself will determine if he meets with his own approval or not. This is called self-approval.

> **The opinion that the individual forms of himself will determine if he meets with his own approval or not.**

If he fails to meet his own approval he will display self-dislike, self-rejection, and self-hatred in various degrees.
If he meets his own approval he will have his own endorsement, validation, sanction and blessing.
Thus, the individual's level of self-worth stems from his level of self-approval. On the previous page I indicated that self-worth and self-esteem are synonymous and interchangeable terms. If the individual's self-approval is low, his sense of self-worth will be low, thus his self-esteem will be low. He will see himself as having little value.
If the individual's self-approval is high, his sense of self-worth will be high, thus his self-esteem will be high. He will see himself as having great value.

> **If the individual's self-approval is low, his sense of self-worth will be low, thus his self-esteem will be low. He will see himself as having little value.**

> **If the individual's self-approval is high, his sense of self-worth will be high, thus his self-esteem will be high. He will see himself as having great value.**

A person with low self-approval will see himself as cheap, depreciated, ordinary, mediocre, inferior, worthless and valueless.
A person with high self-approval will see himself as costly, appreciated, expensive, dear, excellent, noble, precious, priceless, sophisticated, superior, worthy and valuable.

Dr. Nathaniel Branden wrote that self-esteem is a powerful force, and that it is this force that is the experience that we are appropriate to life and the requirements of life.

> **Self-esteem is a powerful force within each of us... Self-esteem is the experience that we are appropriate to life and to the requirements of life.**
> *Nathaniel Branden*

Low self-esteem is a powerful restraining force that keeps people from feeling valid, appropriate and capable of meeting the problems that life throws their way. However, high self-esteem is also a very powerful force that makes people phenomenally successful.

Self-esteem affects:
1. Your goals
Self-esteem is a powerful force that can keep people from pursuing and achieving worthwhile and valuable goals but it can also propel them to pursue and realise great achievements. Without a high level of self-esteem, people are unable to set and achieve valuable goals.
If someone's self-esteem is low, they are unlikely to set significant goals for themself, and even if they do set goals they will abandon them before they are realised, because they have a lack of belief in their own worthiness and abilities. People with low self-esteem have a very meagre sense of what's possible for them.

However, people with high self-esteem set significant goals because they feel worthy and adequately capable of achieving their goals. They are great possibility thinkers.

> **Self-esteem is a powerful force that can keep people from pursuing and achieving worthwhile and valuable goals but it can also propel them to pursue and realise great achievements.**

2. *Your ability to learn and your level of education*

Your level of self-esteem will either enhance or impede your ability to learn. For example, there are many ways in which a child's self-esteem could be negatively affected so that he becomes a slow learner.

One such scenario is when a child is convinced that he is stupid because the teacher called him that. On the other hand, a child who is constantly affirmed by a teacher will progress at a faster rate than those students who are not constantly affirmed. In both scenarios the child's self-esteem is shaped by what others say about him and what he begins to believe about himself.

There exists a great danger that the child can carry his diminished self-esteem into his adult life. His conviction that he is not a good student will prevent him from pursuing any type of self-improvement related to studying and learning. If his self-esteem is low, he will never obtain a tertiary level diploma or degree and all the benefits that come with these certifications.

> **Your level of self-esteem will either enhance or impede your ability to learn.**

According to new research conducted over a 15 year period, at McGill University in Canada, scientists have discovered that people with low self-esteem are more likely to suffer from memory loss as they age. The brain size of older people with low self-esteem was 20% smaller than that of a person with high self-esteem.

The scientists also proved that brain atrophy was not a permanent state and that the brain can be rejuvenated. One way to rejuvenate the brain is to start thinking about positive things and to have a positive mental attitude. It was proven that people who accept declining memory as being a part of ageing experienced declining memory. However, memory loss in old age is not normal and it can be kept at bay by simply saying that it is normal to lead an exceptional and fulfilling life and have excellent memory in old age. It seems almost too simple to believe, but the evidence is overwhelming that the contents of your thoughts will promote growth or decay of your brain.

> **It seems almost too simple to believe, but the evidence is overwhelming that the contents of your thoughts will promote growth or decay of your brain.**

3. Your level of income and material success

People with high self-esteem are generally more successful than other people, especially in the area of wealth-generation. It takes high self-confidence and high self-efficacy to be successful. Self-confidence and self-efficacy are components of self-esteem. Self-efficacy is the measure of how confident you are about your abilities to cope with life's challenges. High self-esteem produces high success. Thomas Carlyle once wrote: 'Nothing builds self-esteem and self-confidence like accomplishment.'
When you are successful, you develop greater self-esteem.

> **Nothing builds self-esteem and self-confidence like accomplishment.**
> *Thomas Carlyle*

Sam Walton, the founder of Wal-Mart once said: "If people believe in themselves, it's amazing what they can accomplish."
The sky is the limit for people who have the calibre of self-esteem that stems from strong self-belief. All the great achievers of the past, as well as the present, first possessed exceptionally high levels of self-esteem, before they were successful. Sam Walton, for example, was able to build the largest retail corporation in the US during his lifetime. How did he do it? He did it by having high self-esteem and, as we saw in the last quote, by building up the self-esteem of

those around him. Through building his own and the self-esteem of others, Sam Walton was able to build a multi-billion dollar enterprise.

> **If people believe in themselves, it's amazing what they can accomplish.**
> *Sam Walton*

Social status is linked to material success. People who are materially successful are able to afford the best education for their children, live in the best homes, drive the best cars, go on the best vacations and generally enjoy an overall higher standard of living. Most people who are materially successful first possessed large amounts of self-esteem before they possessed large bank accounts.

> **Most people who are materially successful first possessed large amounts of self-esteem before they possessed large bank accounts.**

4. Your relationships

People with low self-esteem are less likely to forge healthy relationships. Human beings tend to seek the approval of others, and we go to great lengths to acquire that approval. For example, a teenager who joins a gang does so primarily because he feels that the other gang members approve of who he is and in addition, he is accepted. The teenager is most-likely dearly loved by his family, but his desire for acceptance from the gang members will propel him to form strong bonds with those gang members. His self-esteem is boosted by the acceptance and shared experiences he enjoys with the gang members. The differentiating factor is that he would not feel compelled to join the gang if he saw himself as being worth more than the value that he attains from joining the gang.

Just like the teenager in the example above, we all form relationships based on how we see and value ourselves – our self-esteem. We form relationships with people who will affirm, admonish and accept us, whether the relationship is healthy or not.

> **We all form relationships based on how we see and value ourselves – our self-esteem. We form relationships with people who will affirm, admonish and accept us, whether the relationship is healthy or not.**

Many people also fear being rejected by those close to them. When people fear rejection they act out their fears in the form of arguments, fights, deceit, backbiting, dishonesty, accusations and so forth. When someone's self-esteem is low because of rejection, the relationship takes on immense strain. Harvey Mackay wrote: "Most fears of rejection rest on the desire for approval from other people. Don't base your self-esteem on their opinions."

> **Most fears of rejection rest on the desire for approval from other people. Don't base your self-esteem on their opinions.**
> *Harvey Mackay*

5. Your health

People with low self-esteem are less likely to follow a regular exercise regime, eat healthy and avoid addictive substances such as nicotine, alcohol and drugs. It is general knowledge that healthy eating and regular exercise promote good health of the body and an overall sense of well-being in the mind. Healthy eating promotes healthy brain activity and consequently better decision-making aptitude in an individual. People with high self-esteem value their bodies and make sound decisions related to their daily activities and what they eat, in order to promote longevity, good life-quality and overall happiness. However, people with low self-esteem tend to neglect themselves by not doing what is necessary to promote good overall health, and in many cases, they actually do the things which devalue their worth. Examples of activities through which an individual devalues his own worth are promiscuity, lack of exercise, unhealthy eating habits, smoking, drinking, drug-abuse, exposure to dangerous situations, breaking the law and sometimes deliberately inflicting physical harm on themselves. Whereas people with high self-esteem promote health and longevity through their daily activities, people with low self-esteem commit suicide by instalment. The level of the individual's health is determined by the level of his self-esteem.

> **Whereas people with high self-esteem promote health and longevity through their daily activities, people with low self-esteem commit suicide by instalment. The level of the individual's health is determined by the level of his self-esteem.**

Self-esteem impacts your mental health. Low self-esteem is the very root of neurosis and all the behaviour patterns associated with it. C. George Boeree, professor emeritus at Shippensburg University, identified the following behaviour patterns which are associated with neurosis:
'.. anxiety, sadness or depression, anger, irritability, mental confusion, low sense of self-worth, etc., ***behavioural symptoms*** such as phobic avoidance, vigilance, impulsive and compulsive acts, lethargy, etc., ***cognitive problems*** such as unpleasant or disturbing thoughts, repetition of thoughts and obsession, habitual fantasizing, negativity and cynicism, etc. ***Interpersonally***, neurosis involves dependency, aggressiveness, perfectionism, schizoid isolation, socio-culturally inappropriate behaviours, etc.' [xxxii]
People with high self-esteem tend to have a positive outlook on life, even when things go bad, and this permits them to overcome life's difficulties instead of being overcome. This fact holds especially true for people who suffer from illness. Even people with high self-esteem suffer from illnesses and diseases, but their level of self-esteem, consisting of self-determination, self-belief and self-confidence, gives them the ability to cope with and sometimes defeat illnesses. However, people with low self-esteem usually give up the fight when faced with the adversity that is brought on by sickness and disease.

6. Your posture and appearance

The manner in which you present yourself in public is affected by your level of self-esteem. People with high self-esteem are more likely to carry themselves with poise and charisma. When you have high self-esteem it is easy to walk upright and with your head held high. People with high self-confidence usually dress well. Dressing well does not mean wearing the most expensive clothing, but instead it means dressing according to your budget, body type and the occasion. People with high self-esteem know how to look good without breaking their bank accounts.

People with low self-esteem usually try too hard to impress others and spend unreasonable amounts on designer brands when something else which costs much less would have sufficed. On the other end of the scale there are those who are careless about their appearance because of low self-esteem. When someone displays one or more of the tendencies of dragging their feet, dressing sloppily and are generally untidy on themself, you can be assured that the person has low self-esteem.

7. Your performance

Performance is about your actions and achievements. Performance is relative to yourself and others. We rate our performance against what we've accomplished in the past so that we can establish whether we have become better, worse or remained the same. We rate our performance against the performance of others so that we can establish whether we are better, worse or on par with our competitors. Harvey Mackay wrote: 'Like it or not, life is a series of competitions. You may be competing for a grade, a spot on a team,

a job, or the largest account in town. The higher your self-esteem is, the better you get along with yourself, with others, and the more you'll accomplish.'

Your self-esteem influences your relative performance and the higher your self-esteem, according to Mr. Mackay, the more you'll accomplish.

> **Like it or not, life is a series of competitions. You may be competing for a grade, a spot on a team, a job, or the largest account in town. The higher your self-esteem is, the better you get along with yourself, with others, and the more you'll accomplish.**
> *Harvey Mackay*

Unless people have a strong belief in their ability to accomplish a task or challenge, they will either not take it on or they will fail when trying it. People perform only as well as they believe they can. As mentioned earlier, this is the individual's self-efficacy. If an individual believes that he can perform exceptionally, he most likely will, but if he believes that he cannot do it, he will not do it. People with high self-esteem possess the level of self-belief that acts as a sort of fuel that keeps them going towards their goals, but people with low self-esteem lack this fuel – they do not have self-belief.

8. Your confidence

Confidence is simply behaving in a manner that indicates complete conviction concerning an outcome. Your level of conviction concerning an outcome will determine your level of activity related to realising that outcome. If you belief that the outcome will be achieved, you will confidently act in a manner that indicates that belief. Thus, if you belief that the outcome is unachievable you will not commit any action to it, but if you belief that the outcome is achievable, you will commit the action that is necessary to achieve it.

Confidence is affected firstly, by internal factors (what we see ourselves as capable of doing) and secondly, external factors (the circumstances that influence how things can turn out.) If someone has low self-esteem he will not see himself as being capable within himself to do something, and he will draw back. In addition, if he thinks that circumstances are stacked against him, he will also draw back. However, an individual with high self-esteem will take on a new challenge by leaning on his self-confidence and by looking for the circumstances that promote success.

It was George Bernard Shaw who wrote: 'The people who get on in this world are the people who get up and look for the circumstances they want, and if they can't find them, make them.'

People with high self-esteem get on in this world because they have the inner self-confidence to create the circumstances that they want, especially when they can't find them.

> **The people who get on in this world are the people who get up and look for the circumstances they want, and if they can't find them, make them.**
> *George Bernard Shaw*

9. Your ability to express yourself

People with low self-esteem have difficulties communicating. When you cannot communicate effectively then it also becomes difficult to express yourself. Expressing yourself is all about getting the message of your feelings, thoughts and opinions over to one or more listeners. Low self-esteem makes people question the validity of their own opinions and viewpoints, thus they are less likely to assert or argue for their position. Low self-esteem can also cause people to feel that they are insignificant and that their words and actions will not count. However, people with high self-esteem stand up and are counted. They confidently express their views, even in the light of opposition. Confident self-expression comes from the knowledge that you can make a difference, that you have what it takes to make a difference, and that you must make a difference for yourself and others. When you express your views and opinions you are able to make a difference for yourself and others, be it in a big or small way.

> **When you express your views and opinions you are able to make a difference for yourself and others, be it in a big or small way.**

10. Your ability to deal with problems, challenges and crises

In order to deal successfully with problems, challenges and crises, an individual must call upon his endowments of choice, creativity, cognition and imagination. When an individual has low self-esteem he will be uncomfortable in making tough choices, and he may also not fully utilize his imagination and creativity to conjure up various options to deal with the problem, challenge or crisis. Furthermore, he might not have the confidence to follow his inner convictions and use his cognitive abilities to choose between the various options and/or outcomes.

In order to deal successfully with problems, challenges and crises, an individual must have high self-confidence, self-worth, self-assurance and self-belief. All these attributes come with high self-esteem.

In order to deal successfully with problems, challenges and crises, an individual must have high self-confidence, self-worth, self-assurance and self-belief. All these attributes come with high self-esteem.

11. Your ability to recover from trauma and tragedy

No human being is immune from tragedy and trauma. Bad things happen to people everywhere, all the time. Without a strong sense of self-confidence that comes with high self-esteem, no human can successfully traverse the road of recovery from a traumatic or tragic event. It is the individual's strong self-will coupled with self-confidence, self-belief and hope that will carry him through the journey to recovery, and when the individual possesses these attributes he will most certainly come through his ordeal. However, someone who has low self-esteem will lack the attributes that are necessary to make a smooth transition from trauma and tragedy to recovery.

It is the individual's strong self-will coupled with self-confidence, self-belief and hope that will carry him through the journey to recovery, and when the individual possesses these attributes he will most certainly come through his ordeal.

12. Your creative expression

When you operate from a paradigm of self-doubt it is very difficult to create new things that have not existed before. The individual must dispel with the need to seek the approval of others concerning his creative endeavours. The individual must firstly have his own self-approval as it pertains to what he has created, and he must also possess self-confidence. Self-confidence is an essential trait for creative expression in human beings. When people have low self-esteem they lack the self-approval and self-confidence that is necessary to both give the gift of creativity to themselves and the world and to also enjoy it, without feeling uneasy about how he and his worked will be judged. People with high self-esteem easily create new things without the fear of public ridicule.

> **Self-confidence is an essential trait for creative expression in human beings.**

13. Your ability to deal with conflict

Conflict in human relationships is inevitable. Conflict can be defined as a clash of human wills. When human wills collide, it is necessary for an individual to value his own opinions and abilities in order to communicate and negotiate. In addition, the individual must also have the self-assurance that is necessary to amend his views when needed, without feeling inferior in any way. Thus, the individual must possess inflexibility of confidence but also flexibility of perception if he is to overcome conflict with others. People with low self-esteem do not possess the strength of character that is necessary to approach a conflict-situation and still feel whole even if concessions in ideas and perceptions must be made. People with high self-esteem, however, are able to come out of a conflict-situation still feeling self-assured and self-confident even if they had to make some adjustments to their expectations and perceptions, because their security lies in their ability to be positively influenced even when it is uncomfortable. Their security also lies in their ability to be a positive influence on others.

> **People with high self-esteem are able to come out of a conflict-situation still feeling self-assured and self-confident even if they had to make some adjustments to their expectations and perceptions, because their security lies in their ability to be positively influenced even when it is uncomfortable.**

14. Your ability to invest in others and in yourself

Investing generally entails committing resources into a specific commodity in order to receive a return at a certain point in time in the future. Using the example of financial investments, it can safely be said that people only invest in an asset or commodity which they believe will produce a return. The value of the asset is determined by its projected future return. In human terms, people usually invest in themselves and others based on the projected future return. For human relationships the returns would be companionship, intimacy, collaborative partnerships as well as feeling worthy and accepted by others. It takes patience, perseverance and courage to invest in other people. People will not invest time and effort in a relationship from which they will not receive some sort of return. People with low self-esteem will be reluctant to invest time in worthwhile relationships because they lack the attributes of courage, resilience and perseverance which are necessary to invest in others. Putting in the time and effort necessary to build worthwhile relationships is just too hard and too much trouble for people with low self-esteem. People with high self-esteem easily invest in others because they possess the necessary attributes that are required to navigate the sometimes difficult arena of human relationships.

People with high self-esteem readily invest in their own personal development in order to maximise their inner talents and potentialities, because they have a broader vision of what they could be. However, people with low self-esteem seldom seek to expand themselves because they have a diminished view of their own value and potential. One way to invest in oneself is through education. It was Benjamin Franklin who said: "An investment in knowledge pays the best interest."

Through continuous learning people with high self-esteem invest in themselves and they receive the best interest.

> **An investment in knowledge pays the best interest.**
> *Benjamin Franklin*

15. Your overall happiness

Happiness can be described as the feelings of satiety and fulfilment that stem from the attaining and accomplishing of those things that we hope for and dream about.

> **Man is, properly speaking, based upon hope, he has no other possession but hope; this world of his is emphatically the place of hope.**
> *Thomas Carlyle*

Without something to hope for and things to dream about, we will not have fulfilment and the joy of accomplishment. Hope and happiness are therefore inseparable concepts. An individual will usually hope for those things which he feels, firstly, he is capable of having and, secondly, worthy of having. Thus, it follows that those people who have high levels of self-confidence and self-belief along with strong belief in the plausibility of their dreams will be able to achieve significantly greater accomplishments than people who settle for scraps or easy dreams. It also follows that those people who achieve great successes will tend to be more fulfilled and happy than people who are not pursuing what they would like to have and do not have the self-esteem to back their pursuits.

Self-esteem is a sub-conscious phenomenon. We are usually not aware of the esteem that we have of ourselves. It can however be measured. Self-esteem is usually measured with a questionnaire and the results are recorded on a ruler or grid-type scale. These tests determine the value of certain indicative components of self-esteem. These components are called indicators. Some of the indicators are discussed later in this chapter.

The score of a self-esteem test will indicate if the subject's level of self-esteem is low, average or high. It's unlikely that you will come across an individual who has zero self-esteem or an individual who has a perfect self-esteem. Most people find themselves somewhere between the two extremes of low self-esteem and healthy self-esteem because every human being has negative self-esteem issues in some area of their lives. Even though somebody seems to have it all together, the truth is that they do not really have it all together. It is not as it seems. Usually people conceal these self-esteem issues well, causing others to be totally unaware of the inner turmoil which they experience.

King Solomon wrote concerning these hidden thoughts: 'The heart knows its own bitterness.' Proverbs 14:10 NLT

This is a true description of every single human being who has ever lived and who is living right now. Every human being harbours some negative assessment or thought about their value. A woman's negativity could be related to her lack confidence concerning her appearance, or in the case of a man, his lack of ability to express himself in words – the list is endless. These perceptions of self have a negative impact on a person's self-esteem. Every single human being could do with a self-esteem boost.

The noted psychotherapist, Nathaniel Branden wrote:

'The reputation you have with yourself – your self-esteem – is the single most important factor for a fulfilling life.'

This statement communicates the idea that the value you place on yourself will ultimately determine the heights that you reach in all the areas of your life where you seek fulfilment.

The higher your self-esteem, the greater the probability of success.

Healthy self-esteem is an absolutely necessary component for success in any field of endeavour. With a greater sense of self-worth people tend to be more courageous and resilient. They are more likely to take risks and to pursue the unknown.

People who have very low self-esteem behave in the opposite manner – they are fearful and reluctant to act, they avoid the unknown and would rather embrace mediocrity than take a chance on something that carries a high risk of failure but simultaneously offers a high possible reward.

When we then consider that success is dependent upon a healthy self-esteem, and that most people harbour hidden feelings of a lack of worth in some area of their life, we must embrace the idea that people must then elevate their valuations of themselves – their self-esteem – if they are to be more effective and live more fulfilling lives.

The relevance of self-esteem in an educational environment is of high importance if we intend to raise academic performance levels.

If learners are to perform better, raising self-esteem amongst learners must then become a high priority. In educational circles, there has developed what is called 'the

self-esteem movement' amongst those who belief in its importance as a factor of effective learning amongst learners at schools.
A diminished self-esteem causes you to have a diminished view of your future prospects. Start seeing yourself as bundle of possibilities.

> **A diminished self-esteem causes you to have a diminished view of your future prospects. Start seeing yourself as bundle of possibilities.**

Addressing self-esteem issues

There are four questions one must ask in order to address self-esteem issues, and they are:

1. what are you ***not*** doing that you should be doing?
2. why are you ***not*** doing it?
3. what are you doing that you should not be doing?
4. why are you doing it?

Question 1 will usually consist of habits and behaviour patterns which the respondent will regard as admirable and desirable to have.
Question 3 will usually consist of habits and behaviour patterns which are destructive, such as substance use and abuse and criminal offences etc.
Questions 2 and 4 are always related to value.
In the case of question 2 it will relate to the lack of skill or resources that impact an individual's personal value etc.
In the case of question 4 it will relate to a desire for acceptance from peers or a strong personal need/obsession etc.
All people do what they do, and don't do things because of their self-esteem which is the barometer of personal value. When we have to address these self-esteem issues, we must begin to work through the components of self-esteem and make corrective adjustments in order to raise the person's self-esteem.
It has been mentioned previously that addressing self-esteem issues requires getting rid of some things and also acquiring others. In this next section, you will be introduced

to a list of characteristics and influencers that have a strong bearing and impact on an individual's level of self-esteem.
It seems almost logical that people should simply think of themselves in more positive terms, and then they will develop healthy self-esteem. Unfortunately, raising the individual's self-esteem is not as simple as that because self-esteem is affected by many intersecting areas, or components, of an individual's life. Human beings are complex creatures, and they inhabit this planet with other human beings who are equally complex. An individual's self-esteem is often most affected by what others say to him and the manner in which they act towards him. Someone's self-esteem can be quickly dented by another person who speaks a damaging word or performs a harmful act.
Self-esteem is affected by many areas of an individual's life, some of which he can control and others over which he exercises no control. Following is a list of some of the influencers and indicators of self-esteem and self-efficacy. The list is not meant to be exhaustive and to cover every possible condition, scenario and/or circumstance that an individual may face, but it is sufficiently detailed to cover the most essential components that are necessary for the development of healthy self-esteem.
All the topics start with the letter 'C' so we shall refer to them as '**The 70 Cs of Self-esteem.**'

1. Control
Man is a creature of appetites. Appetites are those cravings which drive our pursuits. Our existence is ensured through our appetites for food, water, sunshine, exercise, rest, escapism, self-fulfilment, companionship and happiness. Without appetites we will not survive and we will not enjoy the good things in life which are worth pursuing. Despite being absolutely necessary, appetites are a two-edged sword because they also have the potential to destroy us. When we are driven by an uncontrolled appetite for something, the consumption of that thing will have an effect that is the opposite of its intended purpose. For example, when you eat too much food you will become obese, and obesity brings with it diseases such as hypertension and diabetes. Someone who consumes excess quantities of alcohol risks damage to his liver and digestive system. Someone who relentlessly

pursues sexual intimacy with many partners not only risks hurting the feelings of his sexual partners but also risks contracting sexually transmitted diseases. There is a real risk of damage to the individual's well-being when his appetites are outside of his control. An individual will have longevity and a good quality of life when he controls his appetites, but he will suffer pain, sickness and loss when his appetites control him.

> **There is a real risk of damage to the individual's well-being when his appetites are outside of his control. An individual will have longevity and a good quality of life when he controls his appetites, but he will suffer pain, sickness and loss when his appetites control him.**

King Solomon wrote that a man without self-control is like a city which has no walls. In the time that King Solomon wrote this verse, most cities were surrounded by protective walls to keep out enemies. Any city which had no walls was open to attack from outside forces. In the same manner, a man without self-control is open to attack from outside forces when he does not exercise control over his appetites.

> **A man without self-control is like a city broken into and left without walls.** Proverbs 25:28 ESV
> *King Solomon*

People with high self-esteem exercise self-control over their appetites because they understand that through an inability to control what you crave you will be digging your own grave.

> **Through an inability to control what you crave you will be digging your own grave.**

Control also refers to managing your temperament. King Solomon wrote: 'A fool always loses his temper, but a wise man holds it back.'
He also wrote: 'A hot-tempered person starts fights; a cool-tempered person stops them.'

Wisdom rests in the ability to exercise control over your temperament because when you are able to control your responses to circumstances, you promote peace and well-being for everyone. However, outbursts of anger and frustration lead to broken relationships.

> **A fool always loses his temper,**
> **But a wise man holds it back.** Proverbs 29:11 NASB
> **A hot-tempered person starts fights; a cool-tempered person stops them.** Proverbs 15:18 NLT
> *King Solomon*

People with high self-esteem express their value when they exercise control over their temperament, because a controlled temper promotes a controlled environment.

2. Charity

Charity is about love. Love is about expressing care and affection towards other people. Jesus of Nazareth said that the greatest commandments pertain to love. Jesus said that the first of these commandments is to love God with all your heart and soul, and the second is to love your neighbour as you love yourself. He also said that treating others in the same manner as you want to be treated is the summarization of all the laws given to the Israelites by Moses and the messages conveyed by the ancient Jewish prophets. From the guidance laid down by Jesus, each of us must care for our neighbour with the same level of care and affection which we desire for ourselves, and in addition, to treat them in a manner that we want to be treated. Your neighbour is not just the person who lives close to you, but anyone you have contact with. Your personal level of affection for yourself must set the bar for the level of affection that you display for your neighbour.

> **Love the Lord your God with all your heart and with all your soul and with all your mind." This is the first and greatest commandment. And the second is like it: Love your neighbour as yourself. All the Law and the Prophets hang on these two commandments.** Matthew 22:37-38 NIVUK

> **Do to others whatever you would like them to do to you. This is the essence of all that is taught in the law and the prophets.** Matthew 7:12 NLT
> *Jesus of Nazareth*

> **Your personal level of affection for yourself must set the bar for the level of affection that you display for your neighbour.**

Charity is also about benevolence and giving. Knowing that you have blessed someone less fortunate than yourself with your resources and talents makes one feel good, and in addition, you make the recipient feel good. King Solomon revealed to us an additional benefit of benevolent charity when he wrote that people who display generosity to the poor are lending to God, and that He will repay them for their kind deeds. Thus, when you bless others, you are twice blessed because firstly, you feel a sense of happiness and secondly, God Almighty is indebted to you. People with high self-esteem readily share of their abundance with others, because there is a greater degree of blessings that stem from giving than from retaining. Expressing charity through giving makes the giver and the recipient feel more valuable.

> **Expressing charity through giving makes the giver and the recipient feel more valuable.**

3. Crises

Clear-air turbulence (CAT) is the rapid and unsteady movement of air and the collision of air pockets, all of which can cause an airplane to shudder, shake and sometimes fall several metres. Turbulence can make a flight very uncomfortable for passengers and crew aboard an airplane. In some cases turbulence can cause fatal crashes. Turbulence cannot be detected and cannot be avoided. Life can be equated to a flight on an airplane, and just as you experience turbulence during a flight you most certainly will experience turbulence in your life. In human terms, these bursts of turbulence are referred to as crises.

According to Oliver Robinson, a life crisis is defined as a period characterized by unstable mental and emotional health, altering the course of their lives and affecting them for a year or longer. [xxxiii]

An individual will experience various crises during his lifetime. These crises will vary in severity and in nature. While growing up, many people will experience an **identity crisis**. This sort of crisis occurs as adolescents are transitioning from childhood into young adulthood and are experiencing many physical and psychological changes. Along with physical changes come new desires, especially sexual desires as well as the sexual identity. They also form their own opinions and ideas, many of which are in contrast to those that they have been taught and believed as children. It is during this stage that the adolescent forms his own self-image. If the adolescent cannot successfully reconcile his perceptions of himself with reality on a psychological level, he will experience an identity crisis. This crisis can last into the individual's adult life if it is not identified and addressed early. In this sense, many teenagers are in crisis with their crisis being manifested as rebellious behaviour, withdrawal, promiscuity, experimentation with harmful substances, anxiety, depression etc.

I read an article recently about Big Ben, the Great Bell of the clock that lies at the north end of the Palace of Westminster, overlooking London. According to the article, The Houses of Parliament's dedicated locksmiths had to be called in when Big Ben's chimes and bongs were sounding six seconds early for about two weeks. After removing a few weights from the clock's pendulum, the locksmiths did admit, however, that they "don't know why it has happened" and that the clock's age means that it "fits every now and then". [xxxiv]

At the time of the incident, Big Ben was 156 years old. It seems that even clocks have fits due to old age. One can call it a *crisis of time*, with an intended pun.

All people have a crisis of time, just like old Big Ben. The crisis of time manifests itself in the form of ageing. With ageing comes sickness and disease, loss of vitality, deteriorating health, deteriorating mobility, weight loss, organ deterioration, loss of control over biological functions and increased dependence on others for assistance. In their forties to early sixties, many people experience a **mid-life crisis**. Men will most likely experience intense emotions related to, but not restricted to work whereas women will experience intense emotions related to, but not restricted to the evaluations of their roles. Mid-life crises can also be triggered by events such as the death of a loved-one, a career change, children growing up and the loss of a spouse through divorce or death.

Some crises are **incidental**, and are usually brought on by an accident or illness. For example, when someone suffers the loss of a limb, or the use of some part of their body due to a stroke or some sort of accident, it is very difficult to deal with the reality of what's happened. The initial trauma will be hard to cope with, but residual trauma can be just as hard. Residual traumas are challenges that follow the initial event. An example of residual trauma is when someone who has become physically disabled has to depend on someone else to bathe, dress and feed them. Learning to use a prosthetic limb and overcoming all the psychological debris of reduced self-esteem are examples of residual trauma. This is very traumatic for someone who was once self-sufficient. I know people who have had to adjust to new lifestyles after tragedy struck, and they were forced to use a prosthetic leg or arm. Despite encountering tragedy in their personal lives, they continue to inspire able-bodied people to live great lives. When life knocks you down so hard that you lose a body part, you can choose to stay down and feel sorry for yourself, or you can get up and prove that it is possible for an individual to be broken but still standing.

> **When life knocks you down so hard that you lose a body part, you can choose to stay down and feel sorry for yourself, or you can get up and prove that it is possible for an individual to be broken but still standing.**

The human spirit has an incredible ability to recover from trauma and crisis. When someone is determined to overcome the crisis and is also willing to seek out help such as counselling, prayer, assistance with resources and moral support, they can triumph over their crisis.

In 1969, in her book titled 'On Death and Dying', Swiss psychiatrist Elisabeth Kübler-Ross postulated a series of emotional stages experienced by the survivors of an intimate's death. These stages are not restricted to coping with death only, but are applicable to coping with any crisis. These stages are progressive, and people may display some or all of the emotions as they are resolving a crisis. The emotional stages are referred to by the acronym DABDA, according to the first letter of each of the five emotions which are:

- denial,
- anger,
- bargaining,
- depression, and
- acceptance.

Denial occurs when someone refuses to accept the news, diagnosis or facts and prefers to hold onto a more acceptable state of affairs or reality.
Anger sets in when the individual comes to the realization that denial is futile, and then lashes out angrily at other people and/or themselves. The individual displays frustration and intolerance and asks questions such as:
"Why is this happening?"
"What did I ever do to deserve this?"
"Why did it not happen to someone else?"
"Who is responsible?"
"Why is life so unfair?"
Bargaining entails negotiating an exchange in order to undo or reverse the crisis. For example, an individual may propose to reform his lifestyle in exchange for an extended life.
Depression occurs when the person becomes discouraged about what he is experiencing and then loses his desire to continue living and also associate with other people. Isolation is a key indicator of this emotional stage.
Acceptance occurs when an individual finally comes to terms with the grief and loss or disappointment. At this emotional stage the person feels strong enough to accept the conditions he finds himself in and deals with it in a mature manner.

There is a pattern that emerges in the above discussion on crises, and it relates to change. Any event that brings about a change from the way things used to be usually acts as a catalyst for a crisis. These changes place pressure on the individual to make adjustments in their perceptions and behaviour. According to Eric Hoffer, every new adjustment is a crisis in self-esteem. This means that those things that usher in a change simultaneously usher in a self-esteem crisis.

> **Every new adjustment is a crisis in self-esteem.**
> *Eric Hoffer*

Having self-esteem that is high does not mean that life will never knock you down. King Solomon wrote: 'A righteous person may fall seven times, but he gets up again. However, in a disaster wicked people fall.'

> **A righteous person may fall seven times, but he gets up again. However, in a disaster wicked people fall.** Proverbs 24:16 GW
> *King Solomon*

This verse is saying that a man of good conduct and strong character can be knocked down, but will rise up stronger, more confident, erect, fixed and established, but a man of weak character who is cruel and criminally minded will be helpless and feeble and will experience injury, distress, misery and unhappiness. Only people who have strong character can survive a life-altering crisis, and still come out feeling good about themselves. If you did not have high self-esteem before a fall, you probably will not have it after a fall. High self-esteem is thus a weapon and resource that you must possess before you face a crisis.

Research has shown that the people who survive crises are the ones who maintain a positive mental attitude, and who feel that they have gained something good from the crisis. Unless you have high self-esteem and high self-confidence, you will not have the mental attitude that is needed to overcome a crisis.

It is undeniably clear that even winners collapse and fall oftentimes when they are pursuing a goal. It is staying down that makes a loser, but the winners are those who get up. Resignation and giving up is for losers, but winners get up every time. An overcomer is not someone who never fails, an overcomer is someone who never gives up.

An overcomer is not someone who never fails, an overcomer is someone who never gives up.

4. Concerns

We all have concerns about what will happen in the future. Sometimes these concerns cause us to display stress and anxiety. We tend to worry about the things over which we feel we have little or no control. Worrying will not give us control over the things which concern us most. We must approach life with the knowledge that we cannot have 100% control over events in our lives. Jesus admonished us to "*not worry about tomorrow, about what you will eat and drink. It is only people who do not believe and trust in God who are concerned about these things.*"

He went on to ask: "*what man by worrying can make himself taller?*" He also said that "*tomorrow has enough troubles of its own.*" These words of Jesus teach us a few valuable lessons.

We must accept that we do not have control over tomorrow. We cannot gain control by worrying (worrying is expending mental energy by persistently thinking about something in negative terms).

People who do not trust God will worry.

We must live fully in the moment, and live in today because tomorrow we will face a myriad of other problems. There is a maxim that reads: 'Yesterday is history, tomorrow is a mystery, today is a gift that's why it is called the present!'

Yesterday is history, tomorrow is a mystery, today is a gift that's why it is called the present!

Appreciate what you have right now. Paul the Apostle gave us a formula for dealing with our concerns when he wrote: '*be anxious for nothing, but through prayer and supplication make all your requests known unto God, and the Lord will keep you in perfect peace.*' Philippians 4:6

Anxiety and worry are the thieves of peace. When your peace is gone, your joy is gone. When your joy is gone, your desire for life is gone. You cannot be effective when you've lost your zest for life. Having a fervent desire to succeed and be effective are innate human traits given to us by God,

whilst anything that steals these desires are not from Him. When your peace is stolen everything else is stolen too. We restore our peace through the method of the prayer when we request divine assistance and providence and also by conducting our lives according to the divine instructions in God's word.
People with high self-esteem dispel all negative concerns which diminish their value from their mind. They appreciate and live fully in the now.

5. Continuity (Coming Through the Storms)
When He delivered The Sermon on the Mount, Jesus of Nazareth taught a few principles and he said that anyone who follows those principles will easily survive life's inevitable storms. He said that the man who follows these principles can be equated to someone who builds a house on a rock and when the storm comes, the house will remain standing. However, anyone who does not follow these principles can be equated to someone who builds his house on sand and when the storm comes, the house will collapse. The storm is a metaphor for those difficult crises that befall all of us. The house that remains standing represents survival, or continuity. The collapsed house represents destruction, which is an inability to stand in the face of the storm.
We have to understand that coming through the storm is not contingent upon what you do when the storm comes and during the storm. Surviving life's storms does not depend on what you do during the storm – it depends on what you do before.

> **Surviving life's storms does not depend on what you do during the storm – it depends on what you do before.**

In the illustration that Jesus gave, we can see that the critical component during the building of the houses was the foundation. The foundation was either solid as represented by the rock, or soft as represented by the sand. The foundation is a metaphor representing the value of the principles on which we build our lives. Principles are the guiding moral laws that we subscribe to. Principles are foundational because they form the primary navigation system by which we make decisions and conduct our lives. Jesus used the example of the foundation of a house in order to convey the idea that our principles are foundational. Principles are not of equal value – some are more valuable and desirable than others. If we build on solid principles then we will survive life's crises, but if we build on soft principles then we will be destroyed by life's crises. The value of your principles dictates whether you will survive or succumb to life's storms.

> **The value of your principles dictates whether you will survive or succumb to life's storms.**

Jesus values you so much that He wants you to come through life's storms.
I will briefly state the principles which he taught his followers. When you practice these principles you will be victorious over the storms that come your way.

1. ***Value yourself.***
   You are the salt of the Earth. Matthew 5:13
   You are the light of the world. Matthew 5:14
2. ***Value others.***
   Love your neighbour, and your enemies. Matthew 5:44
3. ***Value God.***
   Seek first the kingdom of God and his righteousness and all your physical needs such as food, drink and clothing will be met. Matthew 6:33
   Be perfect as God is perfect. Matthew 5:48
4. ***Value reconciliation.***
   Forgive anyone who has harmed you. Matthew 6:14-15
   If someone beats you turn the other cheek. Matthew 5:39
   Settle legal matters as speedily as possible, and before it gets to court. Matthew 5:25
   Settle your disagreements with adversaries before bringing a gift to the altar of God. Matthew 5:23-24
5. ***Value introspection (over criticism).***
   Consider the log in your own eye before you consider the speck in your brother's eye. Matthew 7:3-5

6. ***Value recognition from God instead of men.*** Do not fast, give and pray in a manner that invites compliments from men, but do it in secret so that God can recognize and reward you openly. Matthew 6:3-4, 6, 17-18
7. ***Value today.*** Do not worry about tomorrow's needs, because tomorrow has its own storms. Matthew 6:34

People with high self-esteem readily cultivate the habits that will ensure continuity amidst life's storms.

6. Consistency

The word ***consistency*** means '*to act in the same way continuously.'* For anyone who endeavours to achieve anything, usually there will be something that they must do on a regular basis. For example, the student must regularly study and review his study material if he wishes to pass; an athlete must train and exercise regularly if he wishes to be a winner; the actor must practice his lines and actions if he wishes to give a winning performance and the soldier must practice shooting his rifle if he wishes to come out a winner in a battle. These are just a few examples of routines which people must exercise regularly if they wish to win in life. Unless people persistently exercise, they will not improve their skill, and worse of all they will not emerge as winners in life.

In the book of Proverbs, King Solomon writes:

'If you are lazy, you will never get what you are after, but if you work hard, you will get a fortune.' Proverbs 12:27 GNT

Another translation of this verse reads as follows:

'The lazy man does not roast what he took in hunting,
But diligence is man's precious possession.' Proverbs 12:27 NKJV

If we were to combine these verses, and state them in plain English, they would read as follows:

'If you are lazy you will not prepare your own food that you have worked for and you will never get what you are after, but if you have the precious characteristic of working hard persistently and consistently, which is diligence, you will get a fortune.'

We can see from this combined verse that lazy people will not survive or get what they pursue. However, diligent people will get a fortune. King Solomon also enlightens us concerning what man's most precious characteristic is – it is diligence.

Diligence means *'to be careful and persistent in one's work and efforts; it is conscientiousness, rigour, meticulousness and carefulness.'*

Diligence comes from the Latin word ***diligentia*** which means *'close attention, caution.'*

Diligence is consistency. We have seen that King Solomon warns us that without consistent effort we will never get a fortune. In fact, you cannot achieve and acquire anything worthwhile without consistent effort. If you endeavour to achieve your goals, you must possess the characteristic that separates the winners from the losers. You must possess the most valuable characteristic. All valuable pursuits demand that the pursuer must first have the most valuable characteristic of diligence. In order to possess a thing of value, you must first possess the most valuable characteristic of diligence.

All valuable pursuits demand that the pursuer must first have the most valuable characteristic of diligence. In order to possess a thing of value, you must first possess the most valuable characteristic of diligence.

High self-esteem is not all that is necessary for success. High self-esteem is essential for success, but it is not enough. High self-esteem must be coupled with goals and diligent action in order for success to be achieved.

High self-esteem is essential for success, but it is not enough. High self-esteem must be coupled with goals and diligent action in order for success to be achieved.

People with high self-esteem are exceptionally diligent. They put in the consistent effort that is required for success, and those who desire to be phenomenally successful put in extra effort. Winners put in the extra effort, even when it hurts.

> **Winners put in the extra effort, even when it hurts.**

Phenomenal success is the domain of winners and champions. Winners and champions willingly exercise diligent effort because they possess the valuable characteristic that separates them from the rest of the crowd – they possess diligence.

> **Winners and champions willingly exercise diligent effort because they possess the valuable characteristic that separates them from the rest of the crowd – they possess diligence.**

7. Curiosity

Hosea, an ancient Jewish prophet, wrote:
'My people are destroyed from lack of knowledge.' Hosea 4:6 NIV
The word ***knowledge*** in the original Hebrew text refers to more than mere information - it also refers to '*a desire and willingness to learn and seek out understanding*.' Curiosity is the eager desire to learn, understand and know something. Unless we are constantly curious and deliberately explore our surroundings, we will eventually suffer failure and destruction. Failure and destruction come when people do not seek enlightenment and understanding concerning the things that are worth knowing. However, curiosity concerning those things which destroy people is also dangerous, because not seeking knowledge about what is right and seeking to experience what is wrong are equally destructive. The wrong knowledge can be just as destructive as no knowledge. Hence, all curiosity must be restrained. It is interesting to note that the word ***curiosity*** comes from the Latin word ***curiosus***, which means '*careful*.'
People with high self-esteem are very careful about the knowledge and experiences that they pursue. They also understand the importance of curiosity, because without healthy curiosity, we will never learn, and without learning we will never grow, and without growth we will never become better, and if we do not become better we will not become more effective. Effectiveness is efficacy. Hence we

can see that all self-improvement and self-efficacy have their origins in part, in the attribute of curiosity.
People with high self-esteem have an insatiable desire to learn and to know things. They constantly seek greater understanding of themselves, other people and their surroundings, because it increases their self-efficacy. They understand that curiosity increases their value.

> **All self-improvement and self-efficacy have their origins in curiosity.**

8. Candour

Candour refers to the qualities of openness, transparency and honesty. This word has its origins in the Latin word ***candor*** which means '*whiteness, purity.*'
The characteristics of honesty and openness will open more doors for you than dishonesty and secretiveness ever will. People with high self-esteem are very aware of the consequences of their actions, and they always try to avoid those situations which will put them in a compromising position. When people are caught in compromising positions, they will be dishonest by telling lies. People tell lies to achieve one of two specific goals – to retain or obtain. Every lie and deceptive action is performed to protect something that you don't want to lose or to gain something that you cannot attain through truth. However, in the end, honesty is the best policy. Ironically, you will eventually lose that which you endeavour to hold onto or gain by lying and you will also lose your good name and integrity. In other words, you will lose your esteem and self-esteem. Lies breed distrust, no matter how someone tries to justify the lie. People with high self-esteem protect their integrity at all cost. They remain truthful regardless of the cost. They understand that the difficulty is merely a measure of how much they value their self-esteem. If a man lies to gain $10, then that's the value of his integrity and his self-esteem.
King Solomon wrote: 'Let love and faithfulness never leave you; bind them round your neck, write them on the tablet of your heart. Then you will win favour and a good name in the sight of God and man.'

> **Let love and faithfulness never leave you; bind them round your neck, write them on the tablet of your heart.**
> **Then you will win favour and a good name in the sight of God and man.** Proverbs 3:3-4 NIVUK
> *King Solomon*

Another translation of this verse reads: 'Do not let kindness and truth leave you.' Proverbs 3:3a NASB
When you exercise candour, you automatically become more valuable to those around you because it is a quality that wins the good favour and esteem of men and God. Winners readily exercise the qualities of honesty and openness in order to make themselves more valuable to others.

9. Consummate Professionalism
A consummate professional is someone who is highly skilled, highly conscientious, dedicated, excellent and an expert in what he does. A consummate professional always behaves in the most admirable manner. A consummate professional delivers the highest calibre of work that he possibly can by demanding high quality and distinctive performance from himself.
King Solomon wrote: 'Whatever the activity in which you engage, do it with all your ability.' Another translation of this verse reads: 'Whatever your hand finds to do, do it with all your might.'

> **Whatever the activity in which you engage, do it with all your ability, because there is no work, no planning, no learning, and no wisdom in the next world where you're going.** Ecclesiastes 9:10 ISV
> *King Solomon*

Here King Solomon is advising us to perform any task - whether it be big or small, whether it be for ourselves or others, whether it be for reward or without reward, to the very best of our ability. Doing a task to the best of your ability entails:

1. doing the very best job that you can possibly do,
2. doing it with the highest level of commitment,
3. employing all of your energies to complete the task,

4. seeing the completed task as a reflection of who you are,
5. taking healthy pride in your work,
6. doing the task in an ungrudging manner, and
7. doing the task with inspiration and zest.

When you perform work according to this fashion, you will always feel a high sense of accomplishment and if the task is for reward you will definitely receive a high reward for your efforts.
I want to highlight point number 7, which talks about doing a task with inspiration and zest. This point may be mentioned last, but I consider it to be the foundation of all successful task completion. Inspiration and zest are attributes that make an individual extremely zealous to perform a task. The attributes of mediocrity, lethargy, tardiness and 'dragging-your-feet syndrome' cannot find a place in the life and work of a man who has a zest for life and who is inspired. Being inspired, and having a zest for work and life, drives someone to perform all their tasks with the highest degree of professionalism and excellence.
When I was still a child, and my dad gave me task or a chore to complete, he often watched me as I worked. When he saw me slacking or doing the task half-heartedly, he used to say:
"Get some life in you!"
This statement simply means that you must do things with energy, vitality, passion and enjoyment. I always believed that it also meant that if you're not enjoying what you're doing, at least pretend. The funny thing about pretending to like something is that eventually you actually do like and enjoy what you're doing.

> **Get some life in you!**
> *Leslie H. Heldzinger*

Consummate professionalism is not just a work ethic, it's a lifestyle. When you automatically demand excellence from yourself you will make no exception or compromise, regardless of what you are doing. You will demand excellent performance from yourself, whether your performance relates to your personal life or your career.

> **Consummate professionalism is not just a work ethic, it's a lifestyle.**

People with high self-esteem are the quintessential consummate professionals. They exercise great pride in their work, because they understand that your work – the fruit you have produced - is a reflection of who you are. Quality fruit is produced by quality trees, and in the same way, quality work is produced by quality people and excellent work is produced by excellent people.

10. Centre

People have the tendency to seek and find a sense of security and fulfilment in one key area of their life. That key area differs from person to person. This key area is known as your life-centre, or simply your centre. It is called a centre because it represents the central idea around which your life will revolve. The significance of your centre is that it will have a major influence on most of your decisions and also on your goals. Here are examples of various centres:

- health,
- wealth,
- self,
- family,
- friends,
- work,
- religion,
- learning,
- sport,
- spouse, and
- principles.

All of the centres stated above, with the exception of *principles*, are the type of centres that will lead to frustration in areas that are being neglected or overlooked.
Someone who is ***wealth-centred*** may neglect his family, and possibly cheat family members and friends in the pursuit of his goal.
Someone who is ***self-centred*** will disregard the opinions and feelings of others and can destroy his own life and that

of others in the process. These people display narcissistic tendencies.

Someone who is ***spouse-centred*** may neglect himself and his work responsibilities to please his spouse.

According to Dr. Stephen Covey, the only worthwhile centre is ***principle-centeredness.*** Principle-centeredness speaks about adherence to timeless principles that are changeless. These principles are related to values such as honesty, truth, fairness, reciprocation, kindness, love, respect, honour. Principles also entail The Law of Sowing and Reaping, which speaks about consequences.

People with high self-esteem maintain balance in their lives by following timeless principles, because they understand that a principle-centred life is more valuable than a life that is centred around people and things.

> **People with high self-esteem maintain balance in their lives by following timeless principles, because they understand that a principle-centred life is more valuable than a life that is centred around people and things.**

11. Conduct

Conduct refers to attitude and behaviour. Your behaviour stems from your attitude.

Always conduct yourself in such a manner that your actions are beyond reproach. You can only have behaviour that is beyond reproach if your attitude is beyond reproach.

If you have a bad attitude, you will also display bad behaviour, but if you have a good attitude, you will display good and admirable behaviour. Your behaviour is the truest indicator of your character. Your attitude determines your character. Albert Einstein confirmed this when he said: "Weakness of attitude becomes weakness of character." Einstein was also saying, by implication, that *strength of attitude becomes strength of character.*

> **Weakness of attitude becomes weakness of character.**
> *Albert Einstein*

Attitude is the most influential component in any relationship. The attitudes of the individuals in a relationship, whether it be one of family, friendship, marital or business, will determine the longevity of the relationship.
If people display positive attitudes in their relationships, effectiveness, success and happiness go up. The married couple who display positive and healthy attitudes towards each other will have greater happiness and fulfilment than the couple who continuously display a bad attitude towards each other.
Business will be more productive if employees displayed an attitude of gratefulness for the opportunity of employment, instead of behaving like they're doing the company a favour by showing up for work every day. Many employees are totally unaware of the true reason, or motivation, behind their behaviour when they refuse to perform an instruction given by a manager or employer. People normally refuse to perform instructions because:

1. either they do not know how to perform it – this represents a ***competence*** issue and can be corrected with training;
2. or they feel a strong conviction to not perform – this represents ***conscience*** and relates to the employee's values;
3. or they simply refuse to comply – this is a ***character*** issue and relates to the employee's attitude.

The most destructive of the three behaviours mentioned above, is attitude, which is related to character.
People will be more successful when they develop winning attitudes. Families will be more functional and organizations will be more effective and profitable when their members have more positive attitudes. Zig Ziglar once said:
"Your attitude, not your aptitude, will determine your altitude."

> **Your attitude, not your aptitude, will determine your altitude.**
> *Zig Ziglar*

People with high self-esteem monitor their own attitude and conduct. They behave in ways that engender value in order to become an asset and not a liability to the groups and organizations that they belong to.

> **People with high self-esteem monitor their own attitude and conduct. They behave in ways that engender value in order to become an asset and not a liability to the groups and organizations that they belong to.**

12. Creative Expression

Creativity must be both an escape and a means of expression. Love what you do. Your creative efforts must be performed out of love for something. You must do it because you enjoy the process and the result. You must enjoy the feeling of watching your work unfold into a masterpiece right before your eyes.

Your creative expression must be self-fulfilling. Whatever you do, do it for your own enjoyment, and not only with other people's opinions in mind. If you are happy with your work, in most cases others will be too.

If you do not, or cannot enjoy creating something, then don't do it. When you do something out of passion, you do it to the very best of your ability. Through passion you release your inner creativity, and magic happens.

Creativity is the avenue of expression in any and every sphere of human existence. Creativity is the highest expression of self. When creative self-expression is fuelled, self-esteem is built up, but when it is prohibited or hampered, self-esteem is diminished. Express yourself!

> **Creativity is the highest expression of self. When creative self-expression is fuelled, self-esteem is built up, but when it is prohibited or hampered, self-esteem is diminished. Express yourself!**

Your level of self-esteem will have a strong bearing on your creative expression. People with high self-esteem easily express their creativity with comfort and confidence.

13. Commodiousness

Commodiousness refers to how useful the individual feels, especially as it pertains to the groups and organizations that he belongs to. You can only feel commodious if you are making a useful contribution to the groups and organizations that you belong to. Usually people who are truly commodious reap handsome rewards in terms of remuneration. King Solomon highlighted this truth when he wrote: 'Idle hands make one poor, but diligent hands bring riches.'

> **Idle hands make one poor, but diligent hands bring riches.** Proverbs 10:4 HCSB
> *King Solomon*

The term ***diligent hands*** in this verse refers to more than just the hands of an individual – it refers to '*the employment of all useful capacities resident within the individual, as well as physical labour.'*
If you want to be useful, then make yourself useful. Find ways to apply all your abilities and capacities to perform work worthy of the type of recognition that promotes personal and material value.

> **If you want to be useful, then make yourself useful. Find ways to apply all your abilities and capacities to perform work worthy of the type of recognition that promotes personal and material value.**

14. Counsel

Counsel is about getting guidance and advice from other people. No matter what we endeavour to do, we increase the probability of our success when we seek guidance from others. King Solomon warned us that plans fail when we fail do get counsel, but when we have many counsellors our plans succeed.

> **Plans fail for lack of counsel, but with many advisers they succeed.** Proverbs 15:22 NIV
> *King Solomon*

The seven guidelines for getting counsel are stated below.

The Seven Guidelines for Getting Guidance

1. Humility is the first step towards success.

Only the humble will ask for help. It is counter-intuitive for a proud person to ask for help, guidance, correction and direction. Proud people feel that they will humiliate themselves if they have to ask anyone for anything.

Unfortunately, usually these proud people fail miserably in their endeavours. They *crash and burn.* In order to avoid the *crash and burn syndrome*, you must be willing to humble yourself.

There is a rule that I learnt many years back, and it has served me well. I call it the *Yes-No Rule.* This rule simply says: "If you say 'YES' to one thing, you are also saying 'NO' to something else."

When one applies this rule to seeking advice from people, if you say 'No' to advice, you are automatically saying 'Yes' to failure and ignominy. If you say 'Yes' to guidance, you are saying 'No' to failure and ignominy. King Solomon wrote that pride leads to destruction but humility leads to honour.

> **Pride leads to destruction; humility leads to honour.** Proverbs 18:21 CEV
> *King Solomon*

Many people cut themselves off from the benefits of counsel when they say things like: "I know," and "I know what I'm doing."

These two expressions have been called *famous last words*, and with good reason. Many people who have said these words have not lived to say any other words, and for those who have lived, many have had to hear another famous expression that goes like this: "I told you so."

Anyone who cuts off counsel through their words and actions will eventually suffer because of it. People with high self-esteem always walk on the side of safety by being humble, willing and open to seek out advice and correction.

I have also come to learn, through experience and observation, that it is not only pride that prevents people from reaching out for counsel. I have had the privilege to mentor many school students, and the majority of these students are reluctant to ask questions in class for fear of being seen as stupid by their classmates and teachers. In addition, I've also witnessed many teachers referring to students as being 'stupid.'

The fear of being seen as stupid is a strong motivator in students. Painful memories are also strong motivators which act as deterrents from seeking help in public. The memory of having been called stupid by a teacher can produce terrible psychological scars for students. These two phenomena – fear and painful memories – can keep students from excelling in the classroom and in life. I have discovered that it is only a change in thinking, with regards to what stupidity is, that will reverse these phenomena. In order to correct this mind-set in students, I teach them King Solomon's definition of stupidity. King Solomon wrote: "He who hates correction is stupid." Here, the wise king teaches us that only those who hate correction are stupid. Thus stupidity does not lie in making a mistake – stupidity lies in not seeking or wanting correction to fix your mistake. Anyone who is reluctant to ask a question or to seek out more information in order to take corrective measures is a stupid person. When people have a paradigm shift concerning stupidity, they will be more willing to reach out for help, and they will also be able to correct anyone who uses the word 'stupid' inappropriately when referring to themselves or someone else.

> **Whoever loves discipline loves knowledge, but he who hates correction is stupid.** Proverbs 12:1 NIV
> *King Solomon*

2. Seek out knowledgeable people whom you know, and also those whom you do not know.

Guidance can be found from those whom you know, and you can also contact people who know what you need to know, even if you do not know the person yet. There is great value in having a *go-to person* who can give you direction and guidance. Along with your go-to person, you will also need specialized knowledge from experts.

Who can we seek expert counsel and guidance from?

We can acquire valuable counsel from people who have experience and knowledge about what we desire to achieve. In any field of endeavour you will be able to find someone who can guide you so that you do not make the mistakes that people make in the absence of guidance. In the Book of Job, Job asks his three friends these rhetorical questions: "Is not wisdom found among the aged? Does not long life bring understanding?" Here we receive direction to one source of wisdom - those who are old. Old people have a wealth of experience and knowledge which they will gladly share with a willing listener. We can also ask friends, teachers and other leaders for guidance and advice.

> **Is not wisdom found among the aged?**
> **Does not long life bring**
> **understanding?** Job 12:12 NIV
> *Job of Uz*

The most successful people seek out mentors and coaches to teach, lead and guide them. A good mentor will teach you valuable lessons, but they would normally not push you hard to perform at your best. A mentor can be equated to a personal teacher or private tutor. A coach will be more concerned about peak performance and he will drive you to the very brink of your potential. A coach can be equated to a military drill sergeant.

The wisest man who ever lived, King Solomon, did not become wise by chance. While he was growing up, the young boy, Prince Solomon was taught by his father, King David. The word ***taught*** was translated from a Hebrew word which means '*to shoot arrows; to throw water; to point out* and *to direct, teach and instruct.*' From the meaning of the original Hebrew word, we can see that Solomon was directed, taught, instructed and pointed the way by his father, King David.

King Solomon had valuable mentoring and coaching from a wise and experienced man. You too can obtain valuable mentoring and coaching from an experienced expert, and thereby you will increase your success and self-esteem immensely. Through mentoring and coaching you will become a more valuable person.

> **For I too was a son to my father, still tender, and cherished by my mother. Then he taught me, and he said to me, "Take hold of my words with all your heart; keep my commands, and you will live."** Proverbs 4:3-4 NIV
> *King Solomon*

In addition to making use of coaches, mentors and teachers for counsel, I have espoused the idea that I can learn something from everybody. I have trained myself to try to learn from everybody I meet, because there is always something that the next person knows that I don't. People with high self-esteem are open to this sort of learning. They are always consciously taking in new information from people around them and they learn from it, regardless of the source. The source can be anyone. The source can also be anything or any animal. We can gain wisdom from multiple sources and from all the people around us.

> **I went past the field of a sluggard, past the vineyard of someone who has no sense; I applied my heart to what I observed and learned a lesson from what I saw.** Proverbs 24:30, 32 NIV
>
> **Go to the ant, you sluggard; consider its ways and be wise!** Proverbs 6:6 NIV
>
> **At the window of my house I looked down through the lattice. I saw among the simple, I noticed among the young men, a youth who had no sense.** Proverbs 7:6-7 NIV
> *King Solomon*

3. Seek guidance before you act, not afterwards.
Most people normally seek guidance when things start going wrong. The most successful people seek guidance before they execute any action towards their goals, because advice is more valuable in advance than in retrospect. King Solomon taught that prudent people see danger and take refuge. The word ***prudent*** simply means *'having good judgement; being sensible; being cautious; being advisable.'* Being advisable is about being open to warnings and

corrections. Advisability leads to the avoidance of danger and trouble, but when you are closed off to advice you will walk right into danger.

> **The prudent see danger and take refuge, but the simple keep going and pay the penalty.** Proverbs 22:3 NIV
> *King Solomon*

4. Don't ever stop seeking guidance, even when you've arrived.

Every successful person had to acquire guidance, and the most successful seek guidance even when they've succeeded. Being successful should not stop you from continually seeking the guidance of other people.
Some people who have become successful, materially and otherwise, behave like they hold the franchise on knowledge and wisdom. These are people who believe that they have all the answers simply because they have attained success. King Solomon warned us about such individuals when he wrote: "The rich man's wealth is his strong city, and as a high protecting wall in his own imagination and conceit."
It is only a fool who believes that his material and positional successes are like a high wall which no-one can climb and which is impenetrable. They imagine that their success is sure for all time and that no-one can teach them or reach them. They are conceited.

> **The rich man's wealth is his strong city, and as a high protecting wall in his own imagination and conceit.** Proverbs 18:11 AMP
> *King Solomon*

Anyone who is conceited acts like a *know-it-all.* Anyone who thinks that he knows everything is walking in the domain of self-delusion. Besides, nobody likes a know-it-all because they are simply annoying. People with high self-esteem value the input of others, because they understand that true self-worth does not come from being conceited and thinking that you already know everything that there is to know. On the contrary, people with high self-esteem are comfortable with the knowledge that, despite their outward successes, there is always something new that they can learn. They also understand that when comparing the set of what they know against the set of what they do not know, that the latter is and always will be greater.

5. Put into practice what you've learnt.

When you've been given good advice, make sure that you implement it. Seeking guidance without implementing it is like having a life-jacket but you still jump into the ocean without it. Aristotle wrote: 'For the things we have to learn before we can do them, we learn by doing them.'
It is only through application that true learning occurs.

> **For the things we have to learn before we can do them, we learn by doing them.**
> *Aristotle*

6. Guidance can be found in a good book.

You can learn in 40 minutes what it has taken a man 40 years to learn, simply by reading his book. William Godwin wrote: 'He that loves reading has everything within his reach.' It is through books that the unreachable becomes reachable, and the impossible becomes possible.

> **He that loves reading has everything within his reach.**
> *William Godwin*

7. Consult God for direction in all your affairs, before you consult a man.

Those people who seek God's guidance first, before consulting man, have greater success than people who don't. King Solomon wrote: 'Commit your actions to the LORD, and your plans will succeed.'
Our success in any endeavour is virtually guaranteed when we bring our plans to God and humbly ask Him for His blessings and guidance, through the medium of prayer. Martin Luther, the German theologian, used to say: "I have much to do today, I must pray a little more."

> **Commit your actions to the LORD, and your plans will succeed.** Proverbs 16:3 NLT
> *King Solomon*

15. Challenges

There is an interesting phenomenon that occurs when you set a goal for yourself and are determined to achieve it. All of nature seems to conspire to resist your progress. Life throws one challenge after the other in your way. Challenges are life's obstacles. People with low self-esteem see these challenges as obstacles which are meant to keep them from achieving their goal – a sign that it is not meant to be. However, people with high self-esteem and confidence know that obstacles and challenges are simply life's way of testing your resolve and determination to achieve their goal.

> **People with high self-esteem and confidence know that obstacles and challenges are simply life's way of testing your resolve and determination to achieve your goal.**

Even other people will resist your goals and plans. When you state your goals, those who support you will make themselves known, but those opposed to your goals will also reveal themselves. State your goal and enemies will crawl out of the woodwork. Enemies to your goals are those people who will impede, prevent or postpone the realization of your goals. These people will constantly challenge your progress.

This should not stop you from declaring your goals. Declaring your goals is essential to smoke out your enemies. The enemies to your goals and blessings can be natural and spiritual. Speak your goal and you automatically give them an invitation to make themselves and their plans known. Let your enemies become visible because only a visible insurgent can be eliminated.

Sometimes the enemy is in your camp, and sometimes without. There are those close to you who will oppose you because they propose that you should follow their plan for your life. Say to them:

"Plan your own life, and leave me to plan mine."

Sometimes you will feel that you just don't have the right conditions, abilities and resources to continue working towards your goal. Your challenges may be so immense that you feel like giving up. Don't give up! Always remember that nothing worthwhile was ever achieved under ideal conditions. Also remember that your challenge will never be so great that you have absolutely nothing to work with. The best solution is to make the best of what you have and then work with what you have until something better comes along. Napoleon Hill advises us to start where we stand and *better tools will be found as you go along.*

> **Do not wait: the time will never be 'just right'. Start where you stand, and work with whatever tools you may have at your command and better tools will be found as you go along.**
> *Napoleon Hill*

Body-builders use weights to build muscle tone and strength.
Just like weights provide resistance to a body-builder, so challenges provide resistance for you so that you can be strengthened.

16. Chastity

Social norms and the media place immense pressure on people to be sexually active and promiscuous from a young age. Promiscuity is subtly promoted in movies, daytime soap-operas and other television shows. Many people shape their values around the messages being promoted through these platforms of entertainment, especially young people. Chastity is taboo amongst modern teenagers and young adults. Research has shown that many young people have had several sexual relationships before the age of 18. Premarital sexual relations have become very popular amongst teenagers. Virginity is no longer seen as virtuous, instead it is frowned upon. Albert Einstein once said: "What is right is not always popular and what is popular is not always right."

> **What is right is not always popular and what is popular is not always right.**
> *Albert Einstein*

This statement holds true especially in the arena of sexual conduct. Being chaste may not be popular, but it does not have to be popular to be right. But by what standard can we measure something in order to determine its 'rightness?' There are two standards that we can apply.

The first relates to God's laws. When God gave the Israelites His commandments, the 7th of the 10 Commandments prohibited adultery. Adultery is any sexual act performed with someone who is not your legal spouse. This law forbids any sexual act between two persons who are not legally married, and therefore prohibits sexual relations between people even though they may be consenting adults.

The second measure relates to risk. When you engage in any form of pre-marital sexual activity and promiscuity, you place yourself at risk of contracting and also spreading sexually transmitted infections (STIs) and sexually transmitted diseases (STDs). Any sexually transmitted disease can seriously hamper your quality of life and worse, it can shorten your life.

People with high self-esteem boldly practice chastity and monogamy, because it is the right thing to do. Since the sexual relationship is characterized by intense physical and psychological intimacy between two people, the considerate partner will highly value his/her spouse. People with high self-esteem remain chaste and monogamous because, first and foremost, they value themselves very highly.

17. Cleverness

Intelligence has been highly misunderstood. Most Intelligence Quotient (IQ) Tests measure the subject's mathematical reasoning and analytical thinking. However, statistics have proven that only a small percentage of the population in any country deliver exceptionally high scores in a standard IQ Test. The reason for this is self-explanatory – only a small percentage of the population is naturally gifted in the cognitive areas being assessed, namely logical-mathematical and linguistic abilities.

When you don't do well in these cognitive areas at school, you may be considered stupid. Being considered stupid can really place a damper on your self-esteem.

Howard Gardner, a professor at the Harvard Graduate School of Education at Harvard University, published a book titled

Frames of Mind: The Theory of Multiple Intelligences in 1983 and in his book he suggested that there is more than one type of intelligence and there are different ways by which these intelligences can be measured. He suggested that there are eight intelligences, and then later suggested a 9th sometime after the release of his book. Interestingly, Gardner suggested that the logical-mathematical is just one of the nine possible intelligences which he was able to isolate. Furthermore, he suggested that most people are endowed with a combination of the nine forms of intelligence, although we don't all possess the exact same combinations.

Gardner has included artistic ability, linguistic ability and bodily- kinaesthetic aptitudes as intelligences in their own right. Gardner wrote:

'I balk at the unwarranted assumption that certain human abilities can be arbitrarily singled out as intelligence while others cannot.'

Your cleverness, or intelligence, may not lie in the logical-mathematical arena, but it does lie somewhere. Remember that you are intelligent in some way. Everyone is a genius in some area and in some way, and must therefore be treated like one. Your area of genius is usually that thing that you are naturally good at and that you effortlessly perform better at than other people.

> **Everyone is a genius in some area and in some way, and must therefore be treated like one. Your area of genius is usually that thing that you are naturally good at and that you effortlessly perform better at than other people.**

If you are good at singing, you may be gifted with the intelligence of *musicality*. If you perform well at sports, you are most likely gifted with the intelligence of *fine motor skills*.

People with high self-esteem are able to isolate and celebrate their own unique intelligence without being threatened or feeling inferior to someone else who is more gifted in another area.
IQ testing is performed to determine an individual's intelligence number. A consequence of IQ testing has been that most people believe that one's intelligence is fixed at a certain number. This is a misconception. Your mental capacities have an unlimited potential for growth and expansion. Your mental capacities are expandable and can be stretched like an elastic band. You can grow your intelligence through cognitive exercise just as easily as you can grow muscle strength and volume through physical exercise.

> **Your mental capacities have an unlimited potential for growth and expansion.**
> **Your mental capacities are expandable and can be stretched like an elastic band.**

Research has shown that young children are capable of learning as many languages as they are exposed to, especially during their formative years and early school years. Even as an adult, when you learn a new language, it opens up cortices in your brain which have been unused and the utilization of this additional brain capacity literally makes you smarter. This happens simply by learning an additional language. Imagine what happens when you learn two or more languages ...
Strategy games are very useful to exercise the mind. Chess is a strategy game that teaches discipline, and exercises the individual's strategic, analytical and predictive thinking capacities. Monopoly, the popular money game, is useful for exercising the computational, financial management and creativity capacities of an individual. Scrabble and Boggle are useful to exercise an individual's creativity and communication skills such as vocabulary, spelling and pronunciation.
You can also expand your intelligence by doing puzzles such as building pictures puzzles, completing crossword puzzles, Sudoku and the Rubik's cube. I use the Rubik's Cube extensively in my lecturing sessions. I encourage my

students to learn the Rubik's Cube because it expands your memory, analytical thinking and creative thinking. Learning to solve the Rubik's Cube literally makes you smarter. In addition, understanding the principles involved in solving a Rubik's Cube gives one a better understanding of the principles of life. There is also the added advantage of the confidence boost that everybody experiences when they've mastered the Rubik's Cube. This confidence spills over into other areas of the person's life. It is a timeless truth that mastery in one area of an individual's life produces confidence that leads to mastery in other areas too.

It is a timeless truth that mastery in one area of an individual's life produces confidence that leads to mastery in other areas too.

People with high self-esteem readily expand their intelligence by learning new skills and taking on challenging tasks, puzzles and games. They place their intelligence on a trajectory of ever-increasing value through deliberate action.

People with high self-esteem readily expand their intelligence by learning new skills and taking on challenging tasks, puzzles and games. They place their intelligence on a trajectory of ever-increasing value through deliberate action.

18. Casualty Factor

The Casualty Factor relates to all the hurts and pain from your past. We all carry deep scars which are reminders of past hurts. We carry these injuries and sometimes cry over them for many decades.

Oftentimes the pain from the past lingers and it affects your performance and relationships.

Human beings have a powerful endowment and tool in the form of memory. Memory places pertinent information at your immediate disposal. Memory brings the past into the present. Memory is very useful because it helps you to recall information and experiences so that you don't have to look up the information or learn it again. Memory also has a downside. The downside of memory is that we often recall bad experiences, injuries and pain long after they occurred.

Memory can bring past pain into the present. The memory of past injuries manifests in various aspects of our lives and in various ways.

It can manifest when people enter new relationships, whether it be a new romantic, friendship or business relationship.

A child who has accidentally burnt himself with boiling-hot water from a kettle will always remember the pain from the experience and will also always be very, very careful when dealing with boiling water. The child may become petrified of kettles and steam.

Someone who has been called stupid by a teacher may feel like they do not want to study or learn anything new because the pain of the insult lingers. I have seen this phenomenon amongst students and adults. Whenever the person encounters anything related to learning, his mind switches back to a test or something he failed at and they re-experience the pain of being called stupid by teachers and/or peers.

People enter new relationships with emotional baggage. Emotional baggage is the memory of the pain caused by unpleasant experiences. These are negative residual emotions. If someone has been cheated by a spouse, a friend or a business associate, these experiences make them more distrusting. In many cases, people lash out at others because of negative residual emotions. Many innocent people have to endure explosive emotional outbursts from people who have been hurt by others.

Holding onto yesterday's pain only holds you back. Unfortunately most injuries which occurred in the past, whether they are physical or emotional, cannot be undone. The only way to deal with past injuries is to just deal with them. Leo Buscaglia once asked a very important question relating to dealing with the past, when he said:

"Why hold on to the very thing which keeps you from hope and love?"

Holding onto past injuries keeps us from the things we hope for and the loving relationships we seek.

> **Let go. Why do you cling to pain? There is nothing you can do about the wrongs of yesterday. It is not yours to judge.**

> **Why hold on to the very thing which keeps you from hope and love?**
> *Leo Buscaglia*

Leo Buscaglia advises us to "let it go." Let the past go, so that you can focus on your hopes and your relationships. There is the story of the old professor who told a joke to his students. The entire class laughed in amusement. Again, the professor told the very same joke, and this time less students laughed. The professor repeated the joke several times until nobody laughed. At the end he asked if they didn't keep laughing for old jokes, why do they keep crying for pain and injury for old hurts and injuries?

An athlete who is on the starting line with his competitors at the start of a 100m race looks straight ahead, and not behind. His primary focus is the end point. Nothing else matters. Any athlete who is looking backwards cannot expect to complete or win the race. He may end up running in the wrong direction, or if he adjusts his focus from the rear to the front when the gun's already gone off, he will be at a disadvantage because his competitors will be ahead of him.

> **Never look back unless you are planning to go that way.**
> *Henry David Thoreau*

Just as looking back will slow an athlete down, or cause him to go in the wrong direction and lose the race, any person who is focused on past injuries will either not reach their goal or their speed towards reaching the goal will be impeded.
Remember, to leave the past in the past. Look ahead and you'll stay ahead.

> **Remember, to leave the past in the past. Look ahead and you'll stay ahead.**

19. Corrective Measures

Everybody must take corrective measures in order to promote self-improvement. Self-improvement has also been

called *self-development*, *self-cultivation* and *self-correction.* Corrective measures are those activities that we engage in when we've made a mistake or we fall short of a certain skill-set.
However, sometimes we fail to see our own shortcomings and we focus on the shortcomings of those around us. This is a phenomenon that stems from myopic perception. Myopic perception, as it relates to the self-image, is about having a short-sighted view of your own shortcomings. When we see ourselves as being better than the next person because they have such huge character flaws, and simultaneously we are oblivious to our own bigger shortcomings, then we can easily antagonise the people around us. When it comes to dealing with people, John C. Maxwell advises this: 'Before you put someone on their place, put yourself in their place.'
Putting yourself in someone's place is about getting to understand that person's position and unique vantage point. When you listen to a person's words and arguments in order to attain better understanding, you will be able empathize rather than criticise.

> **Before you put someone on their place,**
> **put yourself in their place.**
> *John C. Maxwell*

In addition to listening empathically, you must also exercise patience when you are tempted to throw accusation bombs all over the place.
People with high self-esteem readily exercise patience and empathic listening in order to gain a greater understanding of someone else's unique vantage point, because it gives them a better picture of who they are dealing with and the circumstances that these people are facing. In a scenario like this, positive self-esteem is actually transferrable from one person to the next. It is only a person with high self-esteem who will permit someone else the freedom to express their views candidly. This is just like giving someone room to move. When you give a person *room to move*, in a proverbial sense, you are adding to their self-esteem, and so there is a transfer of positive self-esteem from one person to another. People who value themselves highly very easily

engender positive feelings and positive self-esteem in other people.
People with high self-esteem also know that they themselves are not perfect - their own shortcomings, experiences and flaws actually seal their mouth from criticism. Jesus of Nazareth taught us that we should remove the plank in our own eye before we point out the speck in someone else's eye. A plank is much bigger than a speck.

> **Why do you look at the speck of sawdust in your brother's eye and pay no attention to the plank in your own eye? How can you say to your brother, "Let me take the speck out of your eye," when all the time there is a plank in your own eye?**
>
> **You hypocrite, first take the plank out of your own eye, and then you will see clearly to remove the speck from your brother's eye.** Matthew 7:3-5 NIV
>
> *Jesus of Nazareth*

The plank and the speck are metaphors for a person's flaws and shortcomings. Jesus was correct when he pointed out, through this teaching, that those with the biggest flaws are usually the most critical of others. Those people who readily criticise others are usually also oblivious to their own flaws and shortcomings.
This is where self-reflection comes in. When we truthfully reflect on ourselves and our behaviour, we will find that there are things about ourselves that we need to correct. Self-correction follows self-reflection. Reflecting on self is a higher-value activity than reflecting on someone else, because it is easier to improve yourself than it is to improve someone else. People with high self-esteem work harder on themselves than they do on others.

> **People with high self-esteem work harder on themselves than they do on others.**

When people concentrate on correcting their own shortcomings, they promote as much peace as one individual can possibly bring about. True self-esteem is not about fixing others, it is about fixing yourself. When you fix yourself, you make yourself more valuable, and you can make the world a more peaceful place. Through self-correction we will have less fights and more peace in the world. So let everyone sweep in front of his own door, and the whole world will be clean, as Johann Wolfgang von Goethe advised us.

> **Let everyone sweep in front of his own door, and the whole world will be clean.**
> *Johann Wolfgang von Goethe*

20. Cognition

The word ***cognition*** comes from the Latin word ***cognitio*** which means *'to perceive, to know, to examine.'*
Cognition refers to any activity related to the mental process of thinking. It refers to the mental activities that we engage in when we are examining things in order to attain understanding and knowledge.

Cognitions are shaping forces which influence the following seven areas of your life:

1. ***ambitions*** (your goals),
2. ***conditions*** (your physical, mental and spiritual state),
3. ***relations*** (your relationships with yourself, other people and God),
4. ***positions*** (your positions and level of authority in groups and organizations),
5. ***perceptions*** (your view of people and things),
6. ***acquisitions***, (what you are able to acquire) and
7. ***situations*** (how you handle life's shifting scenarios).

These are ***The Seven Areas of Cognitive Influence****.*

Your mind is the most powerful problem-solving tool that you have. Without the ability to think you cannot solve any problems. In addition, without your mind, you will not be able to create and achieve goals.
There are seven different types of thinking. Let us explore these types and their respective values.

The Seven Categories (Types) of Thinking

1. Analytical Thinking

This refers to the breaking down of ideas and concepts and studying their relation to each other. Analytical thinking is an investigative process. There is a pattern to everything in life. For example your body has patterns called bio-rhythms; your work has a pattern called work-flow; days have patterns of seconds, minutes and hours which we collectively call time; organizations have pre-defined reporting patterns called procedures and protocols; people have specific modes of actions called behaviour patterns and repetitions of actions called routines; circumstances have patterns that we call ideal conditions; weather has patterns that we call climate. This is just a short list of the many patterns that we are exposed to in life, and analytical thinking investigates these patterns. Some patterns are uniform and others are not. When patterns are studied and analysed, one can observe the presence of anomalies. Anomalies are unusual variations in patterns. The observance of variations in patterns is an absolutely crucial step when we are making corrections and restoring order.

2. Reflective Thinking

The word ***reflect*** comes from the Latin word ***reflectere*** which meant:

- *'to throw back light or an image off a surface;'*
- *'to display an object for what it really is, like in a mirror;'*
- *'to think deeply.'*

Reflective thinking is an evaluative process. Reflective thinking leans heavily on memory. It taps into information stored in the storage vaults of your mind, and then the information is assessed. Through reflective thinking we evaluate our progress related to our goals, by asking questions like:

- is our goal worthwhile?
- is the cost-benefit ratio related to our goals acceptable?
- have we made progress?
- are our purposes and methods still relevant?

Reflection entails thinking really deeply about who you really are, where you come from, where you're positioned and where you're going. It also entails measuring yourself against certain criteria, and looking at yourself realistically – as if you were looking in a tell-all-truth mirror.
Through reflective thinking individuals and organizations reassess their overall vision in order to find relevance and satisfaction.

3. *Strategic Thinking*

Strategic thinking investigates the overall picture and plan of your goals and your pursuits. Strategic thinking considers the following questions:

- what resources will be needed and employed?
- what time and timing is involved?
- what tactical components will be considered?
- what decisions, related to resources, must be made?

The word ***strategy*** comes from the Greek word ***stratēgía,*** which means 'office of general, command, generalship.'
In the past the word *strategy* was most often associated with the science of military command as applied to the overall planning and conduct of warfare. In modern times *strategy* refers to the overall plan of action for achieving a specific goal. Strategic thinking is often referred to as *strategizing.* Without the ability to strategize nobody can formulate and execute workable plans for the solutions of problems or the attaining of a goal.
Strategic thinking is not an isolated process because it entails various other forms of thinking. Strategic thinking can be seen as a tree and the other forms of thinking which it leads to can be seen as its branches.

4. Visionary Thinking

Visionary thinking is a branch of strategic thinking. Through visionary thinking we are able to employ the human endowment of imagination and visualize new possibilities for ourselves and our organizations. Visionary thinking is an envisioning process. When we tap into the power of visionary thinking we can formulate a vision, or future picture, that adequately describes where we are going and what we want to achieve. Visionary thinking is usually

recorded as a vision statement. Vision statements are used extensively in organizations, but they can be used by individuals. People who write their goals on paper have a 97% greater success rate than people who don't write down their goals.
A vision has the ability to empower and excite people. When people are excited they readily and willingly perform in a manner that causes themselves and their organizations to move towards a better version of themselves.

5. Decisive Thinking

Decisive thinking is another branch in the tree of strategic thinking. Decisive thinking relates to decision-making. Decision-making entails selecting from various options, in which direction resources and effort will be employed. Sometimes we are spoilt for choice, and sometimes our choices are limited but we cannot escape the necessity of choice. Since making choices is mandatory, we must possess the ability to assess options in a reasonable manner and then make pragmatic decisions quickly, especially when we are under pressure. Here I want to draw your attention to the word 'quickly.' Decisive thinking is about coming to a decision with speed and then remaining resolutely committed to your chosen course of action. Sometimes, however, decisions cannot be rushed and decisive thinking will also identify those decisions which must be weighed up more carefully.

6. Tactical Thinking

Tactical thinking also branches out from strategic thinking. Tactical thinking deals with specific moves or sequences of actions. Tactics involve a series of proven steps and are recorded as algorithms. An algorithm is simply a proven formula or recipe which describes the components that are needed and lays out instructions for solving a problem in a detailed plan of action. Since there are many different algorithms for different scenarios, tactical thinking identifies which algorithms are most suitable and in which sequence the algorithms will be applied. The **minor tactic**, or secondary tactic, identifies the specific algorithms to be applied and the **major tactic**, or primary tactic, identifies the exact sequence in which the various algorithms will be applied. Winners only use tried-and-tested algorithms.

7. Collaborative Thinking

Collaborative thinking occurs when two or more people share their thinking through the exchange of ideas and concepts. Thus, unlike the six other thinking processes which could take place in isolation, collaborative thinking cannot take place unless two or more people partner together. Other names that can be given to this cognitive process are ***shared thinking***, ***partnered thinking*** and ***co-operative thinking.*** Collaborative thinking is the most powerful and beneficial of all the cognitive processes because it makes the knowledge and skills of each of the contributing members available to the entire group. An additional benefit of collaborative thinking is that the individual is not limited to his own strengths and weaknesses, but he can capitalize on the group's strengths and thereby minimize the effect of his weaknesses. In the absence of collaborative thinking these benefits will not be available to an individual. Through collaborative thinking we gain the following seven benefits:

1. *shared knowledge,*
2. *shared skill,*
3. *shared ideas,*
4. *shared effort,*
5. *support,*
6. *accelerated accomplishment, and*
7. *higher value through synergy.*

These are ***The Seven Benefits of Shared Thinking****.*

Through synergy we gain higher value. The section titled 'Collaborative Effort' in this chapter explains the concept of synergy in greater depth.

Collaborative thinking incorporates all the other thinking processes and disciplines. The goal of all the thinking processes and disciplines is to achieve and improve value – value for the individual and value for the group or organization. The individual is more effective in a group setting than alone, thus synergistic value is higher than singular value. The highest purpose and accomplishment of all forms of thinking should be to achieve synergistic value – the increased value for individuals and the group, amongst inter-dependent collaborators.

> **The goal of all the thinking processes and disciplines is to achieve and improve value – value for the individual and value for the group. The individual is more effective in a group setting than alone, thus synergistic value is higher than singular value. The highest purpose and accomplishment of all forms of thinking should be to achieve synergistic value – the increased value for individuals and the group, amongst inter-dependent collaborators.**

Thinking can be objective or subjective. Objective thinking leans on logical mathematical-type reasoning. Subjective thinking leans on emotions and feelings. People tend to regard themselves as objective when they make decisions and conclusions by suggesting, directly or indirectly, that they have considered all the pertinent information. However, most of human thinking is not logic-based but feeling-based. In his bestselling book titled: *How to Win Friends and Influence People,* Dale Carnegie confirmed this truth when he wrote: 'When dealing with people, let us remember we are not dealing with creatures of logic. We are dealing with creatures of emotion, creatures bristling with prejudices and motivated by pride and vanity.'

> **When dealing with people, let us remember we are not dealing with creatures of logic. We are dealing with creatures of emotion, creatures bristling with prejudices and motivated by pride and vanity.**
> *Dale Carnegie*

This truth expressed by Dale Carnegie exposes one of the two misconceptions related to thinking. The first misconception is that people believe that they are always objective, but in reality they are more subjective in their thinking.

The second misconception is that objective thinking and subjective thinking are conflicting opposites. Although objectivity and subjectivity evaluate information in different ways, they are meant to operate in tandem as two separate tools to evaluate the different aspects of information. Objective thinking and subjective thinking are thus complementary and not opposing processes. When we learn to value objective and subjective assessments we are more adequately equipped to make better decisions.
Men lean more towards objective thinking. The thinking pattern of a man is geared towards identifying a problem and implementing a solution immediately.
Women lean more towards subjective thinking. The thinking pattern of women is geared towards searching for answers that bring emotional balance, even if the answer is totally illogical. Women are also more inclined to seek out the deeper meaning of experiences through soul-searching and introspection, whereas men are not concerned with the nuances of introspection and abstract meanings.

Most people don't win because they don't know how to win. One of the aspects of knowing how to win is knowing how to think like a winner. There is a mind-set, or mental attitude, that is unique to winners, and unless you develop this mind-set you will never be a winner.

> **One of the aspects of winning is knowing how to think like a winner.**

Winners focus their mental energy on three key areas, namely:

1) the future,
2) their goals, and
3) their strengths.

In contrast to winners, losers focus on the exact opposite, namely:

1) the past,
2) their failures, and
3) their weaknesses.

The hallmark of a true winner and champion is the ability to think winning thoughts. Unless you have a paradigm shift with regards to what you focus your mental energy on, you will never be a winner and a champion. People with high self-esteem have a laser-like focus when it comes to their thoughts. They focus only on the three key areas that bring about success and they eliminate the thoughts that losers entertain.

They focus on the future, and not on the past. Winning is always first entertained in the mind before it is achieved. They first embrace the possibility of winning, and then they constantly think about how that possibility can be realised. They utilize their imagination to see themselves achieving and enjoying success.

They also focus on the goal, and nothing else. They know what they want and their minds stay fixed on that purpose without entertaining any deviation.

Then they focus on their strengths. Goals are central to the thought and behaviour patterns of people who succeed. Although they know their own weaknesses, they remain focused on their strong attributes and how these attributes can be improved and fully utilized for the achievement of the goal.

21. Concentrated Activity

Concentrated activity, which is also sometimes called Focused Effort, is the complement of cognition. All cognitive activities are useless if they are not combined with concentrated effort. Cognitive activity and concentrated activity are two different sides of the same coin.

> **Nothing will work unless you do.**
> *Maya Angelou*

There is a common maxim that is frequently quoted in business circles and it goes like this: "The best plan will not work unless you work the plan."

Maya Angelou, the American author and poet, once said: "Nothing will work unless you do."

The wisdom from these quotes lies in the fact that they remind us that our best plans must be accompanied by activity. Concentrated activity must be focused around the completion of a specific goal or task. Your activities must also be concentrated in your field of expertise. King Solomon wrote: 'The one who works his field will have plenty of food.' According to King Solomon, abundance is the reward for *working your field.* When you work on your own field of expertise, your prospects of having plenty increase significantly. If, however, you attempt to work in an area, or field, that is unfamiliar to you, then your chances of failure are high.

> **The one who works his field will have plenty of food.** Proverbs 12:11a NET
> *King Solomon*

The most successful people in the world are those who maintain a very narrow focus with regards to the activities that they expend time and energy on. They are successful because their activities are not scattered. I remember that one of my high school teachers had the habit of referring to any student who lacked focus as a 'scatterbrain.' The truth is that all of us have fallen into the scatterbrain trap at some point in our lives. The most successful people discipline themselves to overcome the distractions and detours which so easily remove us from our path. They exercise a level of concentration that blocks out all internal disruptions such as contrary thoughts and feelings of discomfort and exhaustion. They also block out external disruptions such as noise, mobile phones and other people's opinions. People with high self-esteem practice the habit of combining all cognitive activity with focused activity.

22. Contrasts

The Greek word ***dikhotomia*** means 'a cutting in two' and it is from this word that we get the English word ***dichotomy***. A dichotomy is a separation or contrast between two things. Many areas of human life are dichotomous – they are characterized by contrasts. I call this The Law of Contrasts. The Law of Contrasts refers to the simultaneous presence of opposites in nature. Nature is filled with contrasts and contradictions.

Times and seasons are subject to The Law of Contrasts.

King Solomon observed that every endeavour under the sun is characterized by contrasting seasons (or durations of time).

> **To everything there is a season,**
> **A time for every purpose under heaven:**
> **A time to be born,**
> **And a time to die;**
> **A time to plant,**
> **And a time to pluck what is planted;**
> **A time to kill,**
> **And a time to heal;**
> **A time to break down,**
> **And a time to build up;**
> **A time to weep,**
> **And a time to laugh;**
> **A time to mourn,**
> **And a time to dance;**
> **A time to cast away stones,**
> **And a time to gather stones;**
> **A time to embrace,**
> **And a time to refrain from embracing;**
> **A time to gain,**
> **And a time to lose;**
> **A time to keep,**
> **And a time to throw away;**
> **A time to tear,**
> **And a time to sew;**
> **A time to keep silence,**
> **And a time to speak;**
> **A time to love,**
> **And a time to hate;**
> **A time of war,**
> **And a time of peace.** Ecclesiastes 3:1-8 NKJV
> *King Solomon*

The Book of Ecclesiastes, from which this text was extracted, has been labelled as *King Solomon's Sarcastic Discourse*, because he examines the legitimacy and benefits of common human pursuits by asking deep philosophical questions and then making conclusions that can be considered sarcastic and critical. One of these conclusions was the dichotomous characteristic of seasons. One season is replaced by its dichotomous counterpart. Planting is followed by plucking up; mourning is followed by dancing; weeping is followed by laughter; casting away is followed by gathering and life is followed by death.

The ability to adjust according to the season in which you find yourself is an ability that is inherent in people with high self-esteem. Changing seasons demand changing actions, and contrasting changes demand contrasting actions. You cannot expect to survive and be effective by doing what you did in a previous season that is different to the one in which you find yourself. Coping with contrasts requires that you be dynamic. Being *dynamic* does not refer to changing every day like a schizophrenic who changes his behaviour and displays contrasting personalities. Being *dynamic* is more like being a chameleon that changes its outward appearance according to its environment – the chameleon adapts but it remains a chameleon at its core. In order to cope with contrasting seasons one must adapt like a chameleon. Only people with high self-esteem and self-confidence can alter themselves according to the demands of the environment and circumstances that they find themselves in, whilst still remaining true to themselves. To this end, they adjust their approach and not their true selves.

There are also contrasts between people. Two siblings raised in the same household by the same parents will always display some similarities and some differences. Sometimes the differences are so significant that they are contrasting. This difference between two people is sometimes called the Chalk and Cheese Phenomenon. In order to raise children of contrasting natures, parents must learn to value the uniqueness of each child. Valuing contrasting characteristics amongst siblings will produce people who have high self-esteem and self-confidence because they feel comfortable being themselves. Parents do more harm than good when they make comparisons between siblings when attempting to reprimand or discipline a child by saying something like: "Why can't you be more like your brother?"

Wisdom dictates that we must be sensitive to the contrasting natures of people and value them for their uniqueness. Sometimes, however, contrasting natures amongst siblings cannot be appreciated or tolerated. King David raised two sons, namely Solomon and Absalom. These two brothers were similar in their ability to network and make friends and worthwhile acquaintances. They also shared great ambition – each of them desired to be King David's successor to the throne of Israel. However, they differed in their propensity for violence and war. Absalom was a despot who methodically rallied strong men and formed a defiant militia with the intentions of deposing his father as king and setting himself in King David's place. In contrast, Solomon was a peace-loving individual who understood and valued regal protocols. Ultimately, Absalom received his just reward when he was killed by the military officials who were loyal to King David. Solomon also received his just reward when he was crowned as king over Israel.

The consequences for contrasting personalities between siblings does not always end in the manner that it did for King David's sons. Jesus of Nazareth related the parable of two brothers who were raised in the same home and by the same father. The younger one was disobedient, impatient and intolerant whilst his older brother followed his father's instructions and laboured daily for his father. The younger son demanded his inheritance from his father, who reluctantly agreed to his son's request. This foolish son left and spent all his money on foolish pursuits, and eventually he was forced to return to his father's home as a poor, starving and undernourished derelict. Fortunately this son came to his senses and the story has a good ending. The father valued each of his sons, despite the undeniable fact that they were worlds apart in terms of their characteristics. He also reinforced the inherent value of both sons. This parable, known as the Parable of the Prodigal Son, teaches us two lessons. Firstly, it points out that two siblings can have contrasting personalities and characteristics and consequently parents must exercise wisdom in order to nurture different children in different ways. Secondly, it shows that the prodigal son had to adapt to his new realities when he was bankrupt. As was discussed earlier, he found himself in a season of poverty, which was in contrast to his previous season of prosperity, and so he had to change like a chameleon in order to survive. Inside he was still his father's son, and he knew that. This gave him the confidence and assurance that he will be accepted back. Only constant positive reinforcing of a child's value, by his parents as he is growing up, will give him the self-confidence to make difficult adjustments during difficult seasons. This is especially true when he finds himself in a season that is dichotomous to the one that he was in previously.

Contrasting personalities are not only present in families, but also in groups and organizations. In the Bible we read about a group of men who followed Jesus of Nazareth very closely. They were called the Twelve Disciples. These men all ate at the same tables; they all healed sick people and they all drove out demons because they were all mentored by Jesus Christ. Yet, despite the fact that they were effective in their mission, as an organization, the group was characterised by contrasting ideologies and personalities.

There was a contrast in ideology between Jesus and the disciple called Judas Iscariot. Jesus was building God's spiritual kingdom by declaring God's love for His children, both Jews and gentiles. Jesus had a peaceful agenda and ideology. Judas Iscariot was a traitor and a political rebel who wanted to liberate Israel from Roman captivity by building a military of common citizens. Judas Iscariot had a revolutionary ideology. These two men were part of the same organization but they had contrasting ideologies.

Peter was outspoken and brave. Jesus called him ***Cephas*** which means '*a rock*.' Perhaps Jesus called him by this name because he was a hard man - hard as a rock. It was Peter who drew his knife in defiance when Jesus was being arrested by soldiers and servants of Caiaphas, the high priest. Peter cut off the right ear of Malchus, a servant of Caiaphas. Peter had a violent temper. Despite his propensity for violence, Jesus said to Peter:

"If you love me, feed my sheep." Jesus also said this about Peter: "On this rock I will build my church." Jesus trusted Peter and he knew that Peter possessed the ideal temperament to lead the church in His absence.

Then there was John. John refers to himself as 'the disciple whom Jesus loved.' John was accustomed to lying on the chest of Jesus. John had an affectionate and caring nature. While he was hanging on the cross, it was to John that Jesus declared:

"Look, here is your mother," in reference to Jesus's own mother, Mary. To Mary He said: "Woman, here is your son."

Jesus trusted John. Jesus knew that John's loving and tender nature was well-suited for the task of caring for the woman who gave birth to Him and raised Him.

Peter and John were members of the same organization, yet they possessed contrasting temperaments. Jesus skilfully nurtured and leveraged these contrasting temperaments and found a useful place for both. When people's natures are matched to an assignment, the organization will flourish. In any organization, accurately matching the temperaments and personalities of its people to assignments creates value for the organization. When someone is accurately placed, that person's self-esteem soars to new heights.

Even in modern times, the polarization of individual personalities that was amongst the disciples of Jesus is evident in many organizations, and these organizations must still be effective despite these internal dynamics.

23. Conception

Some people believe that their birth was a mistake. Regardless of whether you were conceived out of wedlock or as the result of a sexual crime, you are not a mistake. Your experiences may not be ideal as compared to other people, but it is ideal for God to be glorified through your life, just as God was glorified by a certain blind man's healing in the bible.

As you read through the following text attempt to grasp all the emotions being experienced by the writer.

> *Behold, I was brought forth in iniquity,*
> *And in sin my mother conceived me.* Psalm 51:5 NKJV
> *Those who hate me without a cause*
> *Are more than the hairs of my head;*
> *Though I have stolen nothing,*
> *I still must restore it.*
> *I have become a stranger to my brothers,*
> *And an alien to my mother's children;*
> *They also gave me gall for my food,*
> *And for my thirst they gave me vinegar to drink.*
> *Those who sit in the gate speak against me,*
> *And I am the song of the drunkards.*
> *You know my reproach, my shame, and my dishonor;*
> *My adversaries are all before You.*

But I am poor and sorrowful;
Let Your salvation, O God,
set me up on high. Excerpts from Psalm 69 NKJV

It is almost impossible to not feel a sense of pity for the writer. The writer is male adult. The writer's pain and anguish leap onto you right off the page of this book. You immediately sense the intensity of his struggle with the shame that is related to his conception and birth. He has been a pariah since he came out of his mother's womb. He has been reviled and despised by his own family and also by strangers simply because of how and when he was conceived. He has had to endure relentless mockery and isolation. His isolation from his own family he equates to that of being treated like an 'alien.'

Wherever he goes he finds people who hate him and are enemies to him. He has reached the point of desperation and he is asking God to save him from the lifelong ridicule, mockery, embarrassment, hatred and isolation that he has had to endure.

One might be tempted to think that the writer is some poor and unknown individual, but the writer was a man of prominence. These words were penned by a king. The king's name was David. David rose to the rank of king from the position of a lowly shepherd. But why would a king present such a desperate plea before God? Why would a king talk about the rejection and isolation that he has endured all his life and ask God to save him from his lifelong ignominy?

In order to understand King David's anguish we must first understand his ancestry.

David was the son of Jesse (Yishai), who was the head of the Sanhedrin which was the supreme court of the Torah Law (God's Laws). Jesse was a prominent and well-admired man who displayed excellence in the knowledge and practice of the Torah Law. Jesse had seven sons with his wife Nitzevet bat Adael. His sons were also well-respected men who continued in their father's traditions of following the Torah Law and they were also devoted military officers. At some stage in his life, Jesse began to entertain doubts about his suitability and credibility as a religious leader of God's people because of a specific entry in Torah Law. Jesse's doubts may have been related to the following instruction given in Mosaic Law:

> *No one born of a forbidden marriage nor any of their descendants may enter the assembly of the Lord, not even in the tenth generation.*
> *No Ammonite or Moabite or any of their descendants may enter the assembly of the Lord, not even in the tenth generation.* Deuteronomy 23:2-3 NIV

Jesse's paternal grandmother was a Moabite woman by the name of Ruth. After having been widowed, Ruth moved to Bethlehem from Moab with her mother-in-law. Under the guidance of Naomi, Ruth's mother-in-law, Ruth married a prominent and wealthy man named Boaz. Boaz was twice Ruth's age - she was forty and he was eighty years old. They were married for one night only because Boaz died the next day, but not before they had an opportunity to consummate their marriage. Although Ruth was once again a widow, she was now also expecting a child from her deceased husband. When the child was born she named him Obed, (Oved) which means *'servant of God.'*

Many people reviled Ruth because she was a Moabite, and they claimed that the death of Boaz was proof of God's disapproval of their union. Obed grew up and truly lived up to the meaning of his name - he was a dedicated servant of Yahweh, the God of the Israelites. Obed was the father of Jesse.

Due to his conviction related to the law about his Moabite ancestry Jesse felt compelled to separate himself from Nitzevet, his wife. This separation included the ceasing of sexual intimacy. In order to attempt to confirm his calling as a leader by Yahweh, Jesse decided to attempt to have a child with his Canaanite maidservant. As a token of loyalty to Nitzevet, the maidservant informed her mistress about Jesse's intentions. Nitzevet then decided to emulate the actions of Leah and Rachel when they swapped places so that Leah could spend the night with Jacob.

Nitzevet swapped places with her maidservant and became pregnant from her husband again. However, Nitzevet did not say a word of her conception until she began to display the obvious physical signs of pregnancy. She kept silent to this point because she wanted to protect and conserve her husband's reputation. The entire plan was to prove that he was wrong to feel unqualified for the priesthood because God still permitted her to conceive a child from him. Eventually Jesse's eighth son was born and his mother named him David, which means '*beloved, darling.*' Nitzevet's other sons wanted to kill her because they thought that she was an adulteress, but Jesse stopped them. However, Jesse still treated young David as an outcast. David had to tend his father's sheep and carry food to his more admirable brothers.

This is where David's pain stems from. He had been conceived under a cloud of deception and he had to pay a dear price for that deception every single day of his life. Just imagine for a moment what would've happened if David had despised himself in the same way that his father, brothers and strangers despised him. He would not have amounted to anything, ever. David chose to look forward to a future of promise instead of a past of pain. He chose to become what he could be and disproved what others thought he could not be. David chose to let his shameful conception and lifelong reproach enable him and not disable him.

> **If you have been conceived in less than desirable circumstances, choose to look forward to a future of promise instead of a past of pain. Choose to become what you could be and disprove what others think you could not be.**

You are not a mistake. God did not make a mistake when you were conceived, regardless of how it happened. People with high self-esteem do not concentrate on a past that they cannot change – they concentrate on a future that they can change. They do not allow themselves to feel self-pity because they know that nobody is a mistake. From beginning to end you are valuable, you were conceived according to God's divine will.

> **From beginning to end you are valuable, you were conceived according to God's divine will.**

24. Comfort Zone

Humans are lazy by nature and intuitively seek out a place of leisure and ease. They are also reluctant to overcome their natural laziness and lethargy. This place of lethargy, leisure and ease is called a comfort zone. Furthermore, your comfort zone is that place where you are not challenging or pushing yourself to do or achieve something. However, in order to achieve anything significant, you must be willing to leave your comfort zone, and when you've left it you must overcome the temptation to return to it. King Solomon described people who do not challenge themselves and push themselves as *sluggards* and *fools.*

Sluggards are always finding excuses to not do things. They are driven by external circumstances and not internal goals.

> **Sluggards do not plow in season; so at harvest time they look but find nothing.** Proverbs 20:4 NIV
> *King Solomon*

Those people who are very happy with circumstances being *just as they are* and are content to remain carelessly at ease are fools. According to King Solomon, this careless ease, or complacency, will destroy them.

> **For the waywardness of the simple will kill them, and the complacency of fools will destroy them.** Proverbs 1:32 KJV
> *King Solomon*

People with high self-esteem understand that they will not achieve anything unless they *get off their butt.* They have to drive themselves relentlessly to overcome the strong forces of complacency and ease. This, however, is often easier said than done because complacency exerts an invisible yet powerful restraining force on us in the same manner that gravity exerts a powerful and invisible force on every object on Earth.

To explain the process of overcoming the gravitational force of complacency we will look at how the National Aeronautics and Space Administration (NASA) solved the problem of overcoming gravity for all the space shuttles used in human spaceflight.

All NASA space shuttles were fitted with two Solid Rocket Boosters (SRBs). These boosters provided the primary propulsion during the first two minutes of the spacecraft's flight. Once the fuel is depleted, a condition called *burnout* is achieved and the boosters are then ejected from the spacecraft. The boosters are fitted with automatically-released parachutes which allow the boosters to reach terminal velocity before they plunge into the Atlantic Ocean where NASA's recovery ships locate and remove them from the ocean. In addition to the boosters, the spacecraft was fitted with a large orange tank, known as the Space Shuttle External Tank (ET). This tank contained liquid hydrogen and liquid oxygen to provide fuel for the three Space Shuttle Main Engines, which resembled open cones and were fitted in the rear-end of the spacecraft. The External Tank was ejected from the aircraft just before it entered into orbit. After the completion of a mission in orbit, the spacecraft would re-enter the earth's atmosphere and be flown as a glider until it landed.

From this example, we can see that the bulk of the spacecraft's fuel requirements were used during lift-off and that very little fuel was needed when the spacecraft returned to Earth and glided to its landing base. The spacecraft used a disproportionately larger quantity of fuel to overcome the earth's gravitational force than it used for the rest of its journey in outer space and to return to Earth.

Overcoming complacency is exactly like trying to lift off from the ground and propel yourself into the air until you exit the earth's atmosphere and enter outer space. You will require more fuel for the initial stage of your journey than for the entire trip. You will require large amounts of fuel to attain lift-off and to continue moving upward. This leads to the question:

'What is the fuel that a human being uses to overcome complacency?'

The fuels are *determination*, *habit* and *self-denial*.

Lack of motivation is a strong restraining force for human beings. Only **determination** can overcome this strong gravitational force. When you are determined to succeed despite all the obstacles that life may throw your way, you place yourself on an upward trajectory of success, in much the same manner as a NASA space shuttle.

Determination also refers to knowing exactly what you want and where you're going. Lack of clear, specific and realistic goals is another strong gravitational force that people must contend with. This lack of adequate goal-setting can only be overcome by the power of determination. Just like a NASA space shuttle always travelled on a predetermined flight-path, with a clear departure point and arrival point, so you must also determine exactly where you are going to.

Habit is the strongest force of human nature. Aristotle, the ancient Greek philosopher implied that we are shaped by our habits when he said that: "We are what we repeatedly do." In order to redefine ourselves, we must then begin by changing what we repeatedly do. By implication, we must overcome the habit of complacency by doing something, on a regular basis, that is the exact opposite of the complacent behaviour. You can only overcome the habit of complacency by replacing it with the habits of responsibility, thoughtfulness, cautiousness, commitment, conscientiousness and directed activity.

Self-indulgence is a strong gravitational force in human spheres. You cannot hope to overcome complacency by indulging your every whim and fancy. King Solomon wrote that a sluggard turns on his bed like a door turns on a hinge, in reference to the self-indulgent nature of complacent people.

> **As a door turns on its hinges, so a sluggard turns on his bed.** Proverbs 26:14 NIV
> *King Solomon*

Self-denial is the only fuel that you can use to overcome self-indulgence. Self-denial entails doing the things that are necessary to be successful. The student must study in order to pass, and he must deny his desire to party with his mates, watch movies and spend time on his smartphone chatting with friends and browsing on-line social networks. In every sphere of life we must deny ourselves some pleasure temporarily in order to gain a greater pleasure in the end. Winners are experts at self-denial. They do what is necessary, even when it's uncomfortable. Winners don't like having to give up the things that they would rather be doing, just like losers, but they make the sacrifice anyway. Winners don't want to do the very same things that losers don't want to do, but winners do it anyway. Self-denial is the trademark of a winner.

> **People with high self-esteem regularly exercise determination, habit and self-denial in order to overcome the strong gravitational force of complacency – they deliberately break free from their comfort zones.**

Once you've overcome the initial strength of these strong forces, and you've attained lift-off, eventually the force of momentum will keep you going. Getting to momentum is the hardest part, but thereafter the journey is much easier. People with high self-esteem push themselves until they reach a stage in their journey where momentum carries them through the rest of the journey to their destination – the point where their goal is realised.

25. Currency

Before you continue reading, take a few seconds to contemplate the answer to the following philosophical questions:
What holds all human relationships together?
What is the glue that binds people together in a mutually fulfilling relationship?
Keep your answer in mind as you read further.

In order to answer the questions above, I will need to explain the concept of a *currency*.
A currency is a standard medium of exchange for the acquisition of goods and services. Every country has its own currency, and some countries, like those affiliated to the European Union, share a common currency. Generally, one cannot engage in any form of trade in a particular country without the use of the standard currency. Up until the 20th century, most countries issued currency that reflected the value of gold that it held in reserve. This was called The Gold Standard. Central banks and reserve banks were required to ensure the integrity of the currency through responsible

minting. Minting is the production of coins and paper currency. The gold was the only medium of exchange between countries. Under The Gold Standard, any citizen holding any form of the country's currency was assured that the currency represented real value – the currency was not the value but rather a representation of the real value. The real value was the gold held in reserve. The underlying value of each coin and note was a quantity of gold. Hence, during the era of The Gold Standard, minted currency could be viewed as being merely an expression of value, and the real valuable currency was gold.

Now we return to the questions at the beginning of this section. Most people would say that the answer to both questions is love. Most people believe that it is love that holds all human relationships together, and that it is love that is the glue which binds people together in a mutually fulfilling relationship.

Answers that have been suggested are: love, admiration, respect and honour. The most common answer is 'love.'

If your answer was 'love' or any of the afore-mentioned possibilities, then I pose this question:

Why does the mother, who loves her drug-addict and criminally-inclined son dearly, kick him out of the house?

Why does a husband, who loves and adores his wife who cheated on him, file for a divorce?

Why does a teenage girl who's fallen pregnant tell her mother the distressing news before she tells her temperamental father, even though she loves both her parents?

When you think really deeply about these questions, you have to begin to investigate options other than love, as the binding force in relationships. The answer to all the questions above is this – trust has been lost. Trust is the most essential component in any relationship. Trust is the life-blood of a relationship.

> **Trust is the most essential component in any relationship.**
> **Trust is the life-blood of a relationship.**

The mother of the drug addict loves him more than words can express, but she cannot trust him at all, hence she's forced to change the terms of the relationship. A sustainable relationship is one in which trust and love are high, but one where trust is low or lacking is unsustainable. We all have someone in our lives that we love but cannot trust and we also have people we love and trust.

When we draw a parallel between the concept of trade under The Gold Standard and interactions between people, we can equate minted currency to love. Remember, the minted currency was a representation of the underlying value, and in the same way the love that we have for people is merely a representation of the underlying value. Love is the minted currency. The gold held in reserve can be equated to trust. The gold represented the true value in The Gold Standard, and likewise trust represents the true value in relationships. Trust is the only true currency in the arena of human relationships. This trust is necessary in our family circles, our friend circles, our work circles and our business circles.

Consider these questions:

Why does a sick man drive pass several doctors in his town, and consults with a doctor on the outside of town?

Why does the housewife drive past several butcheries and supports one that is not the closest to her home?

Why does a woman break off a friendship with her best friend, whom she loves like a sister, for spreading lies about her?

Why does a manager fire the delivery man, whom he really likes, for smashing the company vehicle whilst under the influence of alcohol?

Why does the old lady at the appliance store avoid buying from the tattooed salesman in jeans and prefers to be served by the well-spoken salesman in a formal suit?

Since you now know that trust is the most important currency, you will easily be able to answer: "because of trust," to all these questions.

If we want to establish meaningful relationships in our personal lives and in business, we must be trustworthy and we must be able to identify people who are trustworthy. People with high self-esteem constantly work on their trustworthiness by exercising integrity and promoting a sense of trust and faithfulness.

In addition to building trust with people, you must establish trust with God, the Creator.

YOU ARE VALUABLE

Before you are able to build trust with God, you must first understand God's currency for the valuation of man.
God is the source of the concept of love.
Paul the Apostle wrote: 'the love of God has been poured out within our hearts through the Holy Spirit who was given to us.' Romans 5:5 NASB
John the Apostle wrote: 'Whoever does not love does not know God, because God is love.' 1 John 4:8 NIV
Everything about God is love, and God's currency of value is love. John the Apostle also wrote:
'For God so loved the world that he gave his one and only Son, that whoever believes in him shall not perish but have eternal life.' John 3:16 NIV
There are 3 important facts that emerge from this text, namely:

- God's expression of the value of a human being is conveyed through the currency of love;
- God values each and every person as being equal to the life of His own son, Jesus Christ; and
- God grants eternal life only to those who trust Him (believe).

In this text we can see that God highly values every single human being. That value is equal to the value of His precious son, Jesus Christ.

> **God highly values every single human being. That value is equal to the value of His precious son, Jesus Christ.**

However, despite the assurance that we have of God's high opinion of us because of the love He has, there still needs to be something to back the currency of love in order for the relationship between a man and God to be sustainable. Here too, the underlying currency is trust. Unless you trust God, and He is able to trust you, there is no underlying value.
In the bible we read the story of a very old man who had an old wife who was barren. This man's name was Abraham. God promised Abraham that he will produce an heir in his old age. Despite evidence to the contrary Abraham believed God, and his belief was accounted to him for righteousness. Righteousness is a state where God sees someone as being

in right standing, faithful, trustworthy and pure. Without this belief in God's promises, we can never be valued as 'righteous' by God.

> **Abraham believed God, and it was credited to him as righteousness.** Romans 4:3 NIV
> *Paul the Apostle*

Faith is another word that speaks of *'unquestioning belief.'* Faith is trust. Faith is nothing more than continuous, unwavering and persevering trust in God's word. Faith is the currency by which we value God.

> **Faith is nothing more than continuous, unwavering and persevering trust in God's word.**
> **Faith is the currency by which we value God.**

It is through the currency of trust, also called faith, that we display how much we value God. Without this faith we can never hope to please God and procure His divine favour.

> **And without faith it is impossible to please God, because anyone who comes to him must believe that he exists and that he rewards those who earnestly seek him.** Hebrews 11:6 NIV
> *Paul the Apostle*

As you move on a higher plane of self-value and self-esteem you will need to position yourself as being trustworthy before God and man, and this will bring greater rewards and favour than any other characteristic you may possess. The credibility of an individual and an organization is based solely on how much they can be trusted. When appreciating value is defined as profitability, how profitable we are hinges on how credible we are.

> **The credibility of an individual and an organization is based solely on how much they can be trusted. When appreciating value is defined as profitability, how profitable we are hinges on how credible we are.**

You must also be trusting – trust God and trust people who are worthy of your trust. However, there is a warning about trust. Trust must be earned. It is not earned overnight. Do not be hasty and careless in the giving of your trust. Wisdom dictates that we should test people before we trust them, in the same way that God does.

> **The young trust, the wise test.**
> *Dr. Mike Murdock*

26. Conation

Conation deals with what your life is committed to. Conation is also about what you want to be remembered for – the legacy that you want to leave behind. This we refer to as your core life-focus. The simplest way to determine what your core life-focus is would be to use what I call *The Eulogy Method*. This is a powerful tool which helps people to clarify what's really, really important to them. The method involves imagining yourself as being one of the observers at your own funeral and you picture what you really desire that people will say about you when you die.

How will people feel about you? Will they miss you? Who will attend your funeral and what will they say? Will you be remembered as a taker or contributor? Will they remember a big, tender heart or a heart of stone? Will they remember a smiling individual or a miserable sod? Will they remember someone who changed the community for the better or for the worse? Will they be better or worse for having known you? Will they remember an upholder or a breaker of the country's laws and constitution? Will they remember a loving parent or an abusive drunk? Will they cry tears of sadness for your passing or tears of joy that you're finally gone? Will they remember someone wise or a companion of fools? Will they remember a prospect or a suspect?

Would the eulogies be in alignment with what you desire them to say and think about you? If your answer is "yes" then continue working towards leaving your desired legacy. If your answer is "no" then you need to start making the necessary adjustments in behaviour in order to realise your goal of living up to the thing (or things) which will make your life truly significant and memorable.

An individual's core life-focus can be categorised into one or more of the following seven categories:

1. having a happy family life,
2. becoming wealthy and materially successful,
3. making a positive contribution to society through donations and voluntary work etc.,
4. learning as much as possible in a specific field or area of expertise – religion, the arts, economics, science, history, linguistics, sociology etc.;
5. expressing themself through the creative arts and the performing arts,
6. to become the best in a specific area of expertise,
7. the pursuit of pleasure and fun and/or the destruction of others and/or the building up of others.

Most people would have more than one core life-focus because the foci are all connected. For example, an individual who comes from an impoverished background may want to use category number 4 whereby he will continue learning and studying in order to increase his income thereby moving onto category number 2 so that he can be wealthy enough to elevate his family to a better standard of living thus attaining category number 1.
A successful actress who has worked hard on category 6 and has achieved the fame and fortune of category 2 may want to use her free time and influence to raise awareness and funding for the plight of under-nourished children in third-world countries, thus attaining a category 3 objective.

In order to attain a healthy self-esteem you must do deep introspection with regards to what your core life-focus or life-foci are. Once you've identified your life-focus, begin immediately to start becoming the person you want to be remembered as. This simple process of identifying and working towards your core life-foci will make you feel more self-assured about what's important to you and will produce a level of confidence about the future that will boost your self-esteem like nitrous-oxide boosts a racing car. However, the opposite is also true – when you do not have clarity concerning your core life-focus you can be equated to someone attempting to drive a car forward with their foot on the brake.

27. Constitution

Every country has a constitution. A constitution is a document which spells out a list of principles and values to which a state is committed. Many corporate companies and non-government organizations also have constitutions which state the core-values of the organization. Many people are not aware that every individual can create a personal constitution. Whereas conation deals with your core life-foci, constitution deals with your core life-values. Conation can be described as 'what I want to be' whilst constitution describes the 'what will guide me' part of the journey.

Here is a list of desirable guiding principles:

- honesty and truthfulness,
- justice and fairness,
- integrity,
- love, charity and compassion,
- hard work and dedication,
- equity and equality,
- kindness, sharing and altruism,
- humility and meekness,
- peace and peace-making,
- discretion,
- patience,
- boldness,
- fair judgment,
- civility, decency and politeness,
- patience, and
- loyalty.

It is true that you will have positive results when you practice these principles, but you can also have negative results. Sometimes being truthful when you've made a mistake could cost you a relationship or your job, but in the end the truthful approach is always the best for any situation.

When you espouse these values and principles you are arming yourself with an arsenal of weapons and workshop of tools which will serve you well along life's winding journey.

Consider the consequences of leading a life when you espouse the opposing values and principles of the ones above, namely:

- dishonesty and lies,
- injustice and unfairness,
- corruption,
- hatred, stealing, cruelty and tyranny,
- laziness, disloyalty and unfaithfulness,
- bias, partiality, imbalance and inequality,
- arrogance and pride,
- disharmony, war and instigation,
- indiscretion and carelessness,
- agitation, frustration and intolerance,
- timidity and cowardice,
- unfair judgment and exploitation,
- rudeness and vulgarity,
- impatience, and
- disloyalty and undependability.

28. Conditions

Life is not utopic. We all face a combination of desirable and undesirable circumstances as it pertains to our tri-dimensional being and our circumstances – our conditions. It is easy to accept the good that life offers, but it is not always easy to accept life's lemons. Dale Carnegie recommends that we make proverbial lemonade from our bitter conditions.

> **When fate hands you a lemon, make lemonade.**
> *Dale Carnegie*

To make lemonade from our bitter conditions entails sweetening that which is bitter, but what is the proverbial sweetener that we have to add to our conditions?

> **Happiness and success are the fruits of your disposition and not your position.**
> **Position is where you are, but disposition is how you are.**

The key to happiness and success in life is not our position, but our disposition. It is not where you find yourself, but where you see yourself. Happiness and success are the fruits of your disposition and not your position.

> **I am determined to be cheerful and happy in whatever situation I may find myself. For I have learned that the greater part of our misery or unhappiness is determined not by our circumstance but by our disposition.**
> *Martha Washington*

Our happiness is contingent upon our viewpoint. We need to understand firstly that most bitter conditions are temporary - they are not here to stay.

> **Your problem has not come to stay,**
> **it has come to pass.**

Secondly, we need to understand that we must not begin to entertain negative mental attitudes such as self-pity and self-depreciation when we face difficult times.

> **Feeling sorry for yourself, and your present condition, is not only a waste of energy but the worst habit you could possibly have. Happiness doesn't depend on any external conditions, it is governed by our mental attitude.**
> *Dale Carnegie*

Nick Vujicic was born without limbs. This has not stopped him from being an international speaker, bestselling author, a husband and father. He has turned his disability into an asset. He did not allow his unique challenges to define the scope of his abilities and achievements. Nick could have wallowed in regret and allowed his challenges to restrict his options but instead he leveraged his challenges through determination, self-belief and high self-esteem. Nick may be small in stature but he is a giant in spirit.
Overcoming restrictive conditions is an important step in attaining success in any arena. If we are bitter and we feel self-pity we empower our conditions and circumstances and thereby give them authority over us, but if we are content

and approach life with a positive mental-attitude that lays aside the victim-mentality we can rise above our tough circumstances, just like Nick Vujicic has. This positive mental attitude can only be acquired through firstly, choice – when we choose how we will respond to what has happened to us, and secondly, by heuristic learning – learning from our experiences. Paul the Apostle expressed these two processes when he wrote: "I have learned in whatever state I am, to be content: I know how to be abased, and I know how to abound. Everywhere and in all things I have learned both to be full and to be hungry, both to abound and to suffer need."

> **I have learned in whatever state I am, to be content:**
> **I know how to be abased, and I know how to abound. Everywhere and in all things I have learned both to be full and to be hungry, both to abound and to suffer need.** Philippians 4:11-12 NKJV
> *Paul the Apostle*

You have to work past your personal shortcomings, anxieties, fears, cognitive barriers, and other personal circumstances that hold you back and sometimes hold you captive. You have to work very, very hard at this. Very often those things that challenge us the most are the things inside of us. There is a well-known maxim that says:
"When there is no enemy inside, the enemy outside can do us no harm."
Do not let your own personal perceptions and conditions hold you back from being the phenomenal person that you were meant to be.
Taking positive lessons from our experiences truly empowers us and toughens us, and then we find that we outlive our bitter conditions. It is the strong or toughened person who can rise above his circumstances and conditions. This is what Dr. Robert Schuller meant when he wrote: "Tough times never last, but tough people do."

> **Tough times never last, but tough people do.**
> *Dr. Robert Schuller*

When our plans do not work out well, we should see every failure as a learning opportunity.

29. Criticism

Criticism from others is healthy. Criticism is an alignment selection tool – through criticism you know who is for and against you and who you must stay close to and who you must move away from. An enemy masquerading as a friend is more dangerous than an open enemy.

Many people criticise what they do not understand. Even Jesus's brothers and sisters criticized Him – they did not know that they were in the presence of greatness.

When you make your plans known, those who oppose your objectives will make themselves known. Those who criticise your goals do not understand your vision and purpose. Those who do not understand your vision and purpose will eventually become capable of destroying you and your plans. The constructive critic builds you up and confirms himself as a friend but a destructive critic is bent on just that - destruction. The destructive critic breaks you down and confirms himself as an enemy. As pertains to people who are critical of your goals, those who mind don't matter and those who matter don't mind.

> **Criticism is an alignment selection tool – you know who is for and against you and who you must stay close to and who you must move away from.**
> **As pertains to people who are critical of your goals, those who mind don't matter and those who matter don't mind.**

Unless you are able to give and receive constructive criticism, which is nothing more than feedback, you will always be swayed from left to right by the feelings of hurt and or ecstasy that are evoked from the commentaries of others. Some people are so hurt by criticism that they lash out with violence of the mouth and/or of the body. Some people inflict harm on themselves by seeking solace in drugs and alcohol while others commit suicide. Many lives have been destroyed by people who did not know how to give criticism in a constructive manner. Even when it is given with good intentions criticism can do a great deal of harm. Therefore, the timing of criticism can make all the difference. Timing relates to when people are around or not, public or private, the manner in which the criticism is given and the attitude of the critic. When criticism is being given, acting right is more important than being right, because there is always the risk of saying the right thing in the wrong way.

> **When criticism is being given, acting right is more important than being right, because there is always the risk of saying the right thing in the wrong way.**

For example, when criticism is given in public even though the critic is correct concerning the facts, the critic may place his relationship with the person being criticised at risk, because public criticism and insult are usually one and the same. In this case, a private exchange of views may be more effective. Criticism is only constructive when it adds value to the person being criticised. Criticism adds value when it is done in the right environment, at the right time, with the right attitude and the right motive.

> **Criticism adds value when it is done in the right environment, at the right time, with the right attitude and the right motive.**

People with high self-esteem know how to give and receive criticism in an effective manner. They know when to speak critically and when to keep quiet. When they do speak critically they understand that constructive criticism can be done in a manner that shows genuine concern and sometimes affection toward the person being criticised. When people with high self-esteem are criticised, they are not afraid to admit their shortcomings if they are wrong, but they are also strong enough to defend their own position when they feel that they are right.

The most valuable criticism is self-criticism. Through self-criticism we can measure our behaviour and standards against other people and see if we are behind, on par or ahead of the rest of the pack. This is positive self-criticism. Negative self-criticism produces negative results. Negative self-criticism usually manifests itself as self-condemnation. Self-condemnation is an enemy of self-esteem. Putting yourself down can never produce and engender feelings of high self-worth in an individual.

30. Credit and Capital

Many people abuse financial credit. Modern adults spend more on interest payments to service debt than saving. King Solomon wrote: "The rich rule over the poor, and the borrower is slave to the lender."

When you commit yourself to a credit agreement, you are in effect binding yourself like a slave to a master.

> **The rich rule over the poor, and the borrower is slave to the lender.** Proverbs 22:7 NIV
> *King Solomon*

Many people are overextended when it comes to their credit commitments. When you commit to a credit agreement, you are committing tomorrow's earnings today – you are also spending tomorrow's earnings today. But here's the naked truth – you do not know for sure that you will be able to earn that money tomorrow. The financial system is not designed to be stable. It is just as unstable as a life-raft caught in a storm far out in the ocean. The financial and economic conditions of today will not always remain. If you are buying appliances on credit because you have a good job that pays well, you have no certainty that you will still have that job for the next five years to service that debt. There is no certainty to anything – in fact, the only certainty is uncertainty.

Most people are only one salary cheque away from bankruptcy with no savings to carry them through a financial storm. All over the world, an inability to service credit commitments has forced countless people to apply for bankruptcy protection. Many people lose their homes, cars businesses and other possessions because of an inability to pay their debts. Many people have committed suicide because they could not stand the shame and public disgrace of losing their possessions and good name. Ultimately, taking on credit to buy things is a sign of impatience. The cost of impatience is high interest rates. If you want to avoid the burden of high interest rates and the possible embarrassment of having your goods seized when you cannot pay, you need to follow the rule for acquisitions. The rule for acquisitions is this: if you cannot afford to pay cash for it, you cannot afford it.

> **The rule for acquisitions is this: if you cannot afford to pay cash for it, you cannot afford it.**

I am prepared to concede that houses and cars are just too expensive for the average person to buy with cash. In the case of cars, if you must buy one on credit always ensure that you will be able to service your repayments even if you lose your job or business. You must save sufficient money to cover about 6 -12 months living expenses and credit obligations. If you are buying a home, always buy for a little less than the bank says you can afford, so that you have some extra cash to put on the bond repayment and in this way you will pay off your home-loan sooner.

It is possible to buy a house and a car with cash. I have purchased many homes and vehicles with cash. The key here is to save money every month as if you are already paying off a home-loan or a car-loan. It may take about 2-5 years to save in this manner, depending on how much you are able to save and also the cost of the item you intend to purchase. When you have sufficient money, you have the power to negotiate because cash is king. It always surprises me how willing estate agents and car salespeople are to negotiate when you have cash.

> **When you have sufficient money, you have the power to negotiate because cash is king.**

King Solomon taught that we should not make pledges and commitments which we may not be able to keep, because we will suffer loss in the end.

> **Do not be one who shakes hands in pledge or puts up security for debts; if you lack the means to pay, your very bed will be snatched from under you.** Proverbs 22:26 NIV
> *King Solomon*

Sadly, many people use credit to buy things which impress other people, and most of these items quickly lose value. People of high self-esteem make purchases of value. Making a purchase of value entails buying items which increase in value. People of high self-esteem are patient to save in order to buy what they can afford with cash. People of high self-esteem do not compete with the Joneses to feel good about themselves. They are comfortable in the knowledge that their value does not lie in the acquisition of expensive articles which may bring the occasional compliment but it also brings many sleepless nights when you cannot pay. People of high self-esteem value themselves, their financial security and their assets so much that they will not make a bet with tomorrow's resources today.

> **People of high self-esteem value themselves, their financial security and their assets so much that they will not make a bet with tomorrow's resources today.**

31. Confidence

> **confidence • n 1** faith in someone or something. **2** self-assurance arising from a belief in one's own ability to achieve things.[xxxv]

According to the Oxford English Dictionary confidence entails two aspects of belief:

1. belief in someone or something, and
2. belief in one's own abilities.

The level of belief that we convey towards others through our words and actions is a measure of the confidence that we have in them. This confidence contributes towards that person's self-esteem. If this confidence is low, then our contribution to that person's self-esteem is low, but when this confidence is high then our contribution to that person's self-esteem is high. We must therefore be constantly aware of the power that we have to make or break the next person's self-esteem by what we do and what we say.

> **We must be constantly aware of the power that we have to make or break the next person's self-esteem by what we do and what we say.**

Confidence also relates to our belief in ourselves. This is called self-confidence. Unless you have a strong belief in your own abilities to achieve a goal or overcome a problem, you will never attain success. Confidence is that magical ingredient, which when mixed with our actions, will give us the self-assurance to begin, follow-through and successfully end our endeavours. Henry David Thoreau admonished us of the necessity and rewards of confidence when he wrote: 'If one advances confidently in the direction of his dreams,... he will meet with a success ...'

> **If one advances confidently in the direction of his dreams, and endeavours to live the life which he has imagined, he will meet with a success unexpected in common hours.**
> *Henry David Thoreau*

Success is the reward for self-confidence. This does not mean that people who are self-confident are always successful in all their endeavours. On the contrary, self-confident people suffer the same types of failures as other people, but their confidence lies in the knowledge that they will attain success if they persevere. Consequently, truly self-confident people are not afraid to fail and do things badly until they can do them well. Zig Ziglar once said that: "Anything worth doing is worth doing poorly until you can learn to do it well."

> **Anything worth doing is worth doing poorly, until you can learn to do it well.**
> *Zig Ziglar*

This is how self-confidence is attained ... by doing something the first time, even if you do it badly. Then you do it again, and then again, and again, and again. Every time you do something, you do it a little better than the previous time. With each subsequent attempt you become more proficient, and with greater proficiency comes greater confidence. The proficiency that leads to improved confidence can only be achieved when you leverage the Law of Repetition. The Law of Repetition states that you become better at everything you do repeatedly. You put the Law of Repetition to use through regular practice. The more hours you spend practicing the better you become, and the better you become the more confident you become.

> **The more hours you spend practicing the better you become, and the better you become the more confident you become.**

It is not only sports people who benefit from practice – you can practice to become better at anything you choose. No matter what area you choose to focus on, you can become better. You can be a better lawyer, doctor, public speaker, artist, musician, writer and blogger when you practice often. I have mentioned just a few areas you could focus on to become better, but the list is endless.

Winners place a high value on practice, because it makes them more valuable. People with high self-esteem are not afraid to make the choice and to commit to putting in the time and effort that is necessary to produce the sort of proficiency that leads to unparalleled confidence. They are courageous enough to make the tough choice that others will not. Dr. Rollo May, the American psychiatrist once said: 'The opposite of courage in our society is not cowardice, it is conformity.'

Dr. May was making us aware of the manner in which we have become people who are no longer confident and courageous – we conform to public opinion and do not do what is necessary to achieve what we desire, because we conform.

> **The opposite of courage in our society is not cowardice, it is conformity.**
> *Rollo May*

People with high self-confidence place a high premium on their own abilities which they can depend upon despite life's unexpected twists and turns. Their confidence lies inside and not outside, it is within and not without.

Paul the Apostle reminded us of the benefits of holding firmly onto our confidence when he wrote: "Cast not aside your confidence which has great recompense of reward."

> **So do not throw away your confidence;**
> **it will be richly rewarded.** Hebrews 10:35 NIV
> *Paul the Apostle*

No discussion on self-confidence is complete without noting that self-confidence is a two-edged sword, and it should be exercised with extreme caution. On the one side one could exercise confidence with wisdom, but on the other side one could exercise confidence with foolishness.

Wise confidence can also be called 'justified confidence' and it entails speaking and acting with sound knowledge and discretion with due consideration of the possible outcomes of one's actions.

Wisely confident people think before acting. This thinking encompasses the past, present and future. The past brings in one's experiences and how they relate to possible present applications. The future relates to the most likely outcome if one continues on the selected path. Peter the Apostle described this as a mental process of preparation for action.

> **"Prepare your minds for action..."** 1 Peter 1:13a NASB
> *Peter the Apostle*

The opposite of justified confidence is 'foolish confidence.' Foolish confidence entails speaking and acting with total disregard for the possible disastrous outcomes for oneself and for others. Foolish confidence happens when people lack adequate mental preparation for action.

King Solomon teaches us that foolish confidence can be recognized in an individual by the simultaneous presence of recklessness and overconfidence, whilst the wisely confident person acts out of healthy fear in order to avoid disaster and destruction.

> **The wise person fears and turns away**
> **from evil, but a fool is reckless and**
> **overconfident.** Proverbs 14:6 ISV
> **There is a way which seems right to a man,**

> **But its end is the way of death.** Proverbs 14:21 NASB
> *King Solomon*

Healthy self-esteem can only stem from acting with self-confidence that is wise and justified.

32. Causes

No-one can live an effective life in the absence of goals. Our goals define our dreams and desires, whilst the achievement or non-achievement of our goals has an effect on our sense of self-worth and self-efficacy.
Causes are the worthwhile activities, goals, dreams, aspirations and life purposes which you pursue. No life is complete without one or more worthwhile causes to pursue. These causes can be personal or organizational. Our causes are held as visions of ideal states that we want to achieve. King Solomon wrote: "Where there is no vision the people perish." This means that people suffer failure and destruction when they are not persistently pursuing a worthwhile cause.

> **Where there is no vision the people perish.** Proverbs 29:18 KJV
> *King Solomon*

Happiness and success is not about where you come from, it's about where you're going.
We should never set unrealistic goals, since lack of realisation will most likely lead to diminished self-esteem. When our plans do not work out well, we should see every failure as a learning opportunity.

33. Consciousness Level

How aware are you of what's happening around you? How aware are you concerning your immediate surroundings? Are you alert to dangers and threats? Are you aware of opportunities as they arise?
Without the attribute of keen observation you will always miss information and opportunities to achieve your goals. Wariness is vital for success because most windows of opportunity are small and they never return. Winners are always preparing themselves for the opportunity that arises

unexpectedly. King Solomon wrote: 'The heart of the godly thinks carefully before speaking.' Proverbs 15:28 NLT
Another translation reads as follows: 'The heart of the righteous ponders how to answer.' Proverbs 15:28 NASB
The original Hebrew word for ***answer*** is ***anah*** which refers to '*a verbal answer, a response*.' In this text Solomon is teaching us that we should prepare our responses to situations so that we are ready when they arise.

> **We should prepare our responses to situations so that we are ready when they arise.**

People with high self-esteem operate from an elevated consciousness. They are constantly looking for clues as to what people are thinking and they are continuously keenly aware of how circumstances can change for better or for worse, so that they can respond appropriately.

34. Companionship

Companionship concerns the social circles that we are exposed to. These circles concern family and friends.
Every individual has the authority and power to choose who they can and will associate with. We can build and break off relationships as is needed. We can associate with people who most readily resonate with our own beliefs and lifestyle choices.
Everybody needs someone in whom they can confide. You need someone with whom you can share your feelings, your ideas and your dreams. Sometimes we have more than one confidante. Having someone who will just listen to you when you want to share your deepest feelings can be therapeutic, remedial and liberating. Time spent with a reliable confidante can be worth more than many sessions on a psychiatrist's couch. However, we must choose people who will truly preserve our dignity and value by not broadcasting our deepest concerns to the rest of the world. A confidante must then be someone who firstly, truly loves and cares about you; secondly has your best interests at heart; thirdly is trustworthy; fourth a good listener; and lastly, not a gossip.

Sometimes we have to cut-off some relationships with people who consistently devalue us. Life is too short to entertain nasty people and those who wish to impose their own destructive views and perceptions on us.

Your self-esteem can be built-up or broken down by the people whom you hang out with. People with high self-esteem choose their company very carefully. We all know the expression: 'birds of a feather flock together.' This expression means that people who are the same will always hang out together. There was an ancient Latin phrase that read: 'Talis quis esse putatur qualis ei est sodalitas.'
The English interpretation of this phrase is: 'Tell me your companions, and I will tell you what you are.'
People will always judge you by the company that you keep.

> **Talis quis esse putatur qualis ei est sodalitas. Tell me your companions, and I will tell you what you are.**
> *Latin Maxim*

Epictetus said: "The key is to keep company only with people who uplift you, whose presence calls forth your best."
In order to become a winner you must surround yourself with people who bring out the very best in you – people who call forth your potential and increase your value.

> **In order to become a winner you must surround yourself with people who bring out the very best in you – people who call forth your potential and increase your value.**

35. Collaborators and Competitors

Every environment has a mixture of those who are with you – collaborators, and those who are against you – competitors. It is essential for your success and survival that you know exactly into which category people fall when dealing with them. This is an identification process which entails monitoring the words and activities of those around us. We will find that there are those who are very clear about what their position is, whilst we have to observe others and deduce their position. Sometimes people will switch sides – they may move from collaborator to competitor or vice versa. This occurs because people will not always agree with us and also because people tend to be fickle. Constantly changing one's mind and commitments to friends is a symptom of the human flaw of fickleness of character. In some instances, we should also gain a competitive advantage by aligning ourselves with the competitors of our competitors because the enemy of my enemy is my friend. We gain great personal and business advantages by collaborating with those whose common goal is the overcoming of a common foe.

> **We gain great personal and business advantages by collaborating with those whose common goal is the overcoming of a common foe.**

We must not discount the value of the lessons that we can learn from those who are against us. This lesson applies equally well in our personal lives and in business.

Baltasar Gracián, in The Art of Worldly Wisdom wrote: 'A wise man gets more use from his enemies than a fool from his friends.'

By virtue of Mr. Gracián's definition, I was not wise when I failed to exploit an opportunity to get more use from my enemies. I will briefly expound one of my business experiences to explain what I mean.

Many years ago I made the huge mistake of overlooking the activities of one of my competitors because I had built my business to the level where it had attained the largest market share in that particular industry. Instead of continuously monitoring and analysing my competitor's activities, I ignored them because I assumed that my business position was secure and that my clients would remain loyal regardless of his offering, and especially in light of the fact that he was peddling an inferior line of products. This oversight cost me a great deal of money, because he was able to snatch many clients from me. The result was that I had to again woo my customers in order to rebuild that particular business's turnover to an acceptable level.

> **A wise man gets more use from his enemies than a fool from his friends.**
> *Baltasar Gracián*

> **Love your enemies, for they tell you your faults.**
> *Benjamin Franklin*

Benjamin Franklin advised us to love our enemies, because they tell us our faults. The truly enlightened person is one who can accept the need for criticism. Once we accept the necessity of criticism, we must learn to accept it from diverse sources. Sometimes we can learn our best lessons from unlikely sources, such as our enemies. Life is about education, and we must acquire as much of it as we can, and we must acquire it from friends and enemies.

> **Life is about education, and we must acquire as much of it as we can, and we must acquire it from our friends and our enemies.**

When you become very skilled at identifying your friends and enemies, and how to capitalize on each relationship, you will simultaneously develop greater self-esteem and self-efficacy because you will understand that true collaborators support you no matter what, whilst competitors can promote education and they can help us grow and develop greater degrees of maturity. The knowledge that everybody, including our rivals, are there to contribute positively into our lives is a truly enlightened state of being. High self-esteem is built by knowing what to reap from our friends and also our enemies.

> **High self-esteem is built by knowing what to reap from our friends and also our enemies.**

There is a level of self-esteem that places an individual in the category of godliness, and it is attained when we know that we are the children of God because we exercise unconditional love for our enemies. When you attain this level of self-esteem you are empowered and uplifted because firstly, you are following the instructions of Jesus Christ, secondly because you are doing what is necessary to be the child of God the Father, and thirdly because you are secure in the knowledge of who you are regardless of what your enemy says or does against you.

> **You have heard that it was said, 'Love your neighbour and hate your enemy.'**
> **But I tell you, love your enemies and pray for those who persecute you, that you may be children of your Father in heaven.** Matthew 5:43:44a NIV
> **If you love those who love you, what reward will you get? Are not even the tax collectors doing that?**
> **And if you greet only your own people, what are you doing more than others? Do not even pagans do that?** Matthew 5:46-47 NIV
> *Jesus of Nazareth*

Jesus Christ gave us the formula for the highest form of self-esteem when he delivered The Sermon on the Mount. He encouraged us to love our enemies and to pray for those who persecute us, and in so doing we will be labelled as the children of our Father in Heaven. This is one of the greatest revelations delivered to man through the mouth of Jesus Christ. He revealed to us that God is not just a distant being who wants to impose draconian laws on His creation, but rather that He is a loving God who wants His creation to exercise love for everyone around them - friends and enemies. Jesus also revealed to us that when we do this, that God will value us as His very own children. Yes, by exercising love for our collaborators and our competitors we are included in the family of God - we become greatly valued.

> **By exercising love for our collaborators and our competitors we are included in the family of God - we become greatly valued.**

The highest level of self-esteem you can achieve is knowing that you are a child of Almighty God. God's children are people who exercise love. This knowledge causes Christian people to be so secure in the knowledge of who they are and the value they carry that they will love and treat their enemies and friends equally and with equal love and respect.

The highest level of self-esteem you can achieve is knowing that you are a child of Almighty God. God's children are people who exercise love. This knowledge causes Christian people to be so secure in the knowledge of who they are and the value they carry that they will love and treat their enemies and friends equally and with equal love and respect.

36. Comprehension

Comprehension is understanding. King Solomon once wrote: 'In all your getting, get understanding.' He was teaching us that all our pursuits and activities must be mingled with understanding.

Understanding comes from asking questions. Jesus never volunteered explanations to His disciples unless they asked questions, because as the old maxim goes: "when the student is ready, the master will appear." Asking questions indicates your readiness for learning, but most importantly, it indicates your willingness to learn. Only a willing and ready student can attain understanding.

In life, we are all students because we are always learning new ideas and concepts, whether we are aware of it or not. If our learning does not improve our understanding about life, then our learning has been futile. Our learning must have application value, and that value is determined by the level of increased understanding that we have attained concerning life and all its intricate components. If I don't understand the relevance of what I've learnt, my learning has no value for me. However, when I understand what I've learnt, the value of my learning lies in the fact that I have acquired greater information and knowledge which will help me to navigate the course of my life with greater success.

When I understand what I've learnt, the value of my learning lies in the fact that I have acquired greater information and knowledge which will help me to navigate the course of my life with greater success.

When I teach study skills to students at schools, I encourage them to seek understanding of their materials as they read through it. I insist that they use a dictionary to look-up the meaning of a word that they do not understand, and not to simply overlook the word, because when you overlook the meaning of a single word you can miss the meaning of an entire paragraph. When you don't see the complete meaning, you don't have understanding. When you don't have understanding, you cannot relate information to other people. Albert Einstein once said: "If you can't explain it simply, you don't understand it well enough."
The measure of your understanding of a subject lies in your ability to break it down and explain it in simple terms to someone else, and if you cannot do this, then you don't understand it well enough.

> **If you can't explain it simply, you don't understand it well enough.**
> *Albert Einstein*

Many people are afraid to take on new challenges because they do not understand certain things. They are afraid to venture on the road to success because they feel that there is just too much that they still need to know and learn about how to get to where they want to be. What they are really acting out is the fear of the unknown – they are afraid because they do not have complete knowledge and understanding concerning the future. Most people would be braver to take on the future if they knew exactly what life had in store for them. Unfortunately, we are not meant to have a complete understanding of the future. King Solomon wrote that God has set eternity in the hearts of men, and that no one can find out what God does. The word ***eternity*** was translated from the Hebrew word meaning '*a vanishing point.'* The original verse can be read as follows:
God has set a vanishing point in men's understanding.
This vanishing point is like the horizon – we can only see as far as the horizon and nothing beyond it, but there is something beyond the horizon.

> **He has made everything beautiful in its time. Also He has put eternity in their hearts, except that no one can find out the work that God does from beginning to end.** Ecclesiastes 3:11 NIV
> *King Solomon*

It is clear from King Solomon's words that man was never intended to understand everything, especially what the future holds in store for him.
Everyone wants to move forward. Moving forward means moving into the future and the future lies beyond the vanishing point. This raises the question: "how do we gain sufficient understanding to deal with an unseen and uncertain future?"
We look to Albert Einstein for some wisdom regarding this matter. Einstein said: 'We can not solve our problems with the same level of thinking that created them.'

> **We can not solve our problems with the same level of thinking that created them.**
> *Albert Einstein*

Einstein was saying that if we are to progress beyond our present circumstances, we need to gain a calibre of understanding that is superior to the understanding that led us to where we are.
In order to explain how we make progress in understanding, I will use the example of driving a vehicle at night.
If I were to get into my vehicle to drive to a distant place at night, I will have to drive with the vehicle's lights switched on. However, even with the lights switched on, if my destination is many kilometres away, I will not be able to see my destination from my departure point. At best, I would be able to see about 100 – 200 metres ahead of the vehicle as I drive. As I progress on my journey, I will always be able to see that distance beyond the vehicle. I will always only see the obstacles that lay a few metres close to the vehicle and not those ones beyond the scope of the light and my vision. I will navigate past obstacles as I see them. If I continue driving, whilst seeing just a few metres ahead of me, eventually I will see my destination.

From this illustration we learn a valuable truth concerning understanding – you will never know and understand everything that is coming your way, but you can deal with them as they become visible. Remember that the vanishing point is like the horizon, which is a fixed visual point where Earth and sky meet. Just as it is possible to shift the point of the horizon as you move towards it, so you can shift the vanishing point of your understanding. Only when you move forward can you gain some understanding of what was beyond the vanishing point, because by moving forward you shift the vanishing point.

37. Culmination

Culmination deals with how you intend to die. What do you want your coroner's report to say?

The coroner's report will be a retrospective indicator of how much you valued yourself. This report will tell whether you died of natural or unnatural causes. It will indicate whether you did or didn't place high value on yourself by exposing, in some instances, the lifestyle choices you made while alive. Someone who dies at a very old age and who exercised regularly, never smoked cigarettes, never over-indulged in alcohol, didn't use recreational drugs and was not promiscuous has a higher life-expectancy than anyone who does not practice these disciplines. If one smokes cigarettes, one has a higher likelihood of developing cancer of the throat and lungs. Excessive alcohol intake can cause liver and stomach damage, as well as place you in harm's way when driving, operating heavy machinery and even taking a walk across the street. Drug abuse damages your mental faculties, your nervous system and can lead to death by overdose. Promiscuity places one at risk of contracting sexually transmitted infections and diseases. High self-esteem will compel you to make lifestyle choices that will produce longevity and a favourable lifestyle report when you've passed on.

High self-esteem will compel you to make lifestyle choices that will produce longevity and a favourable lifestyle report when you've passed on.

People with high self-esteem always endeavour to lead very long, productive and exemplary lives. Any individual who truly has high self-esteem will engineer the report of why they died.
Leonardo Da Vinci once said: "While I thought that I was learning how to live, I have been learning how to die."
This quote describes the path of a person with high self-esteem. In the pursuit of maintaining your self-worth through the attaining of the knowledge of how to live well you simultaneously attain the knowledge of how to die well.

> **While I thought that I was learning how to live, I have been learning how to die.**
> *Leonardo Da Vinci*

Through your daily choices you are writing with the ink of deliberate daily action what will not kill you and what you would prefer to kill you. It is every sane person's goal to live a long life, and to die of natural causes. This can only be attained by avoiding those activities and habits which promote unnatural death and by inculcating the habits which truly promote longevity and long life, and then as Da Vinci discovered, you also discover how to have a good coroner's report.

38. Craziness

Craziness is the element of neuroticism displayed by an individual.
Neuroticism is a psychological trait which is characterized by anxiety, fear, moodiness, worry, envy, frustration, jealousy, and loneliness. Individuals who score high on neuroticism are more likely than the average to experience such feelings as anxiety, anger, envy, guilt, and depressed mood. They respond more poorly to stressors, are more likely to interpret ordinary situations as threatening, and minor frustrations as hopelessly difficult. They are often self-conscious and shy, and they may have trouble controlling urges and delaying gratification. Neuroticism is a prospective risk factor for most "common mental disorders", such as depression, phobia, panic disorder, other anxiety disorders, and substance use disorder—symptoms that traditionally have been called neuroses.[xxxvi]

Every individual displays some degree of neuroticism, or craziness. Neuroticism and self-esteem are inversely proportional – as one goes up the other automatically goes down. Someone who displays high levels of neuroticism usually has low self-esteem whilst someone who shows low levels of neuroticism usually has very high self-esteem. Prolonged suffering and stress can make a sane man crazy. One such example is my paternal grandfather who fought on the side of the Allied Forces during WWII. Upon his return to South Africa he had to cope with the stress of dealing with his father's death whilst he was away as well as the physical and psychological effects of combat. He was wounded on the battlefield, but fortunately he survived. As a result of his experiences my grandfather developed what was called "shellshock." The term shellshock has been replaced by post-traumatic stress disorder or PTSD. PTSD is sometimes displayed by war veterans and is characterised by bouts of rage, anger, insomnia, headaches and substance abuse. In my grandfather's case, PTSD displayed itself in the form of violent behaviour, insomnia and excessive smoking. When he experienced a PTSD episode he would pace the hallway of his house, up and down, while his family was sleeping and he would smoke cartons of cigarettes. This is an example of a sane man who displayed severe neuroticism many years after the war, even up to a short time before his death. My grandfather died 45 years after the end of WWII, yet the effect of the traumatic events that he faced during the war lingered with him until his death.

No-one is immune to PTSD. We all have faced tough situations which haunt us continually and affect our behaviour. PTSD is one form of neuroticism which can deliver a strong blow to your self-esteem and self-efficacy. One of the most effective treatments for neuroticism is counselling. One can receive counselling and treatment from a psychologist or a psychiatrist if medicinal treatment is also required.

Albert Einstein once said: "A question that sometimes drives me hazy: am I or are the others crazy?"

Mr. Einstein, as smart as he was, often questioned his own sanity just like most people would sometimes. It certainly is true that we sometimes question the sanity of others. Mental health is just as important as physical health, and any person who endeavours to attain high levels of self-esteem should always work towards minimizing the effect of the neuroticism that we all experience from time to time. Keeping neuroticism in check is thus absolutely essential for the attaining and maintenance of high self-esteem.

> **Keeping neuroticism in check is absolutely essential for the attaining and maintaining of high self-esteem.**

39. Childishness

Holding firmly onto childish immaturity will prevent anyone from reaching adult maturity.

I have often met people who seem to refuse to grow up. These people reason and behave like little children by throwing temper tantrums, acting and reacting silly and uncontrolled when order is required and displaying abnormal selfishness. Childish people are usually throwing their toys out of the cot, proverbially speaking.

Paul the Apostle addressed the maturity that comes with laying off childishness when he wrote: "When I was a child, I talked like a child, I thought like a child, I reasoned like a child. When I became a man, I put the ways of childhood behind me."

> **When I was a child, I talked like a child, I thought like a child, I reasoned like a child. When I became a man, I put the ways of childhood behind me.** 1 Corinthians 13:11 NIV

Becoming a mature man, or woman, requires putting away childish behaviour and customs. People can only attain high self-esteem and self-efficacy when they are mature in their talking, thinking and reasoning.

> **People can only attain high self-esteem and self-efficacy when they are mature in their talking, thinking and reasoning.**

40. Children's Fables

As they grow, all children are exposed to fables, fairy-tales and folklore. When I was growing up, most of these stories were read to us until we could read them ourselves. Today, not only are children exposed to fairy-tales through books but they are also exposed to a plethora of fictional animated movies and television programs.

Although children's fables are entertaining and useful when teaching young children to read, there exists a terrible downside to them. The downside is that it distorts the beliefs of impressionable young minds. This distortion takes place when children really belief that Santa Clause (or Father Christmas), the Easter Bunny, the Tooth Fairy, the Boogeyman and fairy godmothers actually exist. Adults perpetuate and reinforce these flawed beliefs that children have by saying things like:

> "The Boogeyman will get you if you don't sleep now."
> "Santa Clause will bring your gift on Christmas morning."
> "While you sleep the Tooth Fairy will give you money for your tooth."
> "The Easter Bunny left chocolate and marshmallow Easter eggs in the garden."

Adults should constantly be aware of the negative impressions that they are making on children, especially when those impressions are far removed from reality.

It certainly can be argued that most people outgrow belief in the fictitious characters mentioned earlier, but it would be so much better if they did not have to outgrow a false belief that was planted and then had to be uprooted. I belief that the formative years in children should be used to teach them as many languages as possible, as many musical instruments as possible and to develop their reading and cognitive abilities as much as possible, because they do not lack the capacity.

> **The formative years in children should be used to teach them as many languages as possible, as many musical instruments as possible and to develop their reading and cognitive abilities as**

much as possible, because they do not lack the capacity.

Fairy-tales sometimes have an effect that people do not outgrow. In most fairy-tales there is often a knight in shining armour who rescues a beautiful princess and they marry and live happily ever after. Ask any young girl what she wants to be and many of them will answer: "A princess." Many a young girl will grow into womanhood and still want that handsome knight in shining armour who will kiss away all her problems and ride off into the sunset with her.
Unfortunately life is not so easy. You don't always marry the person who made a good first impression. The guy that a girl meets is not always rich, handsome and royal. The girl that a guy meets does not always have rosy cheeks and flowing locks of hair.
In reality you cannot make a wish and everything will magically be better. In reality you cannot cast a spell on your enemies and make magic with a wand. In reality there is no fairy godmother to come to your rescue when people abuse you. In reality stepmothers are not always evil and wicked. In reality people do not always live happily ever after.
Fables, fairy-tales and folklore are detached from reality and by continuously exposing young minds to them we will continue to create adults who are detached from reality.
In order to foster high self-esteem in our children we must expose them to those lessons which are true and which will truly benefit them in childhood and adulthood.

In order to foster high self-esteem in our children we must expose them to those lessons which are true and which will truly benefit them in childhood and adulthood.

I believe that the best source of formative stories is the bible. The written word of God is packed with good stories and laws that will build strong character, high self-esteem and high self-efficacy in children. Moses, the Levite instructed the Israelites concerning the teaching of God's law when he said:

> "Fix these words of mine in your hearts and minds; tie them as symbols on your hands and bind them on your foreheads. Teach them to your children, talking about them when you sit at home and when you walk along the road, when you lie down and when you get up.
> Write them on the doorframes of your houses and on your gates, so that your days and the days of your children may be many in the land the Lord swore to give your ancestors, as many as the days that the heavens are above the earth." Deuteronomy 11:18-21 NIV

One cannot develop high self-esteem that is realistic when one's expectations and beliefs are shaped by unrealistic and fable-like criteria. We must become keenly aware and vigilant regarding the impressionable effect of the media that we expose ourselves and our children to. Learn the stories in the bible in order to remedy and prevent the distorted messages being transmitted to yourself and your loved ones. Being actively vigilant concerning messages that shape perceptions is a trait that is resident in someone with high self-esteem.

41. Crying

Every single day, in every place, people are walking around with sadness and they cry - sometimes their tears are visible and sometimes their tears are hidden. Human beings are complex emotional creatures, and we all experience a wide range of emotions on a daily basis. Sometimes we are happy and sometimes we are sad. Bearing happiness is easy, but sadness is a heavy and burdensome emotion. King Solomon wrote: 'Each heart knows its own bitterness, and no one else can share its joy.'

People walk around with concealed pain, and sometimes this pain can cause bitterness, anger and resentment towards oneself and/or others.

> **Each heart knows its own bitterness, and no one else can share its joy.** Proverbs 14:10 NIV
> *King Solomon*

Sometimes we experience bitterness because of the actions of others, and sometimes we are the engineers of our own bitterness.

The things we cry about have the potential to destroy us if the pain is not dealt with. Even people with high self-esteem experience bitterness and pain caused by circumstances and people, but they do not allow their pain to destroy them. The best antidote for lingering psychological pain is to talk to a professional who can give you guidance and direction in order to cope with your agony.

Nobody is immune to emotional pain and crying, and how you deal with your agony will make the difference between success and failure.

> **Nobody is immune to emotional pain and crying, and how you deal with your agony will make the difference between success and failure.**

42. Condemnation

Very often people condemn themselves because of their circumstances. This is especially true when people face tragic and traumatic circumstances in their lives. For example, a girl who has been raped may blame herself for what has happened to her, or a woman who is being beaten by her husband may blame herself for the abuse.

There is only one thing worse than being condemned by others – it is being condemned by yourself. Self-condemnation is the root and fruit of low self-esteem. Self-condemnation is when you play accuser, judge and executioner against yourself. Self-condemnation is an enemy of self-esteem. If you are constantly putting yourself down with your thoughts and words, eventually your thoughts and words will be manifested. Self-condemnation is the one thing that will prevent anyone from dealing with traumatic events in an effective manner, because it is a barrier which makes progress impossible. Carl Jung confirmed this when he said: 'Condemnation does not liberate, it oppresses.'

If a person is to regain control of their life, they need to take control of the habit of putting themselves down. You cannot win over adversity if you feel that the cause of your failure is within you. When people become the victims of their own

condemnation, they must first overcome that self-condemnation.
You overcome self-condemnation with positive affirmations. In the next chapter there are a few positive affirmations that will help anyone struggling with self-condemnation.

> **Self-condemnation is the root and fruit of low self-esteem.**

People with high self-esteem monitor their thoughts about themselves vigilantly, and they learn to block out any negative thought that may try to take root in their mind.

> **We cannot change anything until we accept it. Condemnation does not liberate, it oppresses.**
> *Carl Jung*

People with high self-esteem do not hold themselves hostage for what has happened in the past and they are constantly moving towards a positive future and away from a negative past. This does not mean that they develop amnesia concerning their past experiences, but rather they see their past experiences as valuable. Their past is valuable because they learn from it and it also becomes a measure against which they can plot their personal growth and progress. All growth and progress comes at the cost of comfort and ease, and when we have to make sacrifices or have our comforts stolen from us we can choose to blame ourselves and remain where we are or we can accept that sometimes bad things happen to everybody, even good people. Self-condemnation is a destructive force which breaks down people's value. People with high self-esteem build themselves up – they do not break themselves down.

> **Self-condemnation is a destructive force which breaks down people's value. People with high self-esteem build themselves up – they do not break themselves down.**

43. Conflict

> **We make war that we may live in peace.**
> *Aristotle*

Members of an organization gathered, as they do once monthly, for a meeting. The members all claim to subscribe to an ethos of brotherly love and forgiveness. Peter* had just entered the door when Ben* approached him and said:
"You are undermining me!" whilst pointing the index finger of his right hand in Peter's face. Peter was shocked at the accusation as Ben continued to voice his disapproval of Peter's alleged behaviour. The encounter soon escalated to a shouting match between two grown men hurling accusations at one another. Finally, when the verbal wrestling ceased, no resolution was reached and the animosity between the two men exists to this day.

"You never listen to me!" shouted Mary* at her husband, John.*
"This was not the spices that I asked you to buy!" she continued shouting aggressively at John as she unpacked the contents of the grocery bag.
"But this is what you wanted," answered John in an irate manner.
"You don't pay any attention to anything I say. Nothing I say is important. Your cars and friends are more important than I am!" Mary continued.
The argument between husband and wife stopped briefly when John reluctantly went back to the supermarket to buy the correct spices, but a cold atmosphere existed between the spouses for many days after the fight.
* Not their real names

The conflict between Peter and Ben; and between Mary and John are two examples of the many conflicts which exist in social settings.

Two distinct patterns can be seen in the above examples, namely:

- that all families, groups and organizations are characterized by various degrees of conflict and disharmony, and
- that the conflict emerges when individuals feel invalidated, misunderstood and ignored – when they feel undervalued.

In my regular interactions with learners at public schools, and people of all ages at various churches, organizations and corporate companies, I have found that there are always differences between individuals on the grounds of personality, ideologies, values, perceptions, goals, fears, interpretations and expectations. These differences sometimes reveal themselves as conflict.
Conflict comes in one or more of three specific forms, namely:

1. cold conflict,
2. vocal conflict, and
3. physical conflict.

Let us explore these types of conflict further.

1. Cold conflict

Cold conflict is characterized by uncomfortable silences, pretence of lack of caring and concern, complacency and lack of interest. The silence which characterizes this form of conflict is merely a brief pause of expression, and thus it is the only form of conflict which eventually escalates to one or both of the two other forms of conflict. The escalation occurs when bottled up feelings need expression.
This sort of conflict often occurs between spouses, in the family environment. My parents had many of these cold conflicts when I was growing up. My mother would instruct me to tell my father something, even though he was in the same room.
This conflict can occur at government level between countries. Post WWII America and Russia entered into what has come to be known as 'The Cold War' when these two super-powers raced for dominance in the areas of nuclear armaments, military size, political influence and space travel, with no formal communication or dialogue between the two countries. In October 1962, during the Cuban Missile Crisis, this non-verbal conflict threatened to escalate into a physical war which could have had far-reaching consequences, not only for the two antagonistic nations but for the whole world. In the aftermath of the failed CIA Operation, now known as The Bay of Pigs Invasion, to overthrow Fidel Castro's government in Cuba, the Cubans had agreed to the erection of Russian nuclear missile launch sites in Cuba in order to prevent another attack on Cuba by the US. In response to

the potential danger, the US set up military blockades to prevent the delivery of any additional armaments to Cuba. The 13-day stand-off exposed the need for direct communication between the US and Russia.
After the threat was neutralized, the Moscow-Washington hotline was established. The direct communication drastically reduced conflicts between the two nations, but only materialized after the threat of active, or physical conflict, had grown out of cold conflict.
Although cold conflict is usually the domain of inaction, people can display aggression in a passive manner. Passively aggressive people are walking time-bombs and conflict with these will usually escalate to a higher conflict.

2. Vocal conflict

> **It is foolish to belittle one's neighbor; a sensible person keeps quiet.** Proverbs 11:12 NLT
> **The words of the reckless pierce like swords.** Proverbs 12:18a NIV
> **Being slow to get angry compares to great understanding as being quick-tempered compares to stupidity.** Proverbs 14:29 ISV
> **A gentle answer deflects anger, but harsh words make tempers flare.** Proverbs 15:1 NLT
> **A hot-tempered person starts fights; a cool-tempered person stops them.** Proverbs 15:18 NLT
> *King Solomon*

Vocal conflict is by far the most common form of conflict. Unlike cold conflict which is expressionless, vocal conflict permits expression and the exchange of thoughts and emotions. With the exception of libel and defamation of character, the constitution of most modern societies permits one person to say what they choose, both to and about another person, without the possibility of litigation and prosecution. This makes vocal conflict an ideal form of conflict.
Everyone has had an argument of some sort with someone else. We use vocal arguments from childhood. A relative told me recently about his 4-year old son who refuses to respond to being called "My Boy" by his dad. He insists on being

called by his first name. He puts up a bitter argument until his dad calls him by his name.

Even non-modern societies have recognized the importance and value of controlled vocal conflict to manage the fragile fabric of society. Indigenous peoples of the Northwest Coast of North America have used a *talking stick* during tribal meetings for many centuries. In a tribal meeting a specially carved stick resembling a totem pole is passed around. Only the person holding the stick is permitted to speak and is guaranteed of no interruption from others in the group.

3. Physical conflict

This is the pinnacle of conflict. It is at this level of conflict where people resort to violence and the use of weapons to defend themselves and/or force their opponents into submission. Throughout history, and even today, this sort of conflict has had the most devastating effect on the world. It leads to physical harm, bloodshed, maiming, disabilities and death of people.

History was written with the blood of the slain – heroes and villains, brave men and cowards, women and children, good and bad, rich and poor.

The bible relates the story of the physical conflict between two brothers named Cain and Abel. [Genesis 4:3-8]

A disagreement between these two brothers resulted in Cain procuring a weapon and then inflicting a fatal wound upon his brother. We do not know if this was their first disagreement, but it certainly was their last.

Physical disagreements do not occur only as one-on-one disagreements and fights but also as many-on-one and many-on-many. Likeminded individuals can join forces to combat and/or resist a person or group.

From the time that Adolf Hitler became the Prime Minister of Germany in 1933, his Nazi Party began to progressively propagate a hegemonic ideal which promoted the Nordic or Aryan race as being superior to people that the Nazis referred to as ***untermenschen*** or '*lower-humans*' such as Jews, Slavs,[xxxvii] Romani, homosexuals, blacks, physically and mentally disabled individuals, Jehovah's Witnesses and political opponents.[xxxviii]

The organized murder, now known as *The Holocaust*, of approximately six million Jews and five million other groups,

by the Nazi Party was a direct consequence of this Aryan ideology. As the Nazi Party sought to unify Europe and purify its inhabitants by military means, the world was cast into a drawn-out conflict which we now call World War II.
When conflict escalates and groups mobilize resources in defence and/or pursuit of a course, the consequences can be far-reaching, historical and truly commemorative.

People will display either the **fight response** or the **flight response** when they encounter conflict.
The flight response is displayed by individuals who automatically avoid the two confrontational conflicts. Flight response is not the absence of conflict but rather a different manner of expressing conflict. Therefore, flight response falls into the category of cold conflict. People who display this response usually come across as softies and as push-overs.
Individuals who automatically display the fight response will approach conflict through vocal and/or physical means. These individuals would make their opinions known by talking and shouting, and in some cases their behaviour escalates to physical fights.

Individuals are not homogenous with regards to characteristics and nature, and hence, they do not all respond in the same manner to similar circumstances. When conflict occurs, this dissimilarity can result in unmatched responses where one individual takes a confrontational stance, whilst the other assumes a non-confrontational position. However, responses might also be matched so that both individuals assume non-confrontational positions or both individuals are confrontational.

Jesus once said: "How terrible it will be for you when everyone says nice things about you, because that's the way their ancestors used to treat the false prophets!" Luke 6:26 ISV
Even Jesus realised that it is a dangerous thing when all people say good things about you, and then he cites the example of the people of old who said good things about bad prophets. It is a given that people will say good things about bad people and they will say bad things about good people, and this is how conflict is bred.

> **It is a given that people will say good things about bad people and they will say bad things about good people, and this is how conflict is bred.**

It was Aristotle who said: "We make war that we may live in peace." Winners understand conflict is an integral part of life and that it is necessary in order to maintain peace and balance in our lives. They also understand that you cannot expect to be liked by everyone, and to get along with everyone. However, when they do encounter conflict they use the conflict to initiate a metamorphosis of the relationship. Ideally, the relationship should grow into something better and more valuable. If the relationship worsens, at least they are better for the experience.

44. Chaos

While you are alive you will always be facing chaotic situations, crises and challenging problems. We all have to accept this as a reality. We must all accept that problems are here to stay and confront them head-on instead of avoiding them or pretending that they do not exist. Henry Ford once said: "Most people spend more time and energy going around problems than in trying to solve them." Problem-solving is not problem-avoidance.

> **Most people spend more time and energy going around problems than in trying to solve them.**
> *Henry Ford*

Focus your energy and cognitive activities on solving the problem and also to learn from it. The measure of a man's self-esteem and self-efficacy is displayed during the moments of crises and challenges. People with high self-esteem and self-efficacy do not despise the presence of problems but are confident that they are capable of overcoming. They seize opportunities to display their abilities and also to learn. This is what Martin Luther King, Jr. meant when he said: "The ultimate measure of a man is not where he stands in moments of comfort and convenience, but where he stands at times of challenge and controversy."

> **The ultimate measure of a man is not where he stands in moments of comfort and convenience, but where he stands at times of challenge and controversy.**
> *Martin Luther King, Jr.*

45. Choices and Consequences

Every human being is born a free moral agent, which simply means that you were born with the power of choice, and that you have the right to choose. Decisions have to be made. Sometimes they don't work out as we have planned, so we must not give up but instead we should make another decision until things work out alright.
Franklin D. Roosevelt once said: "One thing is sure. We have to do something. We have to do the best we know how at the moment. If it doesn't turn out right, we can modify it as we go along."

> **One thing is sure. We have to do something. We have to do the best we know how at the moment.**
> **If it doesn't turn out right, we can modify it as we go along.**
> *Franklin D. Roosevelt*

Choices and consequences are inter-linked. All choices have consequences. They are two sides of the coin of decision. Decisions have to be made in every area of our lives.
The format of decisions is:

1. *circumstance* – where we find ourselves,
2. *choice* – selecting between several options, and
3. *consequence* – the expected and unexpected results of our choices.

Concerning ***consequence***, we do not always know for sure how things will turn out when we make choices, but life will give you one or more of the following four outcomes, namely:

1. *stagnation*,
2. *elevation*,
3. *relegation*, or

4. *termination.*

You either **remain where you** are – this is stagnation, **move forward** - this is elevation, **move backwards** – this is relegation, **or you die** – this is termination.

A person's life-path is not determined by the wonderful plans that he has made, or the circumstances that he was born into or even his social standing. A man's life path is ultimately determined by his choices. A man's quality of life is determined by the quality of his choices. When you make quality choices, you will have a quality life, but when you make bad choices, you will have a bad life.

> **A man's life path is ultimately determined by his choices. A man's quality of life is determined by the quality of his choices. When you make quality choices, you will have a quality life, but when you make bad choices, you will have a bad life.**

Viktor E. Frankl, who was a Jewish neurologist and psychiatrist who was imprisoned in several Nazi concentration camps during World War II, ascribed his psychological strength during those terrible days to his ability to exercise his powers of choice and self-adaptation. Frankl wrote: "Between stimulus and response there is a space. In that space is our power to choose our response." We always have the power of choice to try to change our circumstances. Frankl went on to write: "When we are no longer able to change a situation - we are challenged to change ourselves."
When we exercise our powers of choice, we are either able to change our circumstances or we are forced to change ourselves.

If you want to have a quality life, you must diligently consider the consequences of your choices before you make the choice. When you are making choices, you must ask yourself the following seven questions:

- what results do I desire?

- is what I desire something that is beneficial or destructive?
- what are the possible choices that will lead to beneficial results?
- what will be the results of the choice I am making?
- can I live with the results that stems from my choice?
- what will I be getting and what will I be losing when I make this choice?
- what other choices will I be forced to make if I make this choice?

We all make many choices every single day. Some choices are easy, like choosing what to eat for breakfast, what to wear and what time to leave home for work or school. Other choices are not as easy because they require intense consideration and contemplation. Making the choices concerning one's career and spouse are not easy choices. Choosing your general life-path can be a difficult choice. When you choose to live a truly valuable life, you have to let go of all indulgences that others hold onto. The path that leads to a life of joy, fulfilment and phenomenal success is a tough one, and most people would rather choose the easy way out. For the people who choose to walk the easy road, the choice is also easy.
Jesus Christ warned us that the gate which leads to destruction is broad. The word ***broad*** is a metaphor for '*easy*.' He also said that the gate which leads to life is narrow. In this case, ***narrow*** is a metaphor for '*difficult.*' He added that there are only a few people who find the road that leads to life and phenomenal success – the narrow road.

> **Enter through the narrow gate. For wide is the gate and broad is the road that leads to destruction, and many enter through it. But small is the gate and narrow the road that leads to life, and only a few find it.** Matthew 7:13 NIV
> *Jesus of Nazareth*

The majority of people in this world do not enjoy phenomenal success because they do not want to make the difficult choices and pay the price that is necessary in order to receive the reward of a fulfilling life. If you make the easy choices you will have a difficult life, but if you make the difficult choices you will have an easy life.

> **If you make the easy choices you will have a difficult life, but if you make the difficult choices you will have an easy life.**

People with high self-esteem are not afraid to make the difficult choices, especially when those choices are unpopular. The burden of making the choice for the narrow path is that you will have to walk that path alone. You will walk that path alone because most people would prefer the wide path. People with high self-esteem bravely walk the narrow path, even if it means walking it alone simply because they value themselves so highly that they cannot, and will not, subject themselves to the dangers that exist on the wide road.

This brings us to another aspect of choices, which is *cost.* Cost relates to what you have to give up in order to get what you want. Whenever you say 'yes' to something, you are automatically saying 'no' to something else.

Always be aware of what your choices are costing you and what you will be denying yourself.

> **Whenever you say 'yes' to something, you are automatically saying 'no' to something else.**

The power of choice is a wonderful endowment which has been bestowed upon us by God Almighty, but it can work for you or against you. If you make wrong choices you will pay severe penalties in this life, but if you make right choices you will reap the rewards of phenomenal success. People with high self-esteem make themselves more valuable by making valuable choices - they choose worthwhile and valuable outcomes and are willing to pay the price.

> **People with high self-esteem make themselves more valuable by making valuable choices - they choose worthwhile and valuable outcomes and are willing to pay the price.**

When all is said and done, your life will go where you choices have taken you, so don't ever take the endowment of choice for granted. Use your choices to shape a successful life. A true winner is someone who has used his power of choice to bring about winning circumstances, whilst losers use their power of choice to bring about losing circumstances.

> **Your life will go where you choices have taken you.**

Be a master craftsman with your choices, and mould a meaningful and significant life for yourself. You have the power to do it. Shape and mould a life that you can be proud of. Shape a valuable life by walking valuable paths.

> **Shape a valuable life by walking valuable paths.**

46. Command

Command is leadership.
Leadership begins with self. Self-leadership is a precursor to leading others. Self-mastery and self-ruling are aspects of self-leadership. Self-mastery is more important than leading others. You can have self-mastery without being a leader, but you cannot be a true and effective leader without first having self-mastery. King Solomon pointed out the importance of self-leadership or self-ruling when he wrote: 'He who is slow to anger is better than the mighty, he who rules his [own] spirit than he who takes a city.' Another translation of this text refers to the ruling of one's own spirit as '*self-control*.'

> **Better a patient person than a warrior, one with self-control than one who takes a city.** Proverbs 16:32 NIVUK
> *King Solomon*

Thus self-leadership, self-ruling and self-control are the same concepts.
A person with little self-control and low self-esteem who is placed in any leadership position is a ticking time-bomb. At some point in time that bomb will go off and have devastating consequences for everyone concerned.

- The parent, (home)
- the teacher, (school)
- the manager, chairperson, executive officer, (business, club)
- the politician, (government)
- the religious leader, (church, mosque, temple)
- the influential entertainer, (media)

The leader with low self-esteem will be either completely agreeable or completely un-agreeable. If they are agreeable they will attempt to win the favour and esteem of others by allowing them to walk all over them. On the other hand, if the leader is un-agreeable, he will not let anyone walk over him at all. The leader with high self-esteem knows that doing right is more important than being right, and he will be open to the suggestions of others but still be resolute when it comes to sticking to personal and organizational principles, values and goals. The true leader has a calibre of self-esteem that permits him to not be permanently polarized when it comes to his level of agreeability - he knows when to be agreeable and when not to be.
Let us look at the qualities of a leader with high self-esteem.

A leader with high self-esteem:

- knows his vision and purpose and that of his organization;
- he is comfortable with the knowledge that he cannot do everything himself - he delegates;
- he is not threatened by the ascension of others - he builds leaders not followers;
- he moves confidently towards the future and the fulfilment of organizational goals;
- he encourages others to be their very best;
- he is sensitive to the needs of his followers, he is not selfish and self-centred;
- he is a dedicated learner and reader - he asks questions;
- he uses available resources in a manner that is commensurate with his skill and knowledge;
- he knows that he must have a succession plan in place;
- he wants to share his knowledge and abilities with those who are ready to receive it;

- he corrects mistakes with love and patience;
- he understands who and what are the competition and enemies to his vision and his organization;
- he has a respect for the law – God's Law, taxes etc.
- he builds relationships with other organizations;
- he handles praise and compliments humbly;
- His success does not make him arrogant – he respects his parents, spouse, children, fellow-employees etc.

The leader's skills are not determined by how well he can perform during times of abundance, but really during times of hardship and challenges. This is the time when relationships, commitments, intelligence, knowledge, experience and attitude are tested. A leader with high self-esteem will navigate both good times and bad with unwavering dedication to the realisation of organizational goals without sacrificing values and principles. Truth, honesty and integrity will be the order of the day – lies and deceit will not be the buckets used to empty the ship from the seawater thrust aboard by raging waves.

The 7 Pillars of Leadership are:

1. **Construction**
   Construction is a purpose-clarification function. Construction concerns the reason and purpose for the existence of the organization. Construction also relates to what we are building and creating. Construction addresses such questions as: what impact do we want to make as an organization? What value do we want to transfer to our employees, our partners, our customers and society at large? What are the organization-specific requirements that must be met in order for effectiveness to have been attained?
2. **Direction**
   Direction is goal-setting function. Direction entails the short, medium and long-term goals of the organization. If we look at the pursuit of goals as a journey, direction covers the path or route that we will be taking to get us to our destination, which is the goal that we want to achieve.

Direction addresses such questions as: where are we going? What route are we following?
Leadership and goals are two sides of the same coin – leadership without goals is anarchy and goals without leadership is fantasy.

3. **Relation**
   Relation is a connecting function.
   Relation refers to the relationships, or connections, that we must build and maintain in order to be effective.
   Relation addresses such questions as: who are we going to work with? What individuals, groups and organizations will we partner with? Leadership is a relationship-building function. Leadership also entails an understanding of the different dynamics that apply to human and non-human resources - ***We lead people, but we manage things.***
4. **Instruction**
   Instruction is an information-transmission function. Information has to be transmitted firstly, between people within the organization and secondly, to people outside of the organization. People must be trained and developed. The broader public needs to understand our purpose and relevance within society. Instruction addresses such questions as: how are we going to develop our people? How are we going to prepare and equip our partners in order to build and maintain sustainable relationships?
5. **Delegation**
   Delegation is a task-assignment and role-clarification function. The leader cannot and should not do everything himself. People must be matched with functions for which they are suited, and delegation identifies the terms of suitability of candidates. Delegation also involves stewardship and all that stewardship entails. Delegation addresses such questions as: what must be done and who is the most suitable person to do it? Delegation rests on trust. ***Delegation is trusting and entrusting people with responsibility.***

6. **Decision**
   Decision is a choice-selection function. In any organization, decisions must be made and sometimes the decisions are tough ones. Decision involves choice. Choice is deciding in which direction to employ resources and effort.
   Decision addresses such questions as: what are our options? What can we do and what can't we do? Sometimes the right decision is not popular – the leader is strong enough to make decisions based on facts and not for the procurement of favour.
7. **Succession**
   Succession is grooming function. Succession is about developing more leaders and not followers.
   Succession addresses such questions as: who is willing and suitable to take over? What must the successor know, have and be in order to take the organization further?
   Only secure leaders can groom others into becoming leaders. Leadership is the privilege of individuals with a successive and abundance mind-set.

Command is not about manipulation. The position of leadership that is obtained through manipulation and threats is not true leadership. It is a pseudo-leadership that is unsustainable. Adolf Hitler's command was of this type. He mobilised millions of soldiers through coercion, and although he was successful in the short-term he eventually suffered defeat as the supreme commander of the Third Reich and personal defeat when he committed suicide. He ended his life because he could not bare the thought of falling into the hands of the people on whom he had unleashed a terror which the world had never seen before. Coercive leadership has coercive consequences. In contrast to Hitler's reign of terror, a man small in stature living halfway around the world was able to procure the co-operation of about 300 million people without the use of brute force. This man employed the method of empathic leadership whilst simultaneously denouncing the use of force, even to sway the opinions of their colonial governors. That man was Mohandas Gandhi. Through peaceful protest and consideration he led the people of India through an exodus out of British colonial oppression into a new democracy. His methods proved that leadership through consideration was not only possible but also very desirable. It is therefore not a surprise that the name ***Mahatma***, which means '*the great soul*' has been given to him. This type of leadership demands high self-esteem and immense personal strength, therefore only great souls can exercise empathic leadership. In sharp contrast to coercive leadership, empathic leadership has co-operative consequences.

> **Coercive leadership has coercive consequences. Empathic leadership has co-operative consequences. The latter is more desirable than the former. Empathic leadership demands high self-esteem and immense personal strength.**

47. Commandments

Commandments refer to laws and protocols.
All countries and organizations have laws. Laws are created to maintain stability and order. Without laws, society will come apart at the seams.
Protocols are required behaviour patterns in an organization/or relationship. Protocols relate to how things are done and the hierarchy of command. Protocols state who is answerable to who and who is consulted before who. Protocol also relates to the respect and honour given to an individual.
Study anyone who has failed at anything and you will find that they violated protocol at some point. All failures are stem from a failure to observe protocol.

48. Consideration

Consideration has two aspects, namely:

1. thoughtfulness towards others and thoughtfulness in decision-making, and
2. a return, reward or compensation for one or more actions.

The first aspect of ***consideration*** is '*thoughtfulness towards others and thoughtfulness in decision-making.*'

Thoughtfulness towards others is not only essential for fostering healthy relationships, but it is also commanded by God Almighty.
Jesus of Nazareth taught that we must use the manner in which we want to be treated as the barometer by which we measure how we will treat others. He said that we must treat others in the same way that we want to be treated. He went on to say that this principle was the sum, or gist of the Laws of Moses and the Jewish prophets.

> **In everything, therefore, treat people the same way you want them to treat you, for this is the Law and the Prophets.** Mathew 7:12 NASB
> *Jesus of Nazareth*

In our time, this principle has evolved into a maxim called The Golden Rule. The Golden Rule says: "Do unto others as you would have them do unto you."
Jesus also taught The Law of Reciprocation. Reciprocation is something that is returned or responded, thus this law can also be called The Law of Return or The Law of Response. This Law says that you get back what you give out. Jesus expressed this law this way: "Give, and it will be given to you."
This brings us to the second aspect of consideration which is *'a return, reward or compensation for one or more actions.'*

> **The Law of Reciprocation says that you get back what you give out – people will treat you in exactly the same manner as you treat them.**

Jesus was saying that if you want good attitudes such as patience and understanding from someone, give it first. If you want good emotions such as love and loving kindness, give it first. Eventually what you have given out will be reciprocated, responded and returned. However, the law also works when you give negative attitudes and emotions. When you give attitudes of impatience and intemperance, these will be returned to you. When you give emotions of anger and bitterness, these will be returned to you.

Jesus also taught us about how much will be returned to us when we give. He said: "For with the measure you use, it will be measured to you."
This statement is self-explanatory – the quantity that you give dictates the quantity that you will receive. If you give large amounts of love, you will receive large amounts back, but if you give only a small amount, you will receive only a small amount. The amount of hatred and contempt that you give out will be returned to you in the same amount. So love people and they will love you back but if you hate them, they will hate you and they will give back to you what you have given first in exactly the same quantity.

> **Love people and they will love you back but if you hate them, they will hate you and they will give back to you what you have given first in exactly the same quantity.**

> **Give, and it will be given to you. A good measure, pressed down, shaken together and running over, will be poured into your lap. For with the measure you use, it will be measured to you.** Luke 6:38 NIV
> *Jesus of Nazareth*

The formula given to us by Jesus has a greater application than just helping us build friendships and relationships with people through exemplary behaviour. Another translation of the verse stated by Jesus reads as follows: "So whatever you wish that others would do to you, do also to them, for this is the Law and the Prophets." The Law of Reciprocation suggests the only true formula that we should use to rally people to commit to and help us realise our goals, wishes and dreams. The formula states that if we help others realise their dreams by giving our help and assistance, then they will help us realise our dreams.
Zig Ziglar once wrote: 'You can have everything in life you want, if you will just help other people get what they want.' Mr. Ziglar was simply rephrasing what Jesus had said many thousands of years before. A person of high self-esteem will seek out opportunities to help others realise their goals and

by doing this he will build a list of willing contributors and assistants to his own dream-building efforts.

> **So whatever you wish that others would do to you, do also to them, for this is the Law and the Prophets.** Mathew 7:12 ESV
> *Jesus of Nazareth*

> **You can have everything in life you want, if you will just help other people get what they want.**
> *Zig Ziglar*

A person with high self-esteem is thoughtful towards others and in his decision-making. His thoughts and decisions are directed by his over-arching purpose of being esteemed by others by first esteeming them, and also by realising his visions and goals by first helping others achieve their visions and goals. Genuine, unselfish consideration of others is the foundation for unadulterated self-interest and produces rewards that lead to high levels of self-esteem and self-fulfilment.

49. Compromise

In life we always find that we must negotiate for the things we want. Negotiating involves bargaining, and bargaining is nothing more than coming to an agreement or accord concerning a certain matter. However, before an agreement is reached we sometimes have to give some ground as we take other ground. This is called give-and-take. Give-and-take is simply the process of compromise.

During this process, people often take more than they should or they give more than they should. Dr. Stephen Covey referred to an unbalanced outcome of a negotiation as a *win-lose situation.*

> **When one side benefits more than the other, that's a win-lose situation. To the winner it might look like success for a while, but in the long run, it breeds resentment and distrust.**
> *Stephen Covey*

It is essential that you aim for a win-win situation in all your negotiations. The way to achieve this is to ensure that the outcome guarantees that each party gains equally well.
Zig Ziglar gave us the key to ensuring that we get what we want when he said: "You can have everything in life you want, if you will just help other people get what they want." The key to mutually beneficial outcomes in any negotiation is to help other people get what they want. As you help people get what they want, you will eventually get what you want. This is called a win-win situation.

Compromise also refers to selling-out and betrayal. Many people sell-out on the values and principles that they claim to hold onto.
People with high self-esteem do not compromise on the need for fairness because they always negotiate for the mutual benefit of all, and they also operate from a standpoint where they do not compromise their values and the trust of others.

50. Chronicles – Your History
It is a known fact that people who are experiencing any form of psychological illness tend to dwell on the mistakes and hurts of the past and because of this anyone who is under the care of a psychologist or psychiatrist is encouraged to talk about their past because events in your past shape your perceptions and your perceptions shape every aspect of your life. Your perceptions shape your relationships, what you feel capable of achieving, your career, your personal centres and your goals.
Your childhood experiences and upbringing have a significant influence on shaping your self-esteem and self-efficacy. At home parents play a significant role in shaping their children's self-esteem. A child's school experiences also contribute towards his self-esteem. You will have good and bad memories from your childhood. Some memories are hidden deep in your sub-conscious mind but they will still have an effect on your behaviour.

51. Compliments
It was Abraham Lincoln who said: "Everybody likes a compliment." I agree with Lincoln, but only in part, because

everybody likes *to be given* a compliment. *Furthermore, not* everybody likes *to give* a compliment.
People tend to give compliments because they want one of two things: someone to do something for them or they desire a compliment in return.
People who want to draw you into committing to do something for them will give you the most glorious of compliments, and thereby trap you into committing to some act or deed. King Solomon described this phenomenon as being caught in a net, when he wrote: 'Whoever flatters his neighbour is spreading a net for his feet.' He also wrote that people mask their hearts and evil intentions with their lips.

> **Whoever flatters his neighbour is spreading a net for his feet.** Proverbs 29:5 NIVUK
> **A coating of glaze over earthenware are fervent lips with an evil heart.**
> **A malicious man disguises himself with his lips, but in his heart he harbours deceit.** Proverbs 26:23-24 NIVUK
> *King Solomon*

Using compliments to persuade people to do things is deception. Deception will only be used by people who are not self-confident enough to attain their goals by truth. However, people with high self-confidence and self-esteem do not compromise their values and use deception to manipulate others. Whether you are trying to sell something to someone if you're a salesperson, or if you're trying to convince someone of your idea or just getting your child to do his chores, you must never use the deceptive method of giving false compliments.
Then there are those who give compliments so that they can be complimented in return. This selfish phenomenon was expressed by Francois De La Rochefoucauld when he said: "Usually we praise only to be praised."

> **Usually we praise only to be praised.**
> *Francois De La Rochefoucauld*

Giving praise in order to receive praise is the domain of people with low self-esteem. These are people who constantly crave the praise and recognition of others through compliments and applause. This is a dangerous position to be in, because these compliments are like an addictive drug, and when the addict is not getting his fix he experiences withdrawal symptoms. The withdrawal symptoms of someone who craves constant compliments are manifested as low self-confidence, negative self-talk, frustration, depression, anxiety and an overall feeling of worthlessness. People who feel this way do not face their problems head-on and they do not pursue worthwhile goals because they base their value on the words and actions of others. When these positive words are absent, so is their positive self-esteem. In order to develop high self-esteem one must dispel with the need to constantly be complimented by others. Compliments from other people are a fluctuating external factor of self-esteem and therefore it cannot be depended upon for building self-esteem. Only fixed internal factors can be trusted to build high self-esteem.

Compliments do not only consist of words. We can deliver a sweet compliment through our actions. By permitting effective communication to occur, we give people psychological air. Communication flows easy when people feel understood. Unfortunately, most people talk but they do not truly communicate. We all can benefit from devoting more time into practicing the habits that promote greater communication.
Listed below are ***The Seven Habits Which Promote Effective Communication.***

1. Listen to understand.
2. Pursue understanding the next person first before pursuing being understood.
3. Listen with empathy.
4. Listen to get meaning instead of using the other person's speaking as a chance to formulate your response.
5. Read body language.
6. Do not interrupt the person until they are done speaking.
7. Always remember someone's first name, especially when meeting them for the first time.

> **Remember that a person's name is to that person the sweetest and most important sound in any language.**
> *Dale Carnegie*

People with high self-esteem are very comfortable giving genuine compliments to other people, and they also receive compliments gracefully. Skilful communication is not just about getting your message across – it is also about allowing the other person to get their message across. When we compliment people with words and allow them to communicate their message effectively we are able to connect with them in a way that opens doors of opportunity. Skilful communication produces valuable relationships and valuable relationships in turn produce valuable opportunities.

> **Skilful communication produces valuable relationships and valuable relationships in turn produce valuable opportunities.**

52. Chastisement

> **chastise** •v. reprimand severely
> - DERIVATIVES **chastisement** n.[xxxix]

Chastisement refers to the element of correction, reprimanding and discipline that you were exposed to as a child. If you were regularly disciplined verbally and physically, you are probably a better person because of it, but those who were not have been denied the good characteristics that develop in an individual when they are wisely corrected and chastised.

As you read the next few paragraphs you will begin to understand why all parents must skilfully chastise and discipline their children.

I have been privileged to work with many learners in public schools and I have been able to observe the behaviour of thousands of learners coming from diverse backgrounds. I have discovered that the factors that make a difference in a child's behaviour are the levels of parental chastisement and discipline.

> **The factors that make a difference in a child's behaviour are the levels of parental chastisement and discipline.**

Unless parents actively chastise and discipline their children, we will continue to produce delinquents and criminals who are a burden and liability to society. King Solomon taught us that when we fail to discipline children, we spoil them.

> **Whoever refuses to spank his son hates him, but whoever loves his son disciplines him from early on.** Proverbs 13:24 GW
> *King Solomon*

Spoilt, or undisciplined, children become abominations who cannot be tolerated by their family, friends and society in general. Only through raising children with chastisement and discipline can we create adults who will become contributors to society.

Little children have been endowed with the unique abilities of instant absolution and amnesia. They can continue about their business almost immediately after having been punished. These are mechanisms which permit parents the benefit of exacting discipline without having to fear eternal hatred from their children or permanent harm to the child's self-esteem, if the discipline is done at the right time and in the right way.

When we regularly discipline a small child, we are not stealing that child's self-esteem because they bounce back so easily by forgiving and forgetting. Regular acts of corrective discipline are investments in that child's future. You ensure that your child will have the high self-esteem that comes from being a disciplined individual and a meaningful asset to society when you regularly teach, instruct and discipline him.

It must also be noted that there is a thin line between punishment and abuse. A child should be appropriately punished but in a manner that is not injurious and resulting in maiming, disfigurement and scarring of the child.

Discipline must be done in a loving but stern manner. Loving discipline by a parent may produce momentary discomfort for parent and child but it will produce life-long discipline and high self-esteem in the child as he grows and he becomes an adult.

> **Loving discipline by a parent may produce momentary discomfort for parent and child but it will produce life-long discipline and high self-esteem in the child as he grows and he becomes an adult.**

53. Certainty

> **Two things are certain: death and taxes.**
> *Benjamin Franklin*

Everybody seeks security – a certainty related to one's future. We all desire certainty in our relationships, finances, health, jobs, national economy etc. Two things can be said about certainty:

- the desire for certainty concerning tomorrow is completely natural, and
- human beings spend a great deal of effort to create certainty and security in their lives.

It is a sign of prudence to plan for tomorrow, and no-one should live their life as if tomorrow will either be completely disastrous or completely without disaster. Our plans for tomorrow should always make room for the unexpected. Unexpected circumstances always crop up when they are *unexpected.* This brings us to the dark reality of human life: the unexpected is always lurking around the corner to pounce on you like a prowler in the night, and all your security measures cannot keep you safe. Certainty and safety are illusions. Life's only certainty is uncertainty. We do not have the guarantee that things will always go well and completely as planned, but we do have the guarantee that things will *not* go as planned. Certainty can be best described as an urban legend – everyone talks about it and desires an encounter with it, but no-one can confirm its existence, because in truth, it does not exist. King Solomon taught that tomorrow is guaranteed to no man. You cannot be certain that you will be alive tomorrow. Jesus taught about the man who had a false sense of security when he built large barns to store his wealth – that man died and all his plans and great wealth were wasted.

Human beings need a sense of certainty and security in order to feel happy and safe. We pursue security so that we feel good about ourselves and our future prospects. It is ironic that we pursue security, but security is nowhere to be found.

How then does one remain sane and continue to be happy and cheerful in a world where the odds seem to be set against us? How do we retain that sense of security, which is vital for human psychological well-being in the midst of the storms that batter us consistently?

The answer to this question lies in the source of the question itself: the human psyche. Along with the desire for safety and security which God has placed in the human spirit He has also placed an immense capacity for faith. Faith is the one endowment which balances out fear. Any fear regarding our continued survival in the midst of great threats is countered by our immense faith that things can still work out alright. Faith keeps you sane in an insane world. Paul the Apostle, aptly described faith as 'the substance of things hoped for, the evidence of things not seen.' It is faith that forms the material of the things we desire although the evidence around us seems contradictory to our aims. It is faith that permits us to see the unseen and makes it almost tangible. Without a little bit of faith no-one can continue to hold onto their hopes and dreams because uncertainty is always there to steal your dreams. Faith, however, keeps the dream alive and if you persist you can then laugh in the face of uncertainty. The individual with high self-esteem knows that uncertainty will mock him sometimes, but in the end through the endowment of faith he can persist and then finally have the last laugh, and we all know that he who laughs last laughs best.

54. Cultivating Others

There is an African proverbs that says: 'A person is a person because of other persons.'

The wisdom behind this proverb is profound. It is because of other people that a man can be recognized as an individual in his own right. It is through other people that we become valuable.

> **A person is a person because of other persons.**
> *African Proverb*

We only attain recognition and value as individuals when there is a transfer of value from other people into the life of an individual, and when the transfer has been effected, a '*person will be a person because of other persons*.'
This is a general type of cultivation, whereby an individual is able to learn valuable lessons from all the people that he meets and spends time with. Through this means an individual will learn the habits and characteristics of those people, and become like them. If they are bad persons, he too will become a bad person. If they are good persons, he will become a good person. The calibre and measure of a man's character will be determined by the people who have influenced, through direct and indirect means, that man's life. Influence is a transferring process. Through the process of influence, value is transferred. Through influence one man can attain dignity, recognition and esteem from others. However, he cannot attain those attributes if someone did not first reveal them to him and then taught him how to acquire, use and keep those attributes.

> **The calibre and measure of a man's character will be determined by the people who have influenced, through direct and indirect means, that man's life.**

There is a type of influence that can truly accelerate the value of an individual. King Solomon wrote: '[As] iron sharpens iron, so one person sharpens the wits of another.'

> **[As] iron sharpens iron, so one person sharpens the wits of another.** Proverbs 27:17 GW
> *King Solomon*

King Solomon was teaching us that a man can be sharpened by a friend. An iron tool can sharpen an iron knife so that the knife can be a more effective instrument. In like manner, one man can be made more adequately prepared for the functions he must perform through the sharpening of his friend. In human terms this sharpening process is attained through influence. People are influenced through example and quality education. Example is the model that we represent in our activities. Example is a tacit form of influence. Quality education involves mentoring and coaching, and is a deliberate form of influence. Through the combined means of example and quality education, we can sharpen those around us and also be sharpened by them.

When we consider all the rapid change that is happening around the world, and the need for people and organizations to still remain effective despite changing circumstances, we begin to realize that there is an urgent need for leaders of value everywhere and in every sphere of human social interactions – in the family, in groups and in organizations. Valuable leaders are those who do not simply stick around so that they can milk the organization of all its resources. Valuable leaders are concerned with the common good of all, and not just the lining of their own pockets. Valuable leaders promote value in their people and in their organisations. Valuable leaders understand that it is the primary responsibility of every good leader to develop other good leaders.

Valuable leaders understand that it is the primary responsibility of every good leader to develop other good leaders.

A valuable leader will employ the **R-E-A-C-H Formula**, which was discussed in the chapter titled 'Value Redefined,' in order to identify and teach an individual to become a valuable leader. The leader will also impart the wisdom of The Seven Critical Aspects of Leadership which are discussed in this chapter in the sub-section titled 'Command.'
Only a valuable leader can cultivate and produce other valuable leaders.

Only a valuable leader can cultivate and produce other valuable leaders.

55. Cheerfulness

Cheerfulness is happiness, and happiness is expressed in many different ways. Happiness is joy, laughter, singing and dancing. Material success is useless if its pursuit and also its possession make you miserable. After all, we pursue goals so we can be happy and fulfilled. Andrew Carnegie was one of the richest men in the world during the mid-1900s, and he said: "There is little success where there is little laughter."

The man who has everything but is unhappy, really has nothing. The true value of success, material and otherwise, lies in the happiness that we acquire through our achievements.

> **There is little success where there is little laughter.**
> *Andrew Carnegie*

Being cheerful is about enjoying the fruit of all your hard work. King Solomon wrote: 'The only worthwhile thing for a human being is to eat, drink, and enjoy life's goodness that he finds in what he accomplishes. This, I observed, is also from the hand of God himself.'

> **The only worthwhile thing for a human being is to eat, drink, and enjoy life's goodness that he finds in what he accomplishes.**
> **This, I observed, is also from the hand of God himself.** Ecclesiastes 2:24 ISV
> *King Solomon*

King Solomon was an exceptionally wealthy man, and he said that there is nothing more worthwhile than to consume and find enjoyment in what you have acquired. King Solomon went on to say that the consumption and enjoyment of things comes from the hand of God.

God is a happy individual, and He expresses His joy and cheerfulness through laughter. Thus cheerfulness, joy and laughter originate from God Himself. The psalmist wrote: 'The one enthroned in heaven laughs. The Lord makes fun of them.' Psalm 2:4 GW

God, who is enthroned in Heaven is the creator of all good things, including laughter, joy and having fun. God makes His joy available to anyone who will ask Him for it and abide by His will. Nehemiah, the ancient Jewish leader wrote: 'Don't be dejected and sad, for the joy of the LORD is your strength!'

We see that the joy that comes from God is empowering. When we are able to be cheerful in the midst of the storms of life, we are truly empowered, because the storm does not unsettle us. Having the joy of God is like carrying good weather with you all the time, regardless of the climate conditions.

Paul the Apostle wrote: '... the fruit of the Spirit is love, joy, peace, longsuffering, kindness, goodness, faithfulness, gentleness, self-control.' Galatians 5:22-23 NKJV

Through God's Spirit He infuses His children with cheerfulness and peace along with many other desirable attributes.

> **Don't be dejected and sad, for the joy of the LORD is your strength!** Nehemiah 8:10b NLT
> *Nehemiah*

> **The one enthroned in heaven laughs.**
> **The Lord makes fun of them.** Psalm 2:4 NIV
> *Psalm 2:4*

Being happy is a choice. You and only you can make the decision to be happy. Along with choosing to be happy, you must also make a choice to not saying and doing the things that make you and/or other people unhappy.

Winners are those people who have made a resolute decision to be happy and to spread joy and cheer instead of unhappiness. Although winners also experience moments of sadness, like everyone else, they encourage themselves with positive thoughts and affirmations.

56. Charity

Charity has several meanings. Firstly, it refers to love for others and humanity. Secondly, it refers to generosity and benevolence towards the less fortunate. Thirdly, it refers to acts of kindness towards other people.

Charity is also about giving, and giving is bestowing value. A short while after the African-American educator, Booker T. Washington had become the head of the Tuskegee institute in the state of Alabama, in the United States of America, he went for a walk in a wealthy neighbourhood. As Professor Washington passed the house of a very wealthy family, the lady of the house saw him and assumed that he was one of her husband's hired labourers. She asked him to chop a few logs of wood for her and then take it into the kitchen. Professor Washington humbly and willingly answered: "Yes Ma'am," and then proceeded to do as the lady had instructed him. When Professor Washington entered the kitchen carrying the chopped wood, a servant girl immediately recognized him and she quickly informed her mistress who this 'labourer' really was.

The next day the wealthy lady showed up at Professor Washington's office to apologise. The humble man accepted her apology and proceeded to tell her how he loved showing kindness and generosity towards friends and neighbours. So impressed was the lady with the professor's demeanour that she made a sizeable contribution to the Tuskegee Institute. Furthermore, she convinced many of her wealthy friends to donate large amounts of money to the Tuskegee Institute as well.

This story of Professor Booker T. Washington proves that you get value when you give value. It also proves that kindness is not an expense, it's an investment.

> **You get value when you give value.**
> **Kindness is not an expense, it's an investment.**

People with high self-esteem are not insulted when asked to donate of their time and efforts, because they understand the wonderful rewards that come from an in investment of kindness.

Where love is concerned only actions carries value. If you say that you love me, yet you treat me with disdain and disrespect, your words are worthless. The proof of love is not in words alone. The true proof of love is in action.

57. Channels

When I attended high school, my English teacher, Mrs. Val Davids repeatedly reminded us to expand our knowledge and experiences. She said that most people live their lives in proverbial channels. A channel is a metaphor for the places and people we visited. We walked the same path, to the same place to visit the same people. She also said that most people always read the same magazines and watch the same television shows. Our lives are channelled and predictive.
She encouraged us to seek new knowledge by reading what we have not yet been exposed to. She encouraged us to find new paths. She taught us to seek new channels.
Seeking new channels does not mean that you must break off old relationships and habits, but it does mean that you should explore the world. It is exploration that brings about knowledge. The poet T. S. Elliot reminded us of the unique benefit of exploration when he wrote:
'We shall not cease from exploration, and the end of all our exploring will be to arrive where we started and know the place for the first time.'
It is only through exploration and healthy curiosity to know, that we will eventually gain a better understanding of who we are and where we stand. People with high self-esteem willingly expand their channels – they willingly explore their environment. They see the value of exploration and they add to their own value through exploration.

> **We shall not cease from exploration, and the end of all our exploring will be to arrive where we started and know the place for the first time.**
> *T. S. Eliot*

Breaking from existing channels is also about doing what you've never done before. No learning can ever take place if the student is not willing to do something that he has never done before. The poet Emerson once wrote:
'Unless you try to do something beyond what you have already mastered, you will never grow.'
Unless we reach beyond our current abilities, we'll never acquire and master any new skills.

People with high self-esteem constantly seek new skills to acquire and then they seek to master those which they have already acquired.

> **Unless you try to do something beyond what you have already mastered, you will never grow.**
> *Ralph Waldo Emerson*

58. Creative Purpose

There is something that God has designed you, and only you to do. This is your creative purpose. You attain your creative purpose by practicing those unique gifts and talents which God has given to you to bring joy and fulfilment to your own life and the lives of others.

Abraham Maslow wrote: 'A musician must make music, an artist must paint, a poet must write, if he is to be ultimately at peace with himself.' Only when we exercise the gifts that God has placed in us can we find true harmony, that state which Maslow described as man being at peace with himself.

> **A musician must make music, an artist must paint, a poet must write, if he is to be ultimately at peace with himself.**
> *Abraham Maslow*

People with high self-esteem readily develop their unique talents and abilities. They also seek ways by which they can enrich their own lives and the lives of others by exercising these unique gifts. When they do this, they are living up to their creative purpose.

59. Casting Your Bread Upon the Waters

Goodwill has several meanings. Goodwill is about being benevolent, compassionate and generous. It is also about having a favourable attitude or disposition to a person or group of people. In business terms, goodwill is a phantom asset which is determined by calculating the value of a company's guaranteed future income. Most importantly, goodwill is about having an influence over a person or a group of people without the use of resources such as money and/or assets. Goodwill is about establishing value. First you

value others, and then they value you. When others see you as valuable, you can have an influence on them without any cost to yourself. Creating goodwill is not about being manipulative and deceptive, but rather it is about being truthful and sincere. Goodwill is about building a collaborative, collective and mutually rewarding relationship. Goodwill is about building valuable relationships.
But how does one build goodwill in a relationship?
In his book, Ecclesiastes, King Solomon advises us to cast our bread upon the waters, and it will return. He continues by advising that you should give portions to many people because you do not know what disaster may come upon the land.

> **Cast your bread upon the waters, for after many days you will find it again. Give portions to seven, yes to eight, for you do not know what disaster may come upon the land.** Ecclesiastes 11:1-2 NIV
>
> *King Solomon*

Casting your bread upon the waters is simply a metaphor for creating goodwill and the possible disaster that may come upon the land a metaphor for the unexpected problems that we may encounter. Goodwill does not come by itself. Goodwill is about persistent acts of benevolence and kindness, in word and deed that you display towards people around you. It is about giving to people of your time, effort, resources and assets. This giving is really an investment in other people, so that you can reap future rewards if needed because, as per King Solomon's implied warning - you never know if you will need the help of other people if things go wrong in the land, which refers to problems that you encounter. When people help you because you have been generous and kind to them, your proverbial bread upon the waters is returned to you.
Casting your bread upon the waters is about creating goodwill. Goodwill is about establishing valuable relationships. Without valuable relationships we cannot survive life's difficult storms, and without goodwill we cannot build valuable relationships.

> **Casting your bread upon the waters is about creating goodwill. Goodwill is about building valuable relationships. Without valuable relationships we cannot survive life's difficult storms, and without goodwill we cannot build valuable relationships.**

When you esteem people by being sensitive to their needs and assist them when you are able, you give them value. When you give people value, they will give you value in return. That returned value is goodwill. The measure of the goodwill you receive will be the same measure that you give out. Jesus taught us about establishing goodwill too, but he also makes us aware of the returns that you will get from your generosity. Jesus said:
"For with the same measure that you use, it will be measured back to you."
The quantity that you give will be the same quantity that you can expect. In addition, the quality that you give will be the same quality that you can expect.

> **Give, and it will be given to you: good measure, pressed down, shaken together, and running over will be put into your bosom. For with the same measure that you use, it will be measured back to you.** Luke 6:38 NIV
> *Jesus of Nazareth*

People with high self-esteem continuously build valuable relationships through goodwill. They are always aware of the quality and quantity of their giving, because this sets the bar for the quality and quantity of their receiving. The goodwill that they establish becomes a valuable life-jacket during life's storms, because what you do when things are going well will determine what happens when things go bad.

> **The goodwill that you establish becomes a valuable life-jacket during life's storms, because what you do when things are going well will determine what happens when things go bad.**

60. Care

Care is stewardship. Stewardship is how well you take care of what has been placed in your care. **Excellent care is excellent stewardship.**

> **Stewardship is how well you take care of what has been placed in your care.**
> **Excellent care is excellent stewardship.**
> **Excellent service is excellent stewardship.**

We each have a body over which we are required to exercise stewardship. We also have family members that we must care for. We must exercise stewardship with the time that we are given on this beautiful planet, and we must also exercise stewardship over the planet itself. As adults we must exercise stewardship over our finances and the things that we acquire with our finances. We must also exercise stewardship at the places where we are employed. All of life is an exercise in stewardship.

> **All of life is an exercise in stewardship.**

Stewardship consists of four aspects, which I call **The Pillars of Stewardship**, and they are:

1. ***Responsibility*** (what has been placed into your care).
2. ***Reason*** (why it has been placed into your care).
3. ***Recognition*** (what others observe about your level of care).
4. ***Reward*** (what you get for your level of care).

Although most people despise problems, problems are actually ideal opportunities to show our level of stewardship. Richard Bach once said: "There is no such thing as a problem without a gift for you in its hands. You seek problems because you need their gifts."

Winners embrace problems because they come bearing gifts of opportunity. Through problems you display your value by displaying your level of stewardship. Problems are an opportunity to prove yourself and to improve yourself.

> **Through problems we display your value by displaying your level of stewardship. Problems are an opportunity to prove yourself and to improve yourself.**

Stewardship and its rewards are incremental. You start out by exercising excellent stewardship with little things and you will receive the appropriate recognition and reward. As you display greater levels of excellent stewardship with greater levels of resources, you will receive greater levels of reward. Jesus of Nazareth once said: "Whoever can be trusted with very little can also be trusted with a lot. Whoever is dishonest with very little is dishonest with a lot."
This verse reinforces the idea that all forms of stewardship are incremental, and that people will show the same level of stewardship with a little and with much.

> **Whoever can be trusted with very little can also be trusted with a lot. Whoever is dishonest with very little is dishonest with a lot.** Luke 16:10 GW
> *Jesus of Nazareth*

61. Certification

In order to excel in any field of endeavour, you must study as much as you possibly can in that field. Studying refers to dedicating time and effort to learn the knowledge and skills that are unique to that specific field. Once you have proven your aptitude with regards to knowledge and skill, you will be awarded the relevant certification.

Theodore Roosevelt once said: "A man who has never gone to school may steal from a freight car; but if he has a university education, he may steal the whole railroad." Theodore Roosevelt did not make this statement to encourage people to become certified thieves, but instead, he was opening our eyes to the great possibilities that lie within the reach of an educated man – the educated man can achieve so much more than the uneducated one. Certification enhances your life prospects. You can earn more money and consequently enjoy a better quality of life.

> **A man who has never gone to school may steal from a freight car; but if he has a university education, he may steal the whole railroad.**
> *Theodore Roosevelt*

Without certification you will have little or no credibility.
The sense of accomplishment that one feels after having completed a difficult course is very satisfying. Furthermore, just the knowledge of having obtained your diploma or degree will give your self-esteem a big boost.
Certification is progressive because it occurs over time and not overnight. You do not earn your high school senior certificate on your first day at high school and neither do you earn your bachelor's degree in one semester at a university. People with high self-esteem are patient as they work progressively towards their diploma or degree.
Certification is not final. There is an unhealthy pride that comes with certification and it occurs when people make the mistake of thinking that they have arrived at the pinnacle of knowledge when they obtain a degree or diploma.

> **Certification is progressive**
> **Certification is not final.**

Any pride related to one's superior knowledge should not be in one's advanced skill set relative to other less-informed individuals, but rather in the knowledge that one can now impart knowledge to others. Our knowledge should not be for ourselves. Our knowledge is utilized best when we improve the lives of others and positively impact the world through what we have learnt.
Certification is not final because, statistics have proven two important yet often overlooked facts.
Firstly, all knowledge acquired through a degree or diploma has a maximum lifespan of two years. This means that what you have learnt in terms of knowledge and skill will be outdated in the next 24 months. The only way to overcome obsolete knowledge is to continually learn. Continuous learning will ensure that you are always at the forefront of knowledge and skills related to your field of study and/or career.

Secondly, most of what people are taught at schools, colleges and university is impractical, irrelevant, useless and valueless.
Research has shown that only 20% of what is taught at learning institutions carries any real value. Unfortunately, one must also learn the other 80% in order to receive certification, but the acquisition of this additional knowledge does exercise your mind and this fact can be of comfort to those who do not want to learn what they do not need.
Certification proves your value. When you study and are able to successfully complete a course and are then awarded with a certificate or degree, you prove that you are capable of learning and you also prove that you have mastered your subjects. Thus through studying, you prove your value as a student and also your value related to the subject that you have mastered. A positive consequence that stems from proving your value related to your studies is that you are approved by others. Paul the Apostle wrote these words to Timothy: 'Study and be eager and do your utmost to present yourself to God approved (tested by trial), a workman who has no cause to be ashamed, correctly analyzing and accurately dividing [rightly handling and skillfully teaching] the Word of Truth.'

> **Study and be eager and do your utmost to present yourself to God approved (tested by trial), a workman who has no cause to be ashamed, correctly analyzing and accurately dividing [rightly handling and skillfully teaching] the Word of Truth.** **2 Timothy 2:15 AMP**
> *Paul the Apostle*

Paul the Apostle admonished Timothy to carefully study the word of God so that he can be approved by God. The principle holds true if we seek approval from men – we must study to show ourselves approved. Paul the Apostle continues by writing that you will have no shame when your knowledge is accurate and truthful. Through careful studying, you obtain the sort of value that eliminates the possibility of shame because your knowledge and skills will be accurate and truthful.

Certification proves your value.
Through careful studying, you obtain the sort of value that eliminates the possibility of shame because your knowledge and skills will be accurate and truthful.

Although certification is desirable to add credibility to an individual's knowledge and skill set, it is not always possible for people to attend formal classes in order to up-skill themselves.

Many people who leave high school cannot afford the exorbitant fees charged by tertiary institutions. In first and third world countries, this is a major barrier to certification. Unless an individual comes from an affluent family or his family has made provision through saving for his studies, that individual will have to pay for his studies by working to earn the money to pay for his tuition fees. He can either work while studying or take out a student loan and pay it back after graduating.

For someone who simply cannot find the sort of employment that pays enough to cover the costs of his studies while working, the option of on-the-job training may be a viable option until he has access to greater financial resources. In addition, he could use his free time to earn extra money through direct-selling or by providing a valuable service to people who are willing to pay for his service.

Usually, people who are already working are also raising children, and the added family responsibilities may prevent them from attending formal classes in order to increase their knowledge. Many married people who are raising children simply do not have the spare money and time to commit to evening and weekend classes.

Regardless of your circumstances, you can always increase your skill by reading good books. Reading allows you to keep company with great men, and to enjoy the fruits of a man's many years of experience in just a few minutes. Reading makes you more valuable.

Reading allows you to keep company with great men, and to enjoy the fruits of a man's many years of experience in just a few minutes. Reading makes you more valuable.

People with high self-esteem are constantly learning through formal courses and informal reading. They use every opportunity to make themselves more valuable by acquiring valuable knowledge and skills. People with high self-esteem are never bored because they capitalize on free time to make themselves worthy of the approval of men and God. People with high self-esteem are constantly on an upward spiral of learning and this translates into an upward spiral of personal value.

> **People with high self-esteem are constantly on an upward spiral of learning and this translates into an upward spiral of personal value.**

62. Coping Mechanisms

As we face life's ever-present challenges, we have to find one or more means to deal with and manage those challenges in a calm and rational manner so that we can still attain success by overcoming the challenge. However, human beings are complex creatures and we inevitably take psychological strain under the pressure of challenges and problems. Thus we find that we often have to meet the resource needs that are required to deal simultaneously with problems as well as the residual psychological needs that stem from emotions that build up inside of us. We need to have some sort of psychological pressure-release mechanism.

Being able to unwind and just relax in front of the pool or the television set may be sufficient in some cases.

Sometimes you may need a holiday in order to take your mind off your responsibilities for a short while.

Some people use substances such as drugs, alcohol, cigarettes and hubbly-bubbly pipes to cope.

Very often these substance-based psychological mechanisms can evolve into dependencies and addictions. People don't start using these substances with the intention of becoming addicted, but eventually they do, and they find themselves powerless to resist the urge to go back, again and again, to this substance.

King Solomon wrote: 'As a dog returns to his own vomit,
So a fool repeats his folly.'

> **As a dog returns to his own vomit,**
> **So a fool repeats his folly.** Proverbs 26:11 NKJV
> *King Solomon*

When you exercise your power of choice to seize an addictive substance, eventually that substance will seize you – it will seize control over your power of choice. Anyone who has relinquished his power of choice ceases to be a functional human being and slips into the realm of the animals which are driven by their instincts.

> **When you exercise your power of choice to seize an addictive substance, eventually that substance will seize you – it will seize control over your power of choice. Anyone who has relinquished his power of choice ceases to be a functional human being and slips into the realm of the animals which are driven by their instincts.**

There are times when people should seek help from others to help them cope. Support from relatives and friends can make the difference between winning and losing. When people open up to someone they can trust, the mere fact that they are able to talk about their experiences can be therapeutic. In addition, the person who is listening may have one or more valuable suggestions pertaining to how the speaker may cope with his challenges and feelings in a rational and effective manner.

Getting help from others can sometimes make the difference between life and death. I am always saddened when I am informed about someone who committed suicide, especially when it is a learner at one of the schools where my colleagues and I voluntarily run mentoring and coaching programs.

If that young boy or girl who has committed suicide had just taken a few minutes to talk to someone who could help, they could still have been alive. If they had spoken to someone who could make them see their value, they would be a little more courageous and be able to cope with the immense pressure that they were feeling at that point.

Sometimes people must seek professional guidance and therapy to help them cope effectively. The assistance that is available from suitably trained and qualified counsellors, therapists, psychologists and psychiatrists is invaluable. It is not just crazy people who need psychological and psychiatric help, but instead these treatment alternatives are beneficial for anyone who feels devalued by life and other people. Qualified professionals will help people cope with:

- the feelings that they experience due to life's pressures; and
- undoing the damage caused by harmful behaviour patterns and dependency on harmful addictive substances.

Dr. Abraham Maslow described therapy as 'a search for value.'

From this statement, we can clearly see that the very basis of therapy is to help the patient find value – value in other people, value in a situation, but most importantly value in himself. When a person is able to see his own value, then the very purpose of therapy has been attained, because when someone is enlightened, as if for the first time, to their own immense value, they are given a new lease on life. With this new lease comes a willingness to fight again and to pursue valuable goals. The man who is enlightened to his own value becomes a powerful and unstoppable force – he can cope with life's challenges and courageously takes on new challenges out of choice in order to assert his belief in his own worth and the value of his dreams.

> **We may define therapy as a search for value.**
> *Abraham Maslow*

People with high self-esteem use coping mechanisms to restore and revitalize their psychological and physical strength. They understand that the abuse of coping mechanisms can cause them to sink to levels below their actual value and worth, so they actively avoid succumbing to the momentary pleasures of life that can lead to life-long misery.

> **The man who is enlightened to his own value becomes a powerful and unstoppable force – he**

can cope with life's challenges and courageously takes on new challenges out of choice in order to assert his belief in his own worth and the value of his dreams.

63. Completeness

The world is not utopic – there are no perfect people and no perfect conditions. Nobody is so complete that they are not in need of growth and improvement in one or more areas of their life.

The individual must realise that he is not perfect and that the people around him are not perfect. Nobody is complete. Everybody is imperfect. Imperfect people behave imperfectly, say imperfect things and deliver imperfect work. Humanity consists of imperfect people trying to get by in an imperfect world.

Humanity consists of imperfect people trying to get by in an imperfect world.

If I am to forge healthy relationships with other people, I cannot expect them to display superhuman strength, knowledge and abilities. Most of all, I cannot expect people to be perfect. The most that I can do is to be tolerant of the shortcomings of other people. Without tolerance, I cannot hope for longevity in the relationship. Tolerance of people's shortcomings is essential for the sustained existence of any relationship. Perfectionism is a psychological state which drives people to set very high, often unrealistic goals for themselves and others. Perfectionists are very focused on delivering a superior quality of work.

Perfectionism can be beneficial or detrimental. Perfectionism is beneficial when people produce the highest quality of work possible and people feel a high sense of self-esteem and accomplishment. Perfectionism is detrimental when expectations are unrealistic and people fall short of their targets. Failure to reach targets can cause people to fall into a state of depression.

People with high self-esteem value the contribution of others, but they do not set unrealistic and perfect goals for others. In addition, they refrain from setting unrealistic goals

and delivery standards for themselves. Diverse people have diverse standards of contribution and abilities. People work at different paces and they deliver varying standards of work.
People with high self-esteem value the very best in people and they value the very best that people are able to deliver realistically.

> **People with high self-esteem value the very best in people and they value the very best that people are able to deliver realistically.**

64. Completion
Many people have brilliant ideas. They start out on the journey to realise their dreams and goals, but somewhere along the journey their enthusiasm fizzles and they abandon their pursuits.
It has been said that the most expensive real-estate is the world's graveyards, because these are the places where many unfulfilled dreams are buried along with the dreamers. Many of those dreamers started out to fulfil their dreams, but sadly their dreams died with them. I suppose that it will be impossible to put a value to all those dead dreams, but it can be said with confidence that there are as many dead and buried dreams as there are dead and buried people in the graveyard.

> **It will be impossible to put a value to all those dead dreams, but it can be said with confidence that there are as many dead and buried dreams as there are dead and buried people in the graveyard.**

Jesus once asked this question to a group of people: "For which of you, intending to build a tower, does not sit down first and count the cost, whether he has enough to finish it—lest, after he has laid the foundation, and is not able to finish, all who see it begin to mock him, saying, 'This man began to build and was not able to finish'?" Luke 14:28-30 NKJV

Jesus was warning us about the need to count the cost of your pursuits in advance, and then to pay the full price until completion.

People with high self-esteem do not begin what they cannot afford to complete, but they complete that which is within their means to finish. People with high self-esteem start strong and end strong. In order to start strong, you must have a realistic idea of what the project will cost, and then you must decide if you can afford the cost. Lastly, you must pay the cost until you attain completion. Failure to attain completion of any project leads to public embarrassment. However, successful completion of a project causes people to respect and honour you – they value you greatly.

Failure to attain completion of any project leads to public embarrassment. However, successful completion of a project causes people to respect and honour you – they value you greatly.

65. Compulsions

Human beings are driven by strong irresistible forces to do certain things or behave in a certain way. There are natural compulsions and unnatural compulsions that we have to deal with.

The basic human needs for food, sleep and intimacy with other people are natural compulsions. The afore-mentioned needs are absolutely necessary for survival. In addition, we also have aesthetic compulsions such as looking good and being attractive to members of the opposite sex. Then we have compulsions for self-fulfilment as we pursue goals such as winning an athletic race or becoming someone who is valued and respected by others such as being a doctor, lawyer, corporate leader, successful entrepreneur etc.

We need our compulsions because the basic ones ensure our on-going survival, aesthetic ones ensure that we feel good about ourselves relative to other people and the compulsions of self-fulfilment drive us to fully utilize our inner potential and make something worthwhile and valuable of ourselves.

Our compulsions are meant for good, but sometimes they may drive people to do despicable things to themselves or others.

In school some students cheat because their compulsion to pass is greater than their desire to be truthful and honest. Some people resort to hurting others because they want to assert their own strength – they devalue others so that they can feel some warped sense of self-worth. This is the case when someone uses a firearm to go on a shooting and killing spree in a public place. Unfortunately, there is no place that is really immune to the devastation that is caused by people who cannot control their urges to harm innocent people. In recent months, in 2015 as this book is being completed, there have been reports of such shooting cases in France, the United States of America and in Africa.

Many criminals, such as serial rapists and murderers have an insatiable desire to get to their next victim. They feel a strange sense of power when they are able to take someone else's power of choice, and even their life from them.

People who cannot control their evil urges inflict harm on the innocent.

Unless your compulsion for doing good exceeds your compulsion to inflict harm on the next person, you will be a liability to yourself and to society. You will hurt others and yourself and eventually earn the disdain of people instead of their respect. You will be seen as a pariah that is of no worth and value. People who value the wellbeing of others will earn the respect of others. When you value other people, and subdue your urges to harm someone, even when angered, you will eventually earn their respect in return and be regarded as valuable.

People with high self-esteem relinquish any desire to inflict pain on other people. Their lives are focused on doing good and not evil. The compulsion to do good is a higher value objective than the compulsion to do evil.

> **People with high self-esteem relinquish any desire to inflict pain on other people. Their lives are focused on doing good and not evil.**
> **The compulsion to do good is a higher value objective than the compulsion to do evil.**

66. Collaborative Effort

The word ***synergy*** comes from the Greek word ***sunergós*** which is made up of the word ***sun*** meaning '*together*' and ***ergon*** meaning '*work*.'

Synergy simply means that the whole is greater than the sum of the individual parts. In sociology, synergy refers to the benefit that is attained by combining various individuals, groups and organizations. When people come together and work together, the total output and effectiveness of the combined group is much greater than the sum of the work that the individuals or groups would have produced in isolation. Collaborative effort is more beneficial for everyone than isolated effort. Collaborative effort is synergy. Synergistic value far exceeds individual value.

Below is a description of The Seven Benefits of Synergy (collaborative effort).

The Seven Benefits of Synergy

1. Through synergy, we are able to do much more than we would on our own.

The group's effectiveness in a synergistic partnership far exceeds the effectiveness of the individual's. Helen Keller once said: 'Alone we can do so little; together we can do so much.'

This statement captures the truth about synergy as it relates to our accomplishments – we achieve *so much* if we work together, but alone we achieve *so little.*

Through synergy the value and the quantity of our work is greater than the value and the quantity of work we produce in isolation. True co-operation multiplies effectiveness.

> **Alone we can do so little;**
> **together we can do so much.**
> *Helen Keller*

2. Through synergy, we have a greater reward for our work.

Since we increase our effectiveness through collaborative effort, the resultant reward is greater. Everyone receives a greater reward than he would have on his own. King

Solomon wrote: 'Two are better than one; because they have a good reward for their labour.'
The term ***good reward*** in this verse refers to compensation that is '*fair, agreeable and valuable.*'
Through synergy we receive greater value for our efforts.

> **Two are better than one; because they have a good reward for their labour.** Ecclesiastes 4:9 KJV
> *King Solomon*

3. Through synergy we easily recover from adversity because we have someone to lift us up when we fall.
As we go through life, we encounter circumstances that make us stumble and fall. Falling is a metaphor for being weakened and disabled by adversities and circumstances in such a way that you will need time and resources to recover. Sometimes you can be so severely weakened, you may never recover if you have no help but if you have someone who can assist you with resources and effort, you can easily recover to your former state. King Solomon wrote: 'If either of them falls down, one can help the other up. But pity anyone who falls and has no one to help them up.'
King Solomon warns us that the man who does not have the benefit of a synergistic partnership is in a pitiful state, but he also praises the benefit that comes from synergy. That benefit is help. We have the benefit of someone close-by who can lift us up. Through synergy we gain the value of help.

> **If either of them falls down, one can help the other up. But pity anyone who falls and has no one to help them up.** Proverbs 4:10 NIV
> *King Solomon*

4. Through synergy we benefit from various levels of intimacy.
When we associate and collaborate with others, we enjoy the benefit of intimacy. The type of relationship will determine the level of intimacy. We will not be very open concerning our feelings with everybody we have a conversation with, and we will only have a romantic relationship where there is commitment and trust. Our range of friends and close

associations will meet our needs for intimacy and human contact on various levels. Synergistic social interactions provide us with valuable human contact and intimacy.

> **Synergistic social interactions provide us with valuable human contact and intimacy.**

5. ***Through synergy our personal attributes become useful and are also amplified.***

> **Also, if two lie down together, they will keep warm.**
> **But how can one keep warm alone?** Proverbs 4:11 NIV
> *King Solomon*

King Solomon wrote: 'Also, if two lie down together, they will keep warm. But how can one keep warm alone?'
All of us have a measure of heat in us, but that heat is quickly lost if we lie alone in cold weather. However, the heat that is generated by two people lying next to each other, even when there is no sexual intimacy, is higher than if someone lies alone. In addition the combined heat does not dissipate as fast. In this illustration we see firstly, that the individual's personal body heat becomes useful to both parties, and secondly, the combined heat that is produced is greater than the heat produced by each individual party.
In our illustration, the heat is simply a metaphor which represents our personal attributes such as our inner strengths, unique characteristics, talents gifts and abilities. Through synergistic partnership we are able to tap into our inner strengths and unique endowments. When we do this, we are able to bless others and ourselves because everyone can benefit from the proverbial warmth generated from the hot abilities that we have inside of us.
Just as the heat is magnified in our illustration, the endowments that we put to use in a synergistic environment are also amplified.
Synergy creates opportunities that make the individual's unique endowments useful but in addition, the individual's endowments are amplified for the mutual benefit of

everyone involved. Through synergy our unique attributes become valuable.

> **Synergy creates opportunities that make the individual's unique endowments useful but in addition, the individual's endowments are amplified for the mutual benefit of everyone involved. Through synergy our unique attributes become valuable.**

6. Through synergy we have a strong defence.

Synergy permits the individual the benefit of leaning on the combined strength of everyone in the group. When we are in a synergistic partnership, an insult to one becomes an insult to all. King Solomon wrote: 'A cord of three strands is not quickly broken.'

King Solomon was praising the strength that comes from unity. There is a unique sort of strength that is established when individuals stand together. When one individual in the group is threatened, the entire group comes to his defence.

> **A cord of three strands is not quickly broken.** Ecclesiastes 4:12 NIV
> *King Solomon*

7. Through synergy we are empowered, and not overpowered.

King Solomon wrote: 'Though one may be overpowered, two can defend themselves.'

The maxim 'United we stand, divided we fall,' is attributed to Aesop, the ancient Greek storyteller.

This expression simply means that we will all survive if we stand and fight together, but we will all die if we fight alone. Aesop was simply repeating what King Solomon had said.

It is through synergy that we are able to tap into collaborative power that produces unparalleled levels of safety for everyone in the group. In stark contrast, people who isolate themselves are extremely vulnerable and are usually quickly overpowered by an adversary. King Solomon warned that anyone who isolates themselves from others is raging against all wisdom.

**Though one may be overpowered,
two can defend themselves.** Ecclesiastes 4:12 NIV
King Solomon

Whoever isolates himself seeks his own desire; he breaks out against all sound judgment. Proverbs 18:1 ESV
King Solomon

Through collaborative effort we tap into the amazing abilities that are resident in other people and we also gain access to their resources such as capital, knowledge and skill. Through collaborative effort, what is impossible to do on your own becomes possible because you are not alone.

Through collaborative effort, what is impossible to do on your own becomes possible because you are not alone.

Besides making all contributors and partners more valuable, collaborative effort gives you the benefit of having people to celebrate success with. It is a very satisfying feeling to be able to rejoice and be grateful for the contributions that others have made to bring about the individual's or the organization's success. When we all work together we will all benefit together – we will also all celebrate success together.

When we all work together we will all benefit together – we will also all celebrate success together.

People with high self-esteem continuously forge partnerships in order to attain worthwhile goals through collaborative effort. They do not stand on their own strength alone, but instead they lean on the strength of others too.

67. Christ Jesus

King Solomon wrote: 'the sons of men are snared in an evil time.' Ecclesiastes 9:12 NKJV
The evil is of such a nature that men do not know who they are and how God sees them. To rectify the incorrect perception that men have about themselves and God, the

creator of the universe came down from His throne in Heaven to give us a new hope. Jesus Christ is the creator who was manifest in the flesh.

> **The thief comes only to steal and kill and destroy; I have come that they may have life, and have it to the full.** John 10:10 NIV
> *Jesus of Nazareth*

Jesus was very clear about his mission. He came to give life to people, and to give it in full measure. The word ***life*** comes from the original Greek word ***zōē*** which means:

1. *'the state of one who is possessed of vitality,'*
2. *'the absolute fullness of life, both essentially and ethically,'*
3. *'the same life as God,' and*
4. *'real and genuine life, a life devoted to God and also extending into eternal life.'*

From the definition of *zōē* we can see that Jesus came to give a form of life that is the very same as God has. It is a life of vitality, joy and fullness which extends into all eternity. This is a life of completeness.
Jesus also explained that the *zōē* life does not consist of what one has.

> **Take heed and beware of covetousness, for one's life does not consist in the abundance of the things he possesses.** Luke 12:15 NKJV
> **He who believes in the Son has everlasting life; and he who does not believe the Son shall not see life, but the wrath of God abides on him.** John 3:36 KJV
> *Jesus of Nazareth*

The *zōē* life is not about worldly possessions. An abundance of worldly possessions is not evidence of the *zōē* life.
How then does one attain the *zōē* life?
This life comes through unfailing belief in Christ Jesus. When we belief in Him, and when we confess with our mouths that He is Lord and belief in our hearts that God has raised Him from the dead, we shall be saved. We shall be rescued from mediocrity and low self-esteem.

> **My dear children, for whom I am again in the pains of childbirth until Christ is formed in you.** Galatians 4:19 NIV
> **To them God willed to make known what are the riches of the glory of this mystery among the Gentiles: which is Christ in you, the hope of glory.** Colossians 1:27 NIV
> *Paul the Apostle*

Paul the Apostle explained to us that he was perpetually in pain, as if in labour, so that the mystery of the gospel may be revealed in us. The mystery of the gospel is that we have a hope of glory. The word glory comes from the Greek word ***doxa*** which means:

1. *'a good opinion concerning one, resulting in praise, honour, and glory, splendour, brightness;'*
2. *'magnificence, excellence, pre-eminence, dignity, grace;'*
3. *'a thing belonging to Christ;'*
4. *'a most glorious condition, most exalted state;'*
5. *'the kingly majesty which belongs to him as supreme ruler, majesty in the sense of the absolute perfection of the deity;' and*
6. *'the glorious condition of blessedness into which is appointed and promised that true Christians shall enter after their Saviour's return from heaven.'* [xl]
7. *'the true nature of someone or something.'*

The hope of glory is a hope of attaining God's good opinion and being seen as very valuable by God. It is a hope of attaining splendour, brightness, praise, being exalted, being perfect and being exactly the same as our creator and saviour, Christ Jesus. Man can never be more valuable than his creator. The knowledge that a man can be equally valuable as his creator is truly inspiring and comforting. Being loved by God Almighty and having Christ Jesus formed in you is the highest level of value that any individual can aspire to and attain. Christ formed in you is attaining the zenith of your value. There is no higher state of esteem and self-esteem that an individual can ever reach.

> **Having Christ Jesus formed in you is the highest level of value that any individual can aspire to and attain. Christ formed in you is attaining the zenith of your value. There is no higher state of esteem and self-esteem that an individual can ever reach.**

68. Consecration

> **Man shall not live on bread alone, but on every word that comes from the mouth of God.** Matthew 4:4 NIV
> *Jesus of Nazareth*

Every person must consecrate his life to a being and purpose that is firstly higher than self and secondly, supernatural. Since man is a spirit being wrapped in an exterior of flesh, each man must be cognisant of his eternal spirit and the path that it will travel when his body dies. Jesus of Nazareth said: "Man shall not live by bread alone but by every word that proceeds from the mouth of God."

Reading God's word and obeying it is one of the aspects of leading a consecrated life. We are to feed our spirits with the spiritual food which is God's word just as we feed our bodies with physical food. God's spiritual food strengthens us for this life and the life after death. We must all therefore be committed to the consumption of God's word because through it we are directed and assisted to lead lives that are devoted to our creator.

We all face many challenges and problems as we navigate through any given day and we need to invoke assistance to help us carry on. We have the privilege of invoking divine assistance through the medium of prayer. Prayer is another aspect of leading a consecrated life. Through prayer we are strengthened and we receive supernatural guidance to make right choices. Through the medium of prayer we are able to move the mighty hand of God on our behalf and we are also able to enjoy His awesome protection and security. King David, the ancient Jewish monarch, had a deep relationship with God. This relationship consisted primarily of prayer, praise and worship. In Psalm 91 King David wrote about 'the secret place of the Most High.' He continues by writing: 'I

will say of the Lord, He is my refuge and my fortress: My God, in Him will I trust.'
The *secret place* which David was referring to was the place where he spoke to God – where he declared his faith and trust in God to God Himself. King David also expounds the great benefit that is granted to those who *dwell in the secret place of the Most High* when he writes that they 'shall abide under the shadow of the Almighty.'
Prayer is that secret place and it brings us so close to God that we are directly under His shadow. When we are in God's shadow we are in a place of complete confidence, protection, safety, joy and peace. This protection is a benefit of building a deep relationship with God through the medium of prayer. When we pray regularly we begin to understand who God is and who we are.
Through having a deeply-committed relationship with God Almighty one can attain a high level of self-esteem which is shaped by God's opinion of who we are. This opinion is echoed many times in the bible.

> **Through having a deeply-committed relationship with God Almighty one can attain a high level of self-esteem which is shaped by God's opinion of who you are.**

Words cannot express my immense gratitude to God for the privilege of prayer. As you read the following excerpt from my past, you will see that my own life is a living testament of the power of prayer.

One morning, when I was about four years old, I was eating a biscuit and I suddenly experienced violent seizures. My parents rushed me to hospital. After a thorough examination the medical doctors concluded that I had experienced an epileptic seizure. I was immediately placed on a stringent program of strong medication to combat this life-threatening condition. The seizures still persisted. The medication had an adverse effect at some point and had brought on paralysis of my lower extremities resulting in an inability to walk. Fortunately the paralysis was short-lived but the epilepsy persisted. Every time I suffered a seizure I would suffer simultaneous, irreversible brain damage – so the medical doctors and professors claimed. When I was eight years old, my mother had an encounter with God and became a born-again Christian at an evangelism meeting. She joined a local church and she was taught about the benefits of prayer and having a deep relationship with God. Due to the severity of my condition, I had to stay out of school regularly so that I could go for tests at the hospital where I was being treated. My mother usually took off a few hours from work in order to take me to the hospital. One morning, when I was about nine years old, and about a year after my mother had become born again, she said something to me in the hospital as we were waiting for the nurses and the medical professor to examine me. She said to me that we must pray together so that God can heal me. She spoke with a strong conviction. It was only later in my life that I understood that conviction to be faith. She said the prayer in a manner depicting the true love and concern that only a mother can display. When the medical professor was ready to see us, my mother was seated at the table across from him and I was on the floor playing with my toys. The professor, who was usually quite talkative, was completely silent as he paged back and forth through my medical file and he would occasionally look at me and then at my mother with a perplexed face. He seemed completely bewildered. After approximately 15 minutes of the uncomfortable silence my mother became quite agitated and told the professor to be straight with her about her child's condition and not keep silent. She did not want to be kept in suspense. The professor responded by saying that she did not understand why he was silent. He then proceeded to ask if this was definitely the same child who had been tested a few weeks before. She confirmed that I was the same child, although she did not understand the relevance of the question. The professor then went on to explain that the charts from the previous tests were indicative of a very sickly and worsening child, but that new chart, that day's chart, was one of a completely normal child.

The professor was shocked by the miraculous and sudden turn-around of my medical condition. Ya'weh Rapha (God our Healer) healed me completely.

My medication was gradually decreased, and so were my doctor's visits, until I was given a clean bill of health some time later. I am happy to report that I have never again suffered an epileptic seizure and I have not taken medication for that condition since the day the doctors finally stopped the treatment.

My healing is a testament of the immense power of prayer. It is a testament of the benefit of dwelling in the secret place of the Most High.

In my adult life I have discovered further benefits of prayer. It is a medium by which you can bring your petitions for yourself and others before God. This, however, is a secondary benefit because I see prayer as being more than an opportunity to bring a wish-list to God as if he were Santa Clause during the Christmas season. I have discovered that prayer is the ideal opportunity to give thanks to God for His many blessings and His grace that He bestows upon me and my loved ones daily. I have discovered that through Holy Spirit inspired prayer I am able to tap into the infinite wisdom and infinite power that is resident in God, the Great Creator. This access to supernatural power and wisdom is the exclusive domain of praying people and through it they receive revelation, inspiration, confirmation and edification. Revelation is a deep understanding of both natural and spiritual matters. Inspiration is creative ideas, original thoughts, words of knowledge and prophecy. Confirmation is when you are in complete unison with the Holy Spirit. Edification is when you are strengthened in the spiritual and in the natural.

I bring all my activities before God so that my efforts will be blessed and so that I am Holy Spirit-inspired and enabled. Thus, any success that I may enjoy is as a result of God's grace and provision. Even this book is a testament of God's divine inspiration in my life because I have received all the teaching, guidance, information and understanding, contained herein, from Him.

Staying close to God has surprisingly given me access to creative abilities that I never dreamed of, but I should not be surprised because God is so creative that He conceived and created the entire universe and all its creatures – including you and me.

My secrets have come from God's secret place, and this has given me a level of self-esteem and self-confidence that I have not known before. I have high self-esteem because my value is on an ever-increasing spiral due to my connection to the all-knowing, all-over and all-powerful God. My self-confidence is high, not because it is inwardly directed, but because it is outwardly directed by God's wisdom and guidance.

I advise you to learn to tap into God's magnificent providence through living a life that is consecrated to Him. The joy and successes that you will experience will put your self-esteem and self-confidence on steroids – divine steroids.

> **Learn to tap into God's magnificent providence through living a life that is consecrated to Him. The joy and successes that you will experience will put your self-esteem and self-confidence on steroids – divine steroids.**

69. Costliest Asset

Your costliest asset is your most valuable asset.

Your most valuable asset is not your child or your spouse. Your most valuable asset is not your house. Your most valuable asset is not your car. Your most valuable asset is not your bank balance. Your most valuable asset is not your pension fund. Your most valuable asset is not your investment portfolio.

Jesus of Nazareth asked the question: "For what will it profit a man if he gains the whole world, and loses his own soul? Or what will a man give in exchange for his soul?"

> **For what will it profit a man if he gains the whole world, and loses his own soul?**
> **Or what will a man give in exchange for his soul?** Mark 8:36-37 NKJV
> *Jesus of Nazareth*

Your soul is that eternal part of you that does not die. Losing your soul is a metaphor for losing your eternal freedom. Jesus was asking what a man has gained if he amasses all the wealth that the world can offer but in the end he still loses his eternal freedom. You lose your eternal freedom when you fail to qualify for God's righteous approval and you are eternally separated from God. When you are eternally separated from God, you do not cease to exist, but you continue to exist in an environment of eternal torture and suffering. This will be the punishment for those people who did not value their own souls sufficiently by paying the price for eternal salvation. If you truly value your precious soul, you will pay the required price that produces eternal life, and you will have salvation. But failure to pay the price leads to condemnation.

> **If you truly value your precious soul, you will pay the required price that produces eternal life, and you will have salvation. But failure to pay the price leads to condemnation.**

Before ascending into Heaven, Jesus Christ gave His disciples an instruction to show people the value of their souls and to explain the way of eternal salvation to them. Jesus said: "Go into all the world and preach the gospel to every creature. He who believes and is baptized will be saved; but he who does not believe will be condemned."

> **And He *(Jesus)* said to them, "Go into all the world and preach the gospel to every creature. He who believes and is baptized will be saved; but he who does not believe will be condemned.** Mark 16:15-16 NKJV

Before His crucifixion Jesus met with a man named Nicodemus. Nicodemus was a prominent religious leader and he had covertly sneaked away from under the observation of his fellow religious scholars to meet with Jesus. During this meeting Nicodemus asked Jesus how a man can be born again after Jesus warned him that a man must be born again if he wishes to enter Heaven. Being born again does not refer to a physical rebirth, but instead it refers to a spiritual rebirth. Jesus informed Nicodemus that unless a man is born of water and of the Spirit, he can never see Heaven.

High self-esteem concerning your achievements, your abilities and your limitless potential is still a vain commodity if you do not value your own soul. If you truly value your soul – that eternal part of you that never dies, then you must meet God's requirements as proof that you do not take lightly or for granted what He has given you. Your soul is really the only thing that is truly yours because everything else in this mortal life you will leave behind when you die.

> **Your soul is really the only thing that is truly yours because everything else in this mortal life you will leave behind when you die.**

If you want to add a premium to the value of your soul, and enjoy a loving relationship with God your creator and also the benefit of an eternal life, you can say this prayer:

> *Heavenly Father, Thank you for valuing me so much that you sent your beloved Son Jesus to die on a cross for my sins.*
> *I confess that I am a sinner in need of salvation and I ask for your forgiveness of all my sins.*
> *I confess with my mouth that Jesus Christ is Lord, and I believe in my heart that you have raised Him from the dead.*
> *Come into my heart, and remake me into the valuable person that you intended me to be.*
> *Give me the same eternal life that Jesus has.*
> *Seal me with the precious and valuable blood of Jesus so that I will not return to my old ways.*
> *I thank you now for my salvation.*
> *I thank you that my valuable soul can now enjoy eternal life because of your grace.*
> *Amen.*

Your soul is your most valuable asset. You don't have to lose your soul because of ignorance and/or pride. The most valuable people in God's eyes are those who do not take the value of their own souls and the value of the sacrifice of His son Jesus lightly. If you value your own soul then you will value the opportunity for eternal life that is available to those who take full advantage of the grace shown to all mankind by God, the Creator, by offering them the sort of value that translates into an eternally happy existence.

> **Your soul is your most valuable asset.**
> **If you value your own soul then you will value the opportunity for eternal life that is available to those who take full advantage of the grace shown to all mankind by God, the Creator, by offering them the sort of value that translates into an eternally happy existence.**

70. Confessions

The word ***confession*** comes from the Latin word ***confessus*** which is the past participle of ***confiteri***, from ***con*** which means *'expression of intense force'* and ***fateri*** which means *'admit, acknowledge, declare, avow.'* ***Fateri*** is related to the Latin word ***fari,*** which means *'to speak, to talk, to say.'* Confessions relate to the things we say with intensity, force and belief. Jesus of Nazareth said: 'For the mouth speaks what the heart is full of.'
The word ***heart*** in this verse refers to the mind which is the *'seat of the thoughts, passions, desires, appetites, affections, purposes, endeavours of the understanding, the faculty and seat of the intelligence; of the will and character.'* [xli]

> **For the mouth speaks what the heart is full of.** Luke 6:45c NLT
> *Jesus of Nazareth*

Jesus was warning us that our speech is an indication of the thoughts and beliefs that are resident in our minds. A person's speech is a sure indicator of what he thinks. Confessions are spoken words that uncover the true thoughts, beliefs and convictions of an individual. Our speaking is nothing more than an uncovering of what cannot be seen with the naked eye. Through his speech a man opens his heart and exposes his intimate contemplations. Through our speech we also acknowledge, assert and affirm our beliefs – we reinforce and anchor what we are convinced of. It therefore follows that our confessions are powerful weapons which can make us or break us. We must thus be wary about what we say, because we just may be anchoring an incorrect belief and/or perception.

> **Our confessions are powerful weapons which can make us or break us.**

The one topic about which we all must guard our confessions is about who we are and what we can do. As soon as you hear something negative about yourself proceeding from your mouth you must immediately begin to implement changes in your thought patterns. This is referred to as a paradigm shift.
How does one implement a paradigm shift?
In order to change your thoughts, you must first understand an important principle. When Jesus stated that the mouth speaks what the heart is full of, He was stating a timeless principle. I like to call it **The Principle of Confession.** In this principle lies a hidden secret – a secret that empowers us to forge and mould new thoughts about anything.
Just as what the heart is full of shapes what is in the mouth, so what the mouth is full of can shape what is in the heart. The Principle of Confession works both ways – the mouth can both impress and express what is in the heart. By deliberately changing the things we say about ourselves we ***impress*** new thoughts about ourselves in our minds. Eventually our mouths ***express*** the good and healthy thoughts that we have about ourselves. Your expression will be a healthy confession.

> **Just as what the heart is full of shapes what is in the mouth, so what the mouth is full of can shape what is in the heart. The Principle of Confession works both ways – the mouth can both impress and express what is in the heart.**

People with healthy self-esteem are very vigilant about their confessions. They watch over their words because they understand that words are powerful. The next chapter covers the words, also called '**affirmations**' or '**confessions**' that you can use to build high self-esteem, change your life and be a winner who attains phenomenal success.

Value Is ...

Value is allowing me to do what I love,
And letting me soar like an eagle in the sky above.

Value is treating me kind and fair,
And helping me my burdens to bare.

Value is looking beyond what the eye can see,
It is seeing all I can do and possibly be.

Value is appreciating me, even if we are not alike,
Thru our differences a good partnership we can strike.

Value is to not despise me for what I lack,
But rather, it is about always having my back.

Value is allowing me to shine my inner light,
And letting me stand in a place that for me is right.

Value is lifting me up if I fall,
And not making me feel insignificant and small.

Value is helping me during my time of need,
And nursing my wounds when I suffer and bleed.

Glisson J. Heldzinger

YOU ARE VALUABLE

Know Your Value

There is something that only you can do;
There is somebody that only you can be;
There is a word that only you can speak;
There is an act that only you can perform;
There is a thing that only you can create;
There is a contribution that only you can make,
There is a place that only you can walk;
There is a song that only you can sing;
There is a book that only you can write;
There is a picture that only you can paint;
There is a story that only you can tell;
There is help that only you can give;
There is a need that only you can meet;
There is a unique value that only you can bring:
Know your value,
Grow your value,
Show your value,
Bestow your value.

Glisson J. Heldzinger

Chapter 8

The Power Of Affirmations

Every day, in every way, I'm getting better and better.
Émile Coué

What are affirmations?

Émile Coué was a French pharmacist and psychologist who has been widely accepted as being the father of the method of autosuggestion for the use in psychotherapy, self-healing and self-improvement. Coué developed the method of autosuggestion whilst working in an apothecary, which is similar to a modern-day pharmacy, in Troyes between 1882 and 1910. Coué discovered that when he praised the efficacy of dispensed medication to a patient that the patient's recovery was significantly greater than that of patients to whom he did not comment on the medication. This phenomenon has come to be known as *The Placebo Effect.* Coué first experimented with hypnosis as a tool to cure psychological and physical illnesses, but it produced little success. Eventually Coué began to explore the placebo effect in greater depth. He believed in medication, and he also believed that the mental state of a patient and the patient's faith in the efficacy of the medication affected the effectiveness of medication. Using the power of suggestion, he would praise the medication to create belief and trust concerning the reliability of the medication, in the patient's mind. This was employing the power of *suggestion*. Eventually Coué began to develop a method whereby suggestion could come from the patient himself, calling it *autosuggestion*. Coué believed that patients could cure themselves through their thinking. His philosophy was based on the idea that people could more readily cure themselves from sickness and disease by thinking about being well instead of thinking about being sick.
In his book, titled *Self Mastery Through Conscious Autosuggestion,* Coué described autosuggestion as:

"... an instrument that we possess at birth, and with which we play unconsciously all our life, as a baby plays with its rattle. It is however a dangerous instrument; it can wound or even kill you if you handle it imprudently and unconsciously. It can on the contrary save your life when you know how to employ it consciously." [xlii]

Coué developed a tenet-like statement that reinforced positive mental thoughts in the minds of his patients concerning their overall health and well-being. In Coué's native French, the statement read as follows:

'Toes les ours à tours points de vie je vain de mix en mix.'

In English, this statement reads as follows:

'Every day, in every way, I'm getting better and better.'

Coué recommended that this statement, and others like it, be repeated in a ritualized fashion at least 20 times daily, especially in the morning when waking and at night when retiring to bed.

During the early twentieth century Coué gained international fame for his methods, and his tenet was used in many countries, but mostly in Europe. His mantra-like tenet became known as Couéism.

Couéism gained great popularity in the medical and self-improvement fraternities. In medical fraternities, many doctors who employ the Placebo Effect have achieved significant results by prescribing *trick-medication* to patients. Even though the medication has absolutely no effect on the body and the disease, the patient's belief in the medication brings about healing. In the self-improvement fraternity, philosophical thinkers such as the American clergyman Dr. Norman Vincent Peale and the author Napoleon Hill readily practiced and taught the concept of autosuggestion and its benefits.

Dr. Norman Vincent Peale wrote: 'Watch your manner of speech if you wish to develop a peaceful state of mind. Start each day by affirming peaceful, contented and happy attitudes and your days will tend to be pleasant and successful.'

In the book *Think & Grow Rich*, Napoleon Hill described autosuggestion in the following way:

'AUTO-SUGGESTION is a term which applies to all suggestions and all self-administered stimuli which reach one's mind through the five senses. Stated in another way, auto-suggestion is self-suggestion. It is the agency of communication between that part of the mind where conscious thought takes place, and that which serves as the seat of action for the subconscious mind.' [xliii]

He went on to write:

'AUTO-SUGGESTION is the agency of control through which an individual may voluntarily feed his subconscious mind on thoughts of a creative nature, or, by neglect, permit thoughts of a destructive nature to find their way into this rich garden of the mind.' [xliv]

Napoleon Hill is saying that the ideas and thoughts which an individual entertains will be the ones that will be suggested, or shaped, by what the individual hears, sees, tastes, smells and feels.

As individuals, we can control the suggestions that reach our minds via the five senses through auto-suggestion.

Auto-suggestion is self-administered, according to Émile Coué and Napoleon Hill, and it is the agency through which we deliberately feed our subconscious mind with positive or negative thoughts.

The ancient Greeks understood the power of suggestion and autosuggestion. Using the methods of suggestion and autosuggestion, they taught and practiced many principles which we now refer to as maxims. There were more than one hundred of these Greek maxims and they covered a broad range of topics such as religion, honour, prudence, love, self-knowledge, marriage, relationships, wisdom, education, kindness, judgement, thriftiness, patriotism, self-discipline, old-age and death.

Pythagoras, the Greek philosopher and mathematician who lived from circa 570 BC to circa 495 BC, said:

"Let no one persuade you by word or deed to do or say whatever is not best for you."

He also added:

"God the Father, deliver them from their sufferings, and show them what supernatural power is at their call."

We can see clearly, that Pythagoras understood the 'supernatural power' of auto-suggestion. It has the ability to deliver people from their sufferings.

As one delves deeper into human history, especially in the area of religious and philosophical manuscripts, we discover that knowledge of the power of autosuggestion was around for many centuries before Pythagoras was born.
Joshua, the son of Nun, was an ancient Jewish leader who lived circa 1355 BC to circa 1245 BC. Concerning the Books of the Law, or *torah*, God commanded Joshua to tell the people of Israel:
"This Book of the Law shall not depart from your mouth, but you shall meditate in it day and night, that you may observe to do according to all that is written in it. For then you will make your way prosperous, and then you will have good success." [xlv]
There are seven truths that emerge from this text, namely:

1. the Book of the Law, was not to depart from their mouths, which meant that they (the Israelites) were to confess and affirm it all continuously;
2. they were to meditate, or think about the law all the time,
3. their actions would then be predicated by the law,
4. God gave the Israelites this instruction because He understood that we shape our perceptions, then our behaviour and then our destiny through repetition of positive and uplifting affirmative self-talk,
5. this self-talk can bring about everything that pertains to success but it can also bring about failure,
6. it works for any field of thought, not only religious thoughts,
7. through this process of affirmations the Israelites would bring about their own prosperity and success - positive self-talk, or affirmations, and focussed thoughts which produce positive actions are the only way to achieve prosperity and success.

In the book *Míshlê Shlomoh*, King Solomon, who reigned as the king of Israel from circa 970 BC to circa 931 BC, recorded many 'mashal' which are powerful two or four line short-sayings of wisdom in Hebrew.
These sayings were recorded by King Solomon about 275 years after Joshua died and about 360 years before the time of Pythagoras.

We have these words of wisdom in the book of the bible named Proverbs.
In it, King Solomon comments on the state of a man by writing:
'For as he *(a man)* thinks in his heart, so is he.' [xlvi]
King Solomon was expounding the phenomenal truth concerning the power of thought. Our thoughts shape who we are. All our actions are a manifestation of our thoughts.
King Solomon also wrote:
'The tongue has the power of life and death, and those who love it will eat its fruit.' [xlvii]
Another translation of this text reads as follows:
'The tongue can bring death or life; those who love to talk will reap the consequences.' [xlviii]
King Solomon had an in-depth understanding of the power of speech and thoughts and their consequences many hundreds of years before the Greek philosophers.
He understood that we can produce life or death through the contents of our speech. The things we say to ourselves and to other people will foster death or life. We can produce health and sickness with our speech.

Scientists have begun to understand the power of repeated autosuggestion, and its consequences.
Many volumes of studies have proven that the things you say to yourself repeatedly, even though you may not believe them initially eventually move from your conscious mind into your sub-conscious mind. When an idea has successfully migrated to the sub-conscious cognitive cortices in your brain, you begin to act out those beliefs and thoughts. Your body also manifests those beliefs, as in the case of psychosomatic illnesses.

In the 20th century, a new form of suggestion, called neuro-linguistic programming or NLP, evolved from traditional theories of suggestion. NLP is a thought-influencing process which uses mostly words but can also employ sounds, colours and pictures to influence someone's thinking and behaviour patterns.
The advertising industry uses NLP extensively to influence the perceptions, views, preferences and ultimately the spending patterns of consumers.

Advertising is the process whereby people are skilfully manipulated to desire products and services through the process of sub-liminal messages, suggestions and neuro-linguistic programming. Sub-liminal messages are any form of communication which is designed to pass conscious perception but produces sub-conscious perceptions and responses. Through sub-liminal messaging, advertisers draw your attention, get you to focus and be calm, make you open to suggestions, shape your perceptions, mould your opinions and ultimately influence your spending patterns.

Through daily bombardment of visual images and sounds, people are being programd to behave in a certain manner. To this end, skilful advertising agencies are puppet-masters who control the behaviour patterns of consumers in a very subtle manner. The combined worldwide advertising expenditure by companies and corporations is estimated to add up to several hundred billion dollars annually. These companies and corporations seek to provoke new thinking patterns regarding their products and/or services or reinforce existing thinking patterns.
Many companies and corporations have benefitted immensely from well-planned advertising campaigns, with many of them having extended into several countries through globalization.

Many companies sign up famous people to be brand ambassadors. Celebrity endorsement deals have huge profit spin-offs for companies because people are more prone to buy a product that is promoted by someone they like and admire. This is also a form of subtle programming.
My intention regarding the discussion related to advertising is simply to enlighten people to the sub-conscious programming that they are being exposed to, and to suggest that they can begin to program themselves consciously instead of being programd sub-consciously.

Programming Yourself

How do you program yourself?
The answer is simply *by leveraging the power of autosuggestion.*

You may ask, but how can one leverage the power of autosuggestion?
Positive affirmations are very powerful tools that leverage the power of autosuggestion.
Let us explore what affirmations are, and are not.
An affirmation is an action or process confirming something. It can be a statement that declares that something is true, real and verifiable. It is also a statement that is intended to provide motivation, excitement and emotional support. Affirmations are very useful in shaping a person's thinking patterns and consequently their behaviour.
They are:

- usually short statements,
- positive in nature,
- are most effective when repeated several times daily,
- powerful tools to overcome negative self-talk,
- general or specific – meaning that they can be phrased in a manner that make them applicable for use by anyone, or they can be tailored for your specific situation and/or goals,
- power statements which must be combined with faith, belief and action in order for them to have the desired effect,
- only effective when used for a long period of time, on a daily basis.

They are not:

- abracadabra magic statements that bring about change immediately,
- able to bring about the impossible, like making you grow taller if you are short,
- a substitute for therapy to address deep-seated feelings of low self-esteem brought on by past and on-going life experiences,
- meant to be applied in isolation to your thoughts and actions, because your verbal affirmations, thoughts and actions must be in complete agreement regarding the stated affirmation,
- meant to reinforce the opposite of the suggestion, because some people sub-consciously through the psychological concept called *confirmation bias* actually strengthen their belief in the negative when faced with a positive statement,

- negative references and/or statements of failure, defeat, horror, doom and destruction,
- effective if stated without conviction, power and emotional intensity.

Affirmations

Here are affirmations related to some of the self-esteem influencers and indicators listed in the chapter titled 'Elements of Self-esteem.'
There are general affirmations and I have also included bible-based affirmations for those who want to incorporate biblical promises into their affirmations. I recommend these strongly, especially if you're a Christian.
You can identify the topics which cover the aspects of self-esteem which you need to work on and then you can read them aloud several times daily for a minimum of 63 days.

It takes 3 cycles of 21 days for a thought pattern to settle permanently in your brain and your subconscious mind.
Don't give up until positive changes occur.

Choose the affirmations that apply to you and repeat them aloud several times daily until you begin to see a positive difference in your thinking and behaviour patterns.

I value my physical, mental and spiritual health.
I expose myself only to foods and habits that are healthy for me.
I am valuable no matter what circumstances I find myself in.

I have great worth.
I am expensive, precious and very valuable.
I am a valuable person.
I am very valuable to God, because He loves me.

I am attractive and likeable.
I have many good qualities.
I am a person of good character, good morals, good values and integrity.

I am beautiful, inside and out.
I am charming and attractive.

I am strong enough to ignore negative comments by other people.
I always have good things to say about myself and others.

I have everything I need for a happy and fulfilling life.

I am a healthy, whole and complete person.
God has given me everything for life and godliness.

I am a happy person.
I think happy thoughts.
I spread joy and happiness wherever I go.
Laughter is my medicine.
The joy of the Lord is my strength.

I am always considerate of others.
I am considerate of the circumstances of others.
I value the opinions of others.
I have a good attitude towards others.

I value my happiness.
I am happy and content.
I value everything that I have been blessed with.
I appreciate everything that I have.

I practice healthy habits.
I avoid what is not good for me.

I am a highly creative person.
I have many original and valuable ideas.
I produce excellent work.
My ideas are worthy of recognition.
I use my God-given imagination and creativity to solve problems and express myself.

I think positive and uplifting thoughts.
I shape a bright future and destiny through my thoughts.
I think about things that are true, noble, right, pure, lovely, admirable and praiseworthy.
My mind is stayed on Christ.
I meditate on God's word day and night.
God has given me a sound mind.

I trust my conscience completely.
I follow the soft inner voice of my conscience.
I value the voice of my conscience.

I cope positively with stress and fatigue.
I take breaks when I feel tired and overwhelmed.
I am calm, I am at peace.
God gives me perfect peace because my mind is stayed on Him.

I value the needs of others.
I am compassionate towards others.
I treat others with loving care.
I always look for ways to help those in need.
I share what I have with those who are less fortunate.
I have abundance because God gives to me when I give to others.

YOU ARE VALUABLE

I have a valuable mind.
I have a powerful mind.
I am very smart and intelligent.
I think great and clever thoughts.
I am becoming smarter every day.
I have a special kind of genius.

I value my own curiosity.
I have a curious mind.
I am brave to ask questions about things to enhance my understanding.
I use my mind and my voice to enquire.
I gain understanding through asking questions.

I value my ability for self-improvement.
I am becoming more valuable with every passing day.
I am becoming better every day.
I am growing in knowledge and skill every day.
I work every day towards being a better person.
I apply myself to improve myself continuously.

Change is good, change is necessary - I value change.
I improve myself and my circumstances through the power of change.
I change what I can and graciously accept what I can't.
I value my competence.
I am a highly competent person.
I do everything to the very best of my abilities.
I put all my heart and soul into whatever I do.
Whatever my hands find to do, I do it with all my might.
Whatever I do, in word or deed, I do it as unto God.

I value my ability to exercise self-control.
I exercise control over my thoughts, words and actions.

I value the opinions of others.
I live at peace with all around me.
I value the power of forgiveness.
I forgive others who have harmed me.
I stand strong when challenged.
I am victorious, God gives me victory - He is for me and no-one can be against me.

I value my uniqueness.
I am comfortable being unique.
I value my differences.
I am comfortable being different.
I am comfortable in my own skin.
I am comfortable even if I don't fit in.
I am not conformed to the world – I am transformed by the renewing of my mind in allegiance to God's good, perfect and acceptable will.

I speak only good of others.
I speak only life with my tongue.
I partner and collaborate with people who add to my value.

Chapter 9

Conclusion

Inside-out
In the pages of this book I have taken you on a journey of self-discovery. I have pointed out the relationships which impact the image and value that you have of yourself. I have given you an expanded definition of value in human terms, and defined self-value as self-esteem. I have highlighted the importance of high self-esteem for success and I have shown you many factors that increase or reduce your level of self-esteem and your level of success. The end of this journey is for you to arrive at a point where you know and accept unconditionally just how valuable you truly are and how valuable your dreams, hopes, opinions and contributions are to others. When you begin to see yourself as a person of unlimited potential and worth, it becomes easier to see others in the same light. It also becomes easier to grow your own potential and the potential of others that you associate with. Regardless of the nature of your associations or which organization you belong to, you now have the knowledge and tools to develop yourself and others into winners and exemplary leaders who display high self-esteem and achieve phenomenal success in any area of endeavour.
But this process begins with you – it begins on the inside. In order for things to change, you must first change. You must work very hard on yourself, and when you change, your circumstances will change. All external victories are always preceded by internal victories – it starts with you!

> **In order for things to change, you must first change.**

So start today to see yourself in a new light, and make a commitment to change yourself, and then your circumstances will change. See the new possibilities that you can reach for. Expand the vision you have of yourself and then you will have an expanded vision of what you can achieve. The Roman poet Virgil wrote:
'They succeed, because they think they can.'

Believe that you can – believe that you will – believe that it is possible for you!

> **They succeed, because they think they can.**
> *Virgil*

Set high goals for yourself as you begin to embrace greater possibilities for yourself. Do not be afraid to aim high.
Dr. Norman Vincent Peale once said: "Shoot for the moon. Even if you miss, you'll land among the stars."

> **Shoot for the moon. Even if you miss,**
> **you'll land among the stars.**
> *Dr. Norman Vincent Peale*

Even if you miss the moon, you will land amongst the stars if you aim high. You will become a winner. You will obtain phenomenal success, and you will be setting the bar high – as high as the moon. You will set new standards that others will also want to achieve.

> **Your personal success will inspire others to set higher goals for themselves.**
> **Be the example that others wish to follow.**

When you are highly successful, you become truly valuable. But the essence of this book is not to reach a place where you feel that you have arrived. Instead, it is meant to inspire you to begin a life-long journey of self-discovery and ever-increasing value – value to yourself and value to others.

I thank you for reading this book, and I hope that you have received value from reading it. I trust that you enjoyed reading it as much as I enjoyed writing it. I trust that you will forever see yourself and others in a brand new light, and that your daily message to yourself and others will be –

YOU ARE VALUABLE!

Don't' devalue my value

Don't force me to commit a crime to prove my love and allegiance;
Don't commit a crime against me and claim that it's for love's sake;
Don't claim that you love me, and then act like you hate and despise me;
Don't make me feel less worthy so that you can feel more worthy;
Don't ask me to violate my conscience – if I don't despise crime I'll despise myself.
Don't use me as your punching bag – I'm not here to be beaten;
Don't lie to me – I deserve to always be told the truth and nothing but the truth;
Don't criticise my feelings, thoughts, ideas and opinions – what I think also matters;
Don't expect me to read your mind – use your mouth to convey your thoughts;
Don't expect me to think and act like you do – I am my own person;
Don't criticise me because I am different to you – God made and loves variety.
Don't steal my dreams – they are extremely precious to me;
Don't crucify me when I make mistakes – nobody is perfect;
Don't be a fair weather friend – stick with me through the storms;
Don't pretend to be someone you are not – always be the real you;
Don't break your promises to me – always keep your word;
Don't try to control and manipulate me – I was not born with puppet strings;
Don't play games with my heart – thoughts and feelings are not for sport;
Don't put me on the discount shelf – I am very expensive and valuable;
You and I are of equal value and worth - don't devalue my value.

Glisson J. Heldzinger

Afterthought

The challenge of life is to discover yourself, to find your own value, and then to live to the fullest expression of that value. Life calls on you to put aside mediocrity and to express your greatness.

Truly effective people are those who have discovered and lived up to their own unique value and then expose and develop value in others.

Life calls on you to celebrate your own uniqueness and the uniqueness of others.

Life calls on you to receive a unique reward that is reserved for the givers and sharers.

Life holds a special reward for those who uncover the value of broken people to themselves.

Life calls on you to be the valuable person you were meant to be and then to become a beacon of light to those who have yet to discover their true selves.

In becoming who we are and helping others who they are, we make the world a more valuable place.
Now the question remains – will you heed to life's call?

Discover your value.
Live your value.
Bless others with your value.
Bless others with the knowledge of their own value.

YOU ARE VALUABLE!

About The Author

Glisson J. Heldzinger is a motivational speaker, mentor and coach who has a passion for teaching and bringing out "the inner winner" that is inside of people. By developing innovative learning materials and systems, Glisson is

fulfilling his mission to transform individuals and organizations into being the best they can possibly be and having the best they can possibly have. As a Christian teacher and minister, Glisson loves to enlighten people to the truths contained in the Holy Bible – which he calls 'The Book of Secrets.' In addition, Glisson has a passion for evangelism and praying for the sick.

As part of his social-responsibility strategy, Glisson dedicates many hours of his time to voluntarily teach, mentor and coach students from historically disadvantaged backgrounds.

Glisson currently resides in Johannesburg, South Africa.

Contact Details

For enquiries about Glisson's latest audio and printed materials and programs, please visit the website regularly. For event availability and booking related questions, please direct your enquiries to the office via the e-mail address below.

Website: www.GlissonHeldzinger.com
E-mail: info@glissonheldzinger.com

Feedback

I would love to know what this book has done for you. If this book has made a positive impact on your life please let us know.
You can send your story to: ***mystory@glissonheldzinger.com***

New Books Coming Soon

Valuable Affirmations – *Powerful Phrases to Unleash Your Value*

A pocket-sized, easy-to-carry companion to the book YOU ARE VALUABLE. This little booklet is filled with uplifting and encouraging affirmations that will change your life.

Get It Done - *The Seven Steps of Successful Task Completion*

A step-by-step guide on how to start and complete any task confidently and successfully. Never again will you have to worry about how to manage your tasks.

ma^3 Academic Acceleration Program

Is your child not coping with his/her schoolwork?

Is your child displaying one or more of the following symptoms:

- lack of focus,
- lack of concentration,
- poor grades, and
- an inability to cope adequately with curriculum workloads.

Most high school learners can be equated to ill-trained soldiers who are being sent to war – they are given many weapons and assignments yet they lack the skill to handle their weapons and they lack the discipline necessary to survive in an adversarial environment and this is why most of them suffer and fall along the wayside academically.
Many learners display the following symptoms at high school:

- nervousness, tension and fear,
- lack of confidence,
- lack of the understanding and implementation of proven systems which can be employed to clarify and plot successful task management,
- lack of the understanding of goal-setting,
- lack of basic problem-solving skills,
- lack of the understanding and employment of effective study methods, and
- lack of motivation.

Just Imagine Mentoring© (JIM©) and Glisson Heldzinger Learning Systems© (GHLS©) have developed an amazing mentoring program called:
ma^3 = matric accelerated academic achievement© to prepare and assist learners to cope with secondary (high) school and university. Not only will the tools that learners acquire from these courses equip them to deal effectively and successfully with school and university, they will also acquire above-average skills to deal with adulthood and its many complexities and challenges.
If you wish to give your child a winning edge, enroll him/her for ma^3.

ma^3 = matric accelerated academic achievement© is the ideal solution for parents who are looking to help their children maximize their academic ability. Contact us at ***info@glissonheldzinger.com*** for more information about this exciting program.

ma^3 = matric accelerated academic achievement©

Mentoring & Coaching

Have you been struggling to get to the next level in your personal life, career or relationships?

Are you struggling to overcome an addiction or are you having trouble controlling your temper?
Are you, like many other people worldwide, struggling to realize your dreams, goals, aspirations and resolutions?
Do you need help to create work/life balance and to cope with the changes in your family, such as a new-born baby, or with the responsibilities of a new job or promotion?

If you answered "Yes" to any of the above questions, then you should consider life coaching. Coaching from an experienced mentor and coach can help you make the mental shift and mental leap to overcome the internal and external restraints and constraints that are keeping you from living a truly happy and fulfilled life. With the correct quantity and quality of life coaching, you can transform your life as it is right now into your dream life and RELEASE YOUR INNER WINNER!

Glisson J. Heldzinger, and Just Imagine Mentoring© have created programs that can be implemented in one-on-one settings, group settings and also as an e-program over the internet. These programs can positively impact your life in ways that you've never imagined before.

Contact us at ***info@glissonheldzinger.com*** for more information about our products and services.

Publishing Services

This book has been published by **Joshua Crown Publishing.**[2]
This book is also available as an **eBook** on Kindle and also as an **audio-book** in the Amazon Store.

YOU CAN ALSO BECOME A PUBLISHED AUTHOR

Many people have a dream of someday writing a book, but because they don't know how to convert their idea into an actual book, they never embark on that journey.
If you have such a dream, we have the expertise to convert your dream of becoming a published author into reality.

Joshua Crown Publishing provides a full range of publishing services such as:

- digital capturing of an author's notes,
- manuscript conceptualization,
- proof-reading and editing,
- cover design and legal compliance,
- book printing,
- eBook creation and on-line publishing,
- audiobook creation and on-line publishing,
- book promotion, and
- website creation and development.

If you want to know more about how to publish your fiction or non-fiction book, please do not hesitate to contact us at
info@glissonheldzinger.com for more information.

[2] Joshua Crown Publishing is a subsidiary of the Glisson Heldzinger Group of Companies

Notes

***Chapter 2* – The Beginning And End Of Fulfilment**

[i] Proverbs 19:22a NIV
[ii] Proverbs 22:1b NLT
[iii] Proverbs 4:23 NIV
[iv] Proverbs 4:23 NKJV

***Chapter 3* – People In Our Lives**

[v] Proverbs 18:1
[vi] 1 Samuel 1:11
[vii] Proverbs 31:15
[viii] Proverbs 16:26
[ix] Proverbs 13:22
[x] Proverbs 17:7
[xi] Proverbs 31:24
[xii] Proverbs 1:8-9
[xiii] Proverbs 11:14; 15:22; 24:6
[xiv] Exodus 35:30-35, 36:1-2
[xv] 1 Kings 5:1-12
[xvi] 1 Kings 3:16-27
[xvii] Proverbs 29:4
[xviii] Luke 2:46,47
[xix] Luke 4:16
[xx] Luke 4:15
[xxi] Mark 3:13-19
[xxii] Hebrew 10:25
[xxiii] Ecclesiastes 4:9-12
[xxiv] Proverbs 27:17
[xxv] Ephesians 4:11-12
[xxvi] Proverbs 11:27a NIV
[xxvii] Proverbs 11:12a
[xxviii] Proverbs 3:29 KJV

***Chapter 4* – Lilies And Sparrows**

[xxix] Wikipedia, http://en.wikipedia.org/wiki/Evolution, Retrieved 1 April 2015
[xxx] www.allaboutcreation.org, http://www.allaboutcreation.org/stages-of-man-evolution-faq.htm, Retrieved 1 April 2015

***Chapter 7* – Elements Of Self-esteem**

[xxxi] www.vocabulary.com www.vocabulary.com/dictionary/esteem, Retrieved 1 April 2015
[xxxii] Boeree, Dr. C. George (2002). "A Bio-Social Theory of Neurosis", Retrieved 16 September 2015
[xxxiii] Wikipedia, https://en.wikipedia.org/wiki/Midlife_crisis, Retrieved 16 September 2015
[xxxiv] http://www.telegraph.co.uk/news/politics/11821810/Big-Ben-falls-out-of-time.html, Retrieved 16 September 2015
[xxxv] Paperback Oxford English Dictionary; © Oxford University Press 2001, 2002
[xxxvi] Wikipedia; http://en.wikipedia.org/wiki/Neuroticism, Retrieved 10 June 2015
[xxxvii] Wikipedia, http://en.wikipedia.org/wiki/Causes_of_World_War_II, Retrieved 1 April 2015
[xxxviii] Wikipedia, http://en.wikipedia.org/wiki/Nazi_Party, Retrieved 1 April 2015
[xxxix] Paperback Oxford English Dictionary; © Oxford University Press 2001, 2002

[xl] Strong's Exhaustive Concordance, James Strong, 1990 copyright© by Thomas Nelson Publishers.
[xli] Strong's Exhaustive Concordance, James Strong, 1990 copyright© by Thomas Nelson Publishers.

Chapter 8 **- The Power Of Affirmations**
[xlii] Self Mastery Through Conscious Autosuggestion, Émile Coué (1922), *pg. 19*
[xliii] Think & Grow Rich, Napoleon Hill, *pg. 96*
[xliv] Think & Grow Rich, Napoleon Hill, *pg. 97*
[xlv] Joshua 1:8 NKJV
[xlvi] Proverbs 23:7 NKJV
[xlvii] Proverbs 18:21 NIV
[xlviii] Proverbs 18:21 NLT

www.ingramcontent.com/pod-product-compliance
Lightning Source LLC
Chambersburg PA
CBHW052030090426
42739CB00010B/1849
* 9 7 8 0 6 2 0 7 0 1 6 3 1 *